Know Your SHIPS

Guide to Boats & Boatwatching
Great Lakes & St. Lawrence Seaway

© 2004 – Updated Annually

(No part of this book may be published, broadcast, rewritten or
redistributed by any means, including electronic.)

ISBN: **1-891849-07-7**
ISSN: 0190-5562

Marine Publishing Co. Inc.
P.O. Box 68, Sault Ste. Marie, MI 49783
(734) 668-4734

www.knowyourships.com

Editor & Publisher
Roger LeLievre

Researchers
Jody Aho, Matt Miner, Gerry Ouderkirk,
Neil Schultheiss, Wade P. Streeter, Franz VonRiedel (tugs),
John Vournakis and George Wharton

Founder
Thomas Manse, 1915-1994

Front cover: *Michipicoten* passes
Paul R. Tregurtha in the St. Marys River. *(Roger LeLlevre)*
Back cover: *Walter J. McCarthy Jr.* negotiates the St. Marys River past
Neebish Island. *(Don Coles Great Lakes Aerial Photos – www.aerialpics.com)*

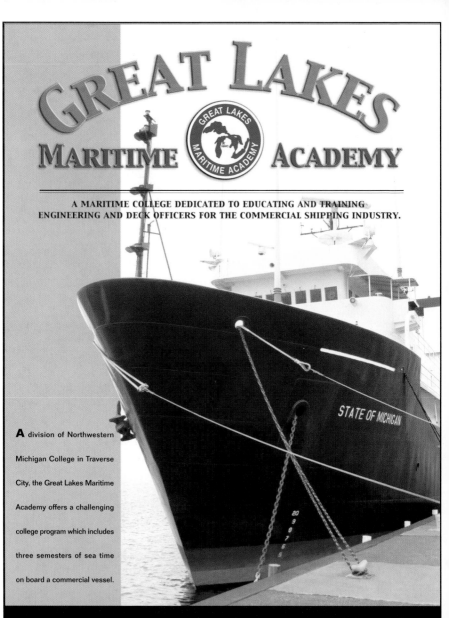

GREAT LAKES MARITIME ACADEMY

A MARITIME COLLEGE DEDICATED TO EDUCATING AND TRAINING ENGINEERING AND DECK OFFICERS FOR THE COMMERCIAL SHIPPING INDUSTRY.

STATE OF MICHIGAN

A division of Northwestern Michigan College in Traverse City, the Great Lakes Maritime Academy offers a challenging college program which includes three semesters of sea time on board a commercial vessel.

1.800.748.0566 ext.**1200**   **www.nmc.edu/maritime**

Sources for the information included herein include the United States Coast Guard, The Lake Carriers' Association, The American Bureau of Shipping, Lloyd's Register of Shipping, Transport Canada, United States Army Corps of Engineers, United States Coast Guard, "Seaway Ships," "Shipfax," "Seaway Review," www.boatnerd.com and publications of the Toronto Marine Historical Society, the Marine Historical Society of Detroit, the Welland Canal Ship Society and the World Ship Society. Listings are accurate as of March 1, 2004.

CONTENTS / '04

An engine-room telegraph awaits its next command.
(Wade P. Streeter)

John D. Leitch and *Roger Blough* cross paths in the St. Marys River. *(Roger LeLievre)*

MICHIPICOTEN

By Jody Aho

The announcement last spring by the Interlake Steamship Co. that it had sold its idle self-unloader *Elton Hoyt 2nd* to Canada's Lower Lakes Towing came with little fanfare, a description that might fit much of this 52-year-old lake boat's career. The 1952 Lake Carriers' Association annual report even fails to highlight the *Hoyt*'s construction, giving it only a casual mention. In addition, the boat's lines have always been

Vessel of the Year

largely utilitarian, lacking the style found in the likes of the *Wilfred Sykes* and others of the same time period, perhaps contributing to the lack of attention paid to the new vessel.

The early 1950s was a time of rapid new-ship construction on the Great Lakes. Even now there are more Great Lakes ships around that were built new or reconstructed in 1952 than in any other year. The 1951-'52 period found the United States at the height of the Korean War, and demand for iron ore resulted in the need for new vessels.

Great Lakes shipyards were already backlogged with orders well into 1953, so Bethlehem Steel Co.

Elton Hoyt 2nd on launch day, 1952. *(Courtesy Jim Luke)*

turned to its own yard in Sparrows Point, Md., to help. In 1951, plans were produced for three new straight-deck bulk carriers. Since they would need to be towed down the East Coast and across the Gulf of Mexico, then up the Mississippi and Illinois rivers and into the Great Lakes, length was a factor. At just 626.6'-long, these new carriers would not be even close to the size of the longest Great Lakes ships of the

Elton Hoyt 2nd in the St. Marys River in 1998. *(Roger LeLievre)*

time. Since bridge heights on the Illinois River restricted the height of vessels, superstructures would be pre-fabricated and carried on deck until the ships arrived in Chicago for final assembly. The first of the trio of hulls was launched at ▶

Michipicoten upbound in the St. Marys River in 2003. *(Jim Hoffman)*

***Michipicoten* arrives at Marquette for her first cargo, May 2003.** *(Lee Rowe)*

Sparrows Point in January 1952, and the other two were completed over the next five months. By mid-November 1952, all three were active on the Great Lakes. Bethlehem kept two for its own needs, naming them *Johnstown* and *Sparrows Point*, after two cities where the company had a major presence. Interlake took delivery of the third, and christened it *Elton Hoyt 2nd*.

After final assembly and sea trials at the American Shipbuilding Co. yard in Chicago, she sailed on her maiden voyage to load iron ore in Superior, Wis. The vessel was fitted with a Bethlehem Steel-built steam turbine plant producing 7,000 horsepower, the benchmark for new ship construction in the early 1950s. Steam was produced by two Foster-Wheeler, oil-fired, water-tube boilers, again commonplace among ships of the time. The *Hoyt* became Interlake's flagship, a distinction she would hold until the new *John Sherwin* came out in May 1958.

Like the other new, large carriers of the 1950s, the *Hoyt* fell into a regular trade route carrying iron ore between Lake Superior and lower-lakes ports. The Great Northern (now Burlington Northern Santa Fe) ore docks in Superior was a common destination for this ship over the years. The ship remains the last to load at the older-style chute docks in Superior, taking the final cargo from Dock No. 1 before it was shut down in 1988.

The *Hoyt*'s shorter length at construction, which helped permit the vessel to enter the lakes, became a liability not long into her career. During the winter of 1956-'57, the *Hoyt* returned to Chicago to receive a 72' midsection, increasing her capacity from 18,800 tons to 22,300 tons. Now 698.6'-long, the lengthening allowed her to carry the equivalent of several more loads of cargo each year.

As the 1970s drew to a close, the *Hoyt* needed additional modifications to allow her to remain competitive. She received a bowthruster and was converted to a self-unloader over the winter of 1979-'80, the latter investment almost certainly prolonging her career given the state of the industry in the next few years. But even having a self-unloading boom doesn't guarantee that a boat would remain active in tough times.

Over the years, the *Hoyt* seemed to be Interlake's favorite to send to the wall when business dropped. She remained in lay-up during parts of the early 1980s. In 1985, she fit out in the spring yet was sent into lay-up from May 14-Aug. 11. While the vessel saw more regular service as the 1980s closed, she entered long-term lay-up again after the 1990 season, not sailing again until 1994. The thriving economy during the rest of the 1990s ensured the ship would keep busy, although carrying a wider variety of cargoes than before. For her last few seasons with Interlake, the *Hoyt* was certified to carry grain and made the run between Superior and Buffalo on several occasions. Coal and limestone were also common cargoes for the boat in this period, and the ship was still used to carry iron ore, often from Marquette to the Rouge Steel plant in Dearborn, Mich. As business slowed again, the *Hoyt* laid up in Superior on Jan. 9, 2001. When she occupied a berth rafted next to her long-idle fleetmate *John Sherwin*, many speculated that she could be in for a similarly long hibernation – 23 years so far. One of her Bethlehem Steel sisters, the *Johnstown*, had long been lost to the scrappers, having the unpleasant distinction of being the first post-World War II laker to be sold for scrap back in 1985. The other, *Sparrows Point*, sailed a dozen busy years in the iron ore trade for new owners, Oglebay Norton, as the *Buckeye*, but did not run in 2003 and faces an uncertain future. ▶

New life rings await installation.

***Michipicoten* on May 24, christening day, at Sarnia, Ont.** *(Neil Schultheiss)*

The *Hoyt*'s idle time turned out to be fairly short. On April 10, 2003, Lower Lakes Towing closed on the transaction, buying the *Hoyt* from Interlake. Its new name, *Michipicoten*, was announced the same day. The name brings back one used previously on the former Pittsburgh Steamship Co. vessel *Henry C. Frick* when she sailed for the Providence Shipping Co., Ltd. from 1964-'72. The new *Michipicoten* underwent a paint job at Fraser Shipyards in Superior, then was towed to Sarnia, Ont., by the tug *Roger Stahl* for more refurbishing and fit out.

The ship's boilers and steam plant proved stubborn, and after several failed attempts, the *Michipicoten* finally set sail on her maiden voyage for her new owners on Friday the 13th, June 2003, a lucky day for the quickly expanding Canadian fleet. Her first trip was a load of iron ore from the Lake Superior & Ishpeming docks in Marquette to the Algoma Steel mill in Sault Ste. Marie, Ont., the run on which the ship spent much of her time in 2003. As her first season with her new owners progressed, the ship found herself on other trips and with a variety of cargoes not unlike her last several years with Interlake.

In a year that saw many favorites sold for scrap, the *Michipicoten*'s return to service was a highlight. In her five decades under the Interlake flag she achieved a better-than-average safety record and proved a reliable workhorse that could be used in a variety of trades. She just never attracted attention for being the prettiest, the biggest, the fastest or the most famous ship to sail the Great Lakes.

Under a new flag and new colors, she was given a revival in a fleet making a name for itself by buying the ships that never were the biggest or newest. Any attention she may have missed out on back in 1952 is coming her way now. Better late than never. ■

Michipicoten unloads at Algoma Steel in August 2003. *(Roger LeLievre)*
Loading a late-winter cargo at Marquette in January 2004 (inset). *(Lee Rowe)*

Joseph H. Frantz, **in Great Lakes Associates' colors, inbound at the Duluth piers. The vessel was chartered last year from Oglebay Norton Marine.** *(Dave Wobser)*

PASSAGES

Changes in the shipping scene since our last edition

As this issue went to press, boatwatchers were anxiously awaiting word on how new port and vessel access restrictions set down by the U.S. Department of Homeland Security and scheduled to take effect July 1 may change the way they pursue their hobby. Marine photographers in particular may bear the brunt of efforts to thwart would-be terrorists on the Great Lakes.

Fleets & Vessels

Also in play this spring was the fate of the Oglebay-Norton Co. of Cleveland, which entered Chapter 11 bankruptcy in February. The 11 vessels operated by the 150-year-old Cleveland firm's marine division were reportedly up for sale or lease, possibly to American Steamship Co.

Pending approval of various regulatory agencies, the Great Lakes Fleet will become part of the Canadian National Railway Co. sometime this year. The vessels involved – *Arthur M. Anderson, Roger Blough, Cason J. Callaway, Philip R. Clarke, Edwin H. Gott, John G. Munson* and *Edgar B. Speer* – will continue to fly the U.S. flag and be operated by Keystone Great Lakes Inc., a Pennsylvania ship-management firm. These seven vessels are all that remain of the once vast United States Steel fleet. ... *Burns Harbor* and *Stewart J. Cort,* the two 1,000-footers once operated by Bethlehem Steel Corp., bought last year by the International Steel Group, now sail under ISG management and logo.

The World War II-era *Richard Reiss*, which sat idle the past two seasons, is now owned by Grand River Navigation Co. ... The 1,000-footer *George A. Stinson* sails as *American Pride* this season. ... Cleveland Tankers' *Saturn* was sold for off-lakes use in late 2003, as was the big tug *Roger Stahl.* ▶

FIRST, AND FINAL LOOKS

The new U.S. Coast Guard cutter *Hollyhock* (above) approaches her home base at Port Huron last fall. She replaces the World War II-era cutter *Bramble*, which will become a marine museum nearby.

(Roger LeLievre)

Saturn heads off-lakes. *(Gerry Ouderkirk)*

One vessel that could have become a marine museum but didn't was the 1959-built steamer *Seaway Queen*, which was sold for scrapping in India late last year. She's shown being towed out of Toronto harbor on the first leg of her long overseas journey Sept. 3, 2003. *(Gerry Ouderkirk)*

The tug *Avenger IV* tows *Lewis G. Harriman* to the scrapper last fall. *(Brian Jaeschke)*

Scrapyard

Missing from the line-up this spring are four steamers long considered favorites of boatwatchers. The *Mapleglen*, *Oakglen* and *Seaway Queen* were towed to breakers in India in late 2003, with *Algosound* set to follow this year. ... The long-idle cement carrier *Lewis G. Harriman*, built in 1923 and last used as a cement storage barge at Green Bay, is scheduled to be scrapped this year at Sault Ste. Marie, Ont., although moves by preservationists to save her continue.

***Algosound* in the Welland Canal.** *(Jimmy Sprunt)*

Lay-up Log

Two Oglebay Norton Marine vessels, *Courtney Burton* and *Buckeye*, did not run at all in 2003 due to lack of demand. They spent the season tied up at Toledo. Fleetmate *Armco* sailed early in 2003, but joined them at the dock in late spring. ... *Edward L. Ryerson* is in the sixth year of lay-up at Sturgeon Bay. ... *John Sherwin* is now in her 23rd year of inactivity at Superior (she has now been laid up for half her life). ... *Algobay*, sidelined possibly for good at the end of the 2002 season, is laid up at Toronto while *Algontario* remains out of service at Thunder Bay. The idle *Algoisle* was towed to Hamilton in 2003, and may see service in 2004. ... *Kinsman Independent* is entering her second year of retirement at Buffalo. ... The former carferries *Viking* and *Arthur K. Atkinson* await uncertain futures at Marinette, Wis., and DeTour, Mich., respectively. ... Continuing in their roles as cement storage vessels are *E.M. Ford* (Saginaw), *J.B. Ford* (Superior), *C.T.C. #1* (South Chicago) and *S.T. Crapo* (Green Bay). The latter was officially converted to a barge in 2003.

MARINE MILESTONES
By Jody Aho

10 Years 1994 / The 1,000-foot *Indiana Harbor* set a new record for a single-trip Eastern coal shipment, 60,578 net tons. The record still stands.

Following the previous year's increased allowable draft levels, the St. Lawrence Seaway adopted 740'-long x 78' wide as the new maximum vessel dimensions that could safely transit the Seaway's locks, up from the previous 736' 6" x 76' which had been in place since 1984.

Massive ice jams caused considerable headaches for early season shipping at Duluth and in the St. Clair River. *Ernest R. Breech* and *Herbert C. Jackson* were two of the vessels stuck off Duluth April 12–15, while the powerful *Stewart J. Cort*'s rare appearance after winter lay-up at Erie helped with stuck traffic in the St. Clair River.

Pontiac downbound in 1972. *(Tom Manse)*

20 Years 1984 / The *Atlantic Huron* entered service for Canada Steamship Lines.

E.G. Grace became the first of the World War II Maritime class vessels sold for scrap. The *Grace* last sailed in 1976 and had a history of engine trouble which helped lead to her early demise. The year was another in which far more ships went to

Atlantic Huron in the St. Marys River in 2003. *(Roger LeLievre)*

the scrapyard than were added to Great Lakes fleets. Besides *E.G. Grace, B.F. Affleck, Eugene W. Pargny, Eugene P. Thomas, Pontiac* and *Saginaw Bay* made the one-way trip to the scrapyard.

James E. Ferris shows off her handsome lines Aug. 23, 1971, downbound in the St. Marys River. *(Roger LeLievre)*

30 Years / 1974

The tanker *Saturn* entered service as the first of three vessels built for Cleveland Tankers in the '70s. Other new vessels this year included *Algosoo* (the last traditional-style laker built with pilothouse forward and engines aft), *Wolverine* and *H. Lee White*.

Incan Superior began an 18-year career carrying railroad cars between Thunder Bay, Ont., and Superior, Wis., in July. She was sold for off-lakes use in late 1992.

Roy A. Jodrey sank in the St. Lawrence River after running aground in the Thousand Islands-area on Nov. 21, 1974. The 640-foot self-unloader was built for Algoma Central Railway in 1965.

The beautiful steamer *James E. Ferris,* built in 1910, arrived in Buffalo with her last cargo in October. The 465-foot straight-decker was one of the smallest vessels to operate on the Great Lakes into the mid-1970s.

40 Years / 1964

John T. Hutchinson and *Richard J. Reiss* became the first Maritime-class vessels to be converted to self-unloaders. Of the 16 members of this class, only four others have been converted to self-unloaders. The others were the *Frank Purnell* (later *Robert C. Norton*), *Crispin Oglebay* (part of which is now the *Canadian Transfer*), *George A. Sloan* (now *Mississagi*) and *J. Burton Ayers* (now *Cuyahoga*).

The 1960s were tough years for overseas scrap tows from the Great Lakes. One such vessel, the *Fayette Brown*, was wrecked off Anticosti Island in the Gulf of St. Lawrence on Dec. 10, 1964, after departing the Great Lakes on her scrap tow.

50 Years / 1954

After a flurry of activity during the previous several years, more of this year's shipyard work shifted toward reconstruction. The tankers *Imperial Woodbend* and *Imperial Redwater* were converted to dry straight-deck bulk carriers and renamed *Golden Hind* and *R. Bruce Angus*, respectively. Completion of an oil pipeline between Superior and Sarnia made these 3-year-old tankers obsolete.

▶

George M. Humphrey upbound in 1978. *(Roger LeLievre)*

George M. Humphrey was the only new U.S. laker built this year. She sailed through the 1983 season, then was sent for scrap in 1986. *Oakglen*, a favorite of boatwatchers until sold for scrap in 2003, entered service as *T.R. McLagan*.

75 Years 1929 Lake Michigan was an especially dangerous place during an eight-week period in the fall of 1929. The self-unloader *Andaste* sank on Sept. 9 with her crew of 25. On Oct. 22, the carferry *Milwaukee* sank with her crew of 47 during 75 m.p.h. winds. A week later, the passenger vessel *Wisconsin* sank with nine of the 68 passengers and crew aboard. Finally, on Oct. 31, the steamers *Senator* and *Marquette* collided, resulting in the *Senator* sinking with nine of her crew of 29.

William G. Clyde and *Myron C. Taylor* entered service as fleetmates in the Pittsburgh Steamship Co. just 12 days apart, on Aug. 15 and Aug. 27, respectively. Their careers would follow similar paths: both were converted to self-unloaders between 1956 and 1961, both were repowered, and both were sold to Grand River Navigation in late 2000. They remain in service today as the *Maumee* and *Calumet*. The *Clyde* had one extra name change, to *Calcite II*, which she bore from 1961-2000.

Myron C. Taylor before her 1956 conversion to a self-unloader. We know her today as Calumet. *(Tom Manse)*

Calumet inbound Maumee Bay near Toledo in 2002. *(Jim Hoffman)*

75 SEASONS OF SERVICE

Maumee visits the Welland Canal in 2003. *(Roger LeLievre)*

Sisters still: *Maumee* and *Calumet* spend winter lay-up together at Sarnia. *(Neil Schultheiss)*

Night view of the *Maumee*. *(Wade P. Streeter)*

GREAT LAKES GLOSSARY

AAA CLASS – Vessel design popular on the Great Lakes in the early 1950s. *Arthur M. Anderson* is one example.

AFT – Toward the back, or stern, of a ship.

AHEAD – Forward.

AMIDSHIPS – The middle point of a vessel, referring to either length or width.

ARTICULATED TUG-BARGE (ATB) – Tug-barge combination. The two vessels are mechanically linked in one axis, but with the tug free to move, or articulate, on another axis. *Jacklyn M / Integrity* is one example.

BACKHAUL – The practice of carrying a revenue-producing cargo (rather than ballast) on a return trip from hauling a primary cargo.

BARGE – Vessel with no engine, either pushed or pulled by a tug.

BEAM – The width of a vessel measured at the widest point.

BILGE – Lowest part of a hold or compartment, generally where the rounded side of a ship curves from the keel to the vertical sides.

BOW – Front of a vessel.

BOWTHRUSTER – Propeller mounted transversely in a vessel's bow under the waterline to assist in moving sideways. A sternthruster may also be installed.

BRIDGE – The platform above the main deck from which a ship is steered / navigated. Also: PILOTHOUSE or WHEELHOUSE.

BULKHEAD – Wall or partition that separates rooms, holds or tanks within a ship's hull.

BULWARK – The part of the ship that extends fore and aft above the main deck to form a rail.

DATUM – Level of water in a given area, determined by an average over time.

DEADWEIGHT TONNAGE – The actual carrying capacity of a vessel, equal to the difference between the light displacement tonnage and the heavy displacement tonnage, expressed in long tons (2,240 pounds or 1,016.1 kg).

DISPLACEMENT TONNAGE – The actual weight of the vessel and everything aboard her, measured in long tons. The displacement is equal to the weight of the water displaced by the vessel. Displacement tonnage may be qualified as light, indicating the weight of the vessel without cargo, fuels, stores; or heavy, indicating the weight of the vessel loaded with cargo, fuel and stores.

DRAFT – The depth of water a ship needs to float. Also the distance from keel to waterline.

FIT-OUT – The process of preparing a vessel for service after a period of inactivity.

FIVE-YEAR INSPECTION – U.S. Coast Guard survey, conducted in a drydock every five years, of a vessel's hull, machinery and other components.

FLATBACK – Lakes' slang for a non self-unloader.

FOOTER – Lakes' slang for 1,000-foot vessel.

FORECASTLE – (FOHK s'l) Area at the forward part of the ship and beneath the main cabins, often used for crew's quarters or storage.

FOREPEAK – The space below the forecastle.

FORWARD – Toward the front, or bow, of a ship.

FREEBOARD – The distance from the waterline to the main deck.

GROSS TONNAGE – The internal space of a vessel, measured in units of 100 cubic feet (2.83 cubic meters) = a gross ton.

HATCH – An opening in the deck through which cargo is lowered or raised. A hatch is closed by securing a hatch cover over it.

HULL – The body of a ship, not including its superstructure, masts or machinery.

INTEGRATED TUG-BARGE (ITB) – Tug-barge combination in which the tug is rigidly mated to the barge. *Presque Isle* is one example.

IRON DECKHAND – Mechanical device that runs on rails on a vessel's main deck and is used to remove and replace hatch covers.

JONES ACT – U.S. cabotage law that mandates cargos moved between American ports to be carried by U.S.-flagged, U.S.-built and U.S.-crewed vessels.

KEEL – A ship's steel backbone. It runs along the lowest part of the hull.

LAID UP or **LAY UP** – Out of service.

MARITIME CLASS – Style of lake vessel built during World War II as part of the nation's war effort. *Richard Reiss* is one example.

NET REGISTERED TONNAGE – The internal capacity of a vessel available for carrying cargo. It does not include the space occupied by boilers, engines, shaft alleys, chain lockers, officers' and crew's quarters. Net registered tonnage is usually referred to as registered tonnage or net tonnage and is used to figure taxes, tolls and port charges.

RIVER-CLASS SELF-UNLOADER – Group of vessels built in the 1970s to service smaller ports and negotiate narrow rivers such as Cleveland's Cuyahoga. *David Z. Norton* is one example.

SELF-UNLOADER – Vessel able to discharge its own cargo using a system of conveyor belts and a moveable boom.

SLAG – By-product of the steelmaking process which is later ground and used for paving roads.

STEM – The extreme forward end of the bow.

STEMWINDER – Vessel with all cabins aft.

STERN – The back of the ship.

STRAIGHT-DECKER – A non-self-unloading vessel. *Edward L. Ryerson* is one example.

TACONITE – Processed, pelletized iron ore. Easy to load and unload, this is the primary method of shipping ore on the Great Lakes and St. Lawrence Seaway. Also known as pellets.

TRACTOR TUG – Highly maneuverable tug propelled by either a Z-drive or cycloidal system rather than the traditional screw propeller.

Vessel Index

Arthur M. Anderson at Duluth on its first trip of the 2003 season.
(Glenn Blaskiewicz)

Vessel Name / Fleet Number	Vessel Name / Fleet Number	Vessel Name / Fleet Number
BBC Shanghai IB-8	Boland, John J. A-9	Cadillac S-28
BBC Spain IW-1	Bonnie B. III M-13	Calanus III............................C-4
BBC Texas IB-8	Bounty..................................V-5	Caledonia C-5
BBC Venezuala...................IB-8	Bowes, Bobby......................D-4	California G-22
Beauty K. IC-8	Boyd, David.........................G-26	Callaway, Cason J......................G-21
Beaver A-13, U-7	Boyer, Willis B. MU-20	Callie M. M-9
Beaver D...............................M-13	Bramble...............................MU-25	Calumet L-17
Beaver Islander..................B-7	Brandon E............................C-25	Canadian M-16
Beaver State M-1	Breaker.................................S-30	Canadian Argosy M-16
Bee Jay G-5	Brenda L...............................F-6	Canadian Empress S-23
Beeghly, Charles M. I-6	Bristol Bay U-3	Canadian Enterprise U-13
Bernier, J.E. C-4	Brochu..................................F-3	Canadian Leader U-13
Betsiamites L-12	Buccaneer............................W-1	Canadian Mariner U-13
Bide-A-Wee S-19	Buckeye State......................B-15	Canadian Miner U-13
Billmaier, D.L. U-2	Buckeye................................O-3	Canadian Navigator U-13
Birchglen C-2	Buckley.................................K-8	Canadian Olympic U-13
Biscayne Bay U-3	Buckthorn............................U-3	Canadian Progress U-13
Bittern C-4	Bufe, B.W. U-2	Canadian Prospector U-13
Black, Martha L...................C-4	Buffalo..................................A-9	Canadian Provider U-13
Block, Joseph L. C-10	Bum Dong IP-3	Canadian Ranger U-13
Block, L.E.............................B-3	Bunyan, Paul U-2	Canadian Sailor..................E-16
Blough, Roger G-21	Burns Harbor I-9	Canadian Trader U-13
Blue Dog S-15	Burro A-10	Canadian Transfer U-13
Blue Heron..........................U-10	Burton, Courtney O-3	Canadian Transport U-13
Blue Heron V.......................B-11	Busch, Gregory J.................B-18	Canadian Venture I-7
Bluewater U-5	Busse, Fred A. D-9	CanMar Bravery IC-2
Bluewing..............................IN-1		CanMar Endurance.............IC-2
BMI-105................................B-3	**C**	CanMar Glory IC-2
Boatman No. 3 ....M-13	C.T.C. No. 1 ....H-2	CanMar Honour...................IC-2
Boatman No. 6 ....M-13	C.T.M.A. Vacancier L-11	CanMar Pride.......................IC-2
Bogdan.................................IN-2	Cabot IO-4	CanMar Spirit.......................IC-2

Stone-laden *Peter R. Cresswell*, assisted by the Gaelic tug *Carolyn Hoey*, inbound on Detroit's Rouge River. *(Wade P. Streeter)*

USCG *Mackinaw* at Bay Shipbuilding for a refit, summer 2004. *(Chris Winters)*

Vessel Name / Fleet Number		Vessel Name / Fleet Number		Vessel Name / Fleet Number	
CanMar Triumph	IC-2	Chief Wawatam	P-13	Cuyahoga	L-17
CanMar Valour	IC-2	Chinook	M-19	Cygnus	C-4
CanMar Venture	IC-2	Chios Charity	IH-3		
CanMar Victory	IC-2	Chios Harmony	IH-3	**D**	
Cantankerous	E-15	Chios Pride	IH-3		
Cap Streeter	S-15	Chios Sailor	IH-3	Daldean	B-13
Cape Hurd	C-4	Chippewa	A-13	Dalhousie Princess	P-10
Cape Roger	C-4	Chippewa III	G-9	Dalmig	H-8
Capetan Michalis	IU-1	Chris Ann	H-11	Danicia	B-3
Capricorn	IB-1	Cicero	IO-4	Daniel E.	E-9
Capt. Shepler	S-11	Cinnamon	IN-1	Daniella	IJ-5
Captain George	F-7	City of Algonac	D-1	Dapper Dan	M-16
Captain George	MU-9	City of Milwaukee	MU-26	Darrell, William	H-12
Caravelle II	R-1	Clarke, Philip R.	G-21	Darya Devi	IK-1
Carey, Emmet J.	O-9	Claudia	IE-2	Dauntless	M-15
Caribou Isle	C-4	Clifford, A.E.	S-16	David Allen	N-10
Caribou	M-7	Clipper Eagle	IP-4	Daviken	IV-2
Carl M.	M-16	Clipper Falcon	IP-4	Dawn Light	R-4
Carlee Emily	K-4	Clyde	G-8	Dean, Americo	D-4
Carleton, George N.	G-17	Coastal Cruiser	T-6	Dean, Annie M.	D-4
Caro	IO-7	Cobia	MU-32	Dean, Elmer	G-1
Carol Ann	K-9	Cod	MU-8	Dean, Wayne	D-4
Carola	II-3	Cohen, Wilfred M.	P-13	Debbie Lyn	M-2
Carolina Borealis	C-22	Coleman	B-9	Debra Ann	H-11
Carrol C. I	M-13	Colinette	M-13	Deep See	B-15
Cartier, Jacques	C-30	Colombe, J.E.	U-7	Defiance	A-8
Cashin	II-1	Colorado	G-22	Delaware	G-22
Cast Prominence	IC-2	Columbia	MU-30	Demolen	U-2
Cast Prospect	IC-2	Columbia Star	O-3	Denise E.	E-9
Catharina-C	IC-5	Columbus	P-12	Derek E.	E-9
Cavalier des Mers	C-28	Columbus, C.	IH-2	Des Groseilliers	C-4
Cavalier Grand Fleuve	C-28	Commodore Straits	U-13	Des Plaines	C-1
Cavalier Maxim	C-28	Condarrell	M-13	Deschenes, Jos.	S-17
Cavalier Royal	C-28	Confederation	N-12	Desgagnes, Amelia	T-14
CEC Crusader	IC-11	Constructor	D-8	Desgagnes, Anna	T-14
CEC Faith	IC-11	Cooper, J.W.	C-26	Desgagnes, Catherine	T-14
CEC Fighter	IC-11	Cooper, Wyn	F-5	Desgagnes, Camilla	T-14
CEC Future	IC-11	Cormorant	F-2	Desgagnes, Cecelia	T-14
CEC Hunter	IC-11	Cornelius, Adam E.	A-9	Desgagnes, Jacques	T-14
CEC Mirage	IC-11	Cornett, J.A.	H-7	Desgagnes, Mathilda	T-14
Cedargeln	C-2	Cornwallis, Edward	C-4	Desgagnes, Melissa	T-14
Celebrezze, Anthony J.	C-20	Corsair	A-13	Desgagnes, Petrolia	T-14
Celene	IE-2	Cort, Stewart J.	I-9	Desgagnes, Thalassa	T-14
Cemba	C-9	Cotter, Edward M.	B-17	Desgagnes, Vega	T-14
Cemex Conquest	H-2	Coucoucache	L-12	Desgagnes, Maria	T-14
CGB-12000	U-3	Cove Isle	C-4	Desjardins, Alphonse	S-17
CGB-12001	U-3	Cowley, Leonard J.	C-4	Detector	MU-1
Challenge	G-25	Crapo, S.T.	I-4	Detroit	N-8
Champion	C-11, D-13	Creed, Frederick G.	C-4	Devine, Barnery	W-7
Changi Hope	IS-9	Cresswell, Peter R.	A-5	Diamond Belle	D-7
Channel Cat	M-19	Crio	IO-7	Diamond Jack	D-7
Charlevoix	C-12	Croaker	MU-2	Diamond Queen	D-7
Charlie E.	I-7	Crystal Spirit	IB-3	Diamond Star	R-5
Chem Bothnia	IC-7	CSL Asia	IC-17	Dimitris Y	IT-3
Cheraw	U-2	CSL Atlas	IC-17	Ditte Theresa	IH-6
Cherokee	B-2, L-6	CSL Cabo	IC-17	Dobrush	IC-12
Cheryl-C	IC-5	CSL Laurentien	C-2	Dona	A-3
Chicago III	C-13	CSL Niagara	C-2	Donald Bert	M-2
Chicago's First Lady	M-18	CSL Spirit	IC-17	Donald Mac	G-17
Chicago's Little Lady	M-18	CSL Tadoussac	C-2	Dongeborg	IW-2
Chi-Cheemaun	O-10	CSL Trailblazer	IC-17	Donner, William H.	K-1
Chief Shingwauk	L-16	Curly B.	L-6	Dorothea	IL-3
				Dorothy Ann	I-6

Vessel Name / Fleet Number	Vessel Name / Fleet Number	Vessel Name / Fleet Number
Dover Light E-1	Empire Sandy N-2	Famille DuFour II F-1
Dover M-2	Empire State L-6	Famille DuFour F-1
Doxa D IB-4	Empress II E-12	Federal Agno IW-3
Dr. Bob T-2	Empress III E-12	Federal Asahi IA-5
Drechtborg IW-2	Empress of Canada E-11	Federal Baffin IF-3
Dredge No. 55 ....M-1	Empress E-12	Federal Bergen IM-1
Drummond Islander II M-1	Enchanter IB-6	Federal Danube IF-3
Drummond Islander III E-3	English River L-2	Federal Elbe IA-7
Drummond Islander IV E-3	Enterprise 2000 ....E-13	Federal Ems IA-7
Duc d' Orleans D-11	Environaut G-7	Federal Franklin IF-3
Duga L-12	Epinette II L-15	Federal Fuji IV-2
Duluth C-7	Erich M-15	Federal Hudson IF-3
Duluth G-19	Ericson, Leif M-7	Federal Hunter IF-3
Durocher, Ray D-13	Erie West M-13	Federal Kivalina IF-3
	Escort II S-7	Federal Leda IA-7
E	Escort B-3	Federal Maas IF-3
Eagle Island A-12	Escorte L-12	Federal Mackinac IF-3
Eagle S-14	Escuminac N-1	Federal Manitou IF-3
Echo Des Mers E-4	Esperanza R-8	Federal Margaree IF-3
Eclipse N-4	Essayons C-8	Federal Matane IF-3
Ecosse N-1	Evening Star S-15	Federal Oshima IF-3
Edelweiss I E-5	Everlast M-11	Federal Polaris IV-2
Edelweiss II E-5	Excellent Pescadores IS-6	Federal Progress IF-3
Edith J. E-7	Express Progress IP-1	Federal Rhine IF-3
Edna G. MU-14	Eyrarbakki W-3	Federal Rideau IF-3
Eileen C. I-1		Federal Saguenay IF-3
Elikon IH-5	**F**	Federal Schelde IF-3
Elise D. R-8	Fairchem Vanguard IF-1	Federal Seto IF-3
Elizabeth W-2	Fairchild U-2	Federal Shimanto IF-8
Elm ID-2	Fairlane IJ-5	Federal St. Laurent IF-3
Emerald Isle B-7	Fairlift IJ-5	Federal Venture IF-3
Emerald Star R-5	Fairload IJ-5	Federal Welland IF-3
Emery, John R. O-9	Faith D-12	Federal Weser IA-7
Emily-C IC-5	Falderntor IK-4	Federal Yoshino IF-8

City of Milwaukee, Arthur K. Atkinson and *Viking* at Betsie Bay (Frankfort/Elberta, Mich.) in fall 1982, after the end of the Ann Arbor carferry operations. *(Marc Vander Meulen)*

Vessel Name / Fleet Number		
Federal Yukon	IF-3	
Felicity	S-11	
Ferbec	C-2	
Fischer Hayden	G-19	
Flinders, Capt. Matthew	M-10	
Flinterbaltica	IF-5	
Flinterbelt	IF-5	
Flinterbjorn	IF-5	
Flinterborg	IF-5	
Flinterbothnia	IF-5	
Flinterdam	IF-5	
Flinterdijk	IF-5	
Flinterduin	IF-5	
Flintereems	IF-5	
Flinterhaven	IF-5	
Flinterland	IF-5	
Flintermaas	IF-5	
Flintersky	IF-5	
Flinterspirit	IF-5	
Flinterstar	IF-5	
Flinterzee	IF-5	
Flinterziji	IF-5	
Flo-Mac	M-13	
Florida	G-22	
Ford, E.M.	I-4	
Ford, J.B.	L-3	
Forest City	G-28	
Fort Saint Jean II	C-32	
Fort Dearborn	C-15	
Forte	IB-1	
Fourth Coast	D-3	
Fox, Terry	C-4	
Frantz, Joseph H.	G-18	
Fraser	MU-12	
Frederick, Owen M.	U-2	
Fret Meuse	IH-4	
Frida	IJ-4	
Friendship	P-11	
Frigga	IB-8	
Frontenac II	O-5	
Frontenac	C-2	

G

G.L.B. No. 1	P-13	
G.L.B. No. 2	P-13	
G.T.B. No. 2	G-2	
Gaillard, Col. D.D.	B-9	
Galactica 001	G-3	
Gardiner, Joyce K.	N-9	
Gaynor, William C.	M-1	
Gemini	A-5	
General Blazhevich	IC-12	
General Brock III	S-4	
General	D-13	
Georgian Clipper	H-9	
Georgian Queen	P-2	
Georgian Storm	S-32	
Georgiev, Kapitan Georgi	IN-2	
Giant	II-1	
Gillen, Edward E. III	E-7	
Glenada	T-7	
Glenevis	M-13	

Vessel Name / Fleet Number		
Glenora	O-5	
Goki	P-13	
Goldeneye	IS-4	
Goodtime I	G-12	
Goodtime III	G-13	
Gott, Edwin H.	G-21	
Gouin, Lomer	S-17	
Goviken	IV-2	
Grampa Woo III	G-15	
Grand Baie	A-4	
Grand Island	P-5	
Grande Mariner	IA-3	
Grant, R.F.	L-12	
Grayling	U-4	
Great Blue Heron	B-11	
Great Lakes	K-7	
Great Lakes Trader	V-1	
Greenstone	U-7	
Greenwing	IN-1	
Grenfell, Sir Wilfred	C-4	
Greta V	M-13	
Gretchen B	L-18	
Grey, Earl	C-4	
Greyfox	U-8	
Griffon	C-4	
Grue des Iles	S-17	
Gull Isle	C-4	
Gunay A	ID-1	

H

Haida	MU-23	
Halifax	C-2	
Hamilton Energy	U-13	
Hammond Bay	L-13, U-2	
Hanlan, Ned	MU-17	
Hanlan, Ned II	C-18	
Hannah 1801	H-2	
Hannah 1802	H-2	
Hannah 2801	H-2	
Hannah 2901	H-2	
Hannah 2902	H-2	
Hannah 2903	H-2	
Hannah 3601	H-2	
Hannah 5101	H-2	
Hannah, Daryl C.	H-2	
Hannah, Donald C.	H-2	
Hannah, Hannah D.	H-2	
Hannah, James A.	H-2	
Hannah, Kristin Lee	H-2	
Hannah, Mark	H-2	
Hannah, Mary E.	H-2	
Hannah, Mary Page	H-2, S-7	
Hannah, Peggy D.	H-2	
Hannah, Susan W.	H-2	
Happy Ranger	IB-6	
Happy River	IB-6	
Happy Rover	IB-6	
Harbor Master	R-10	
Harbor Town	H-4	
Harbour Princess 1	H-5	
Harbour Star	M-29	
Harriman, Lewis G.	P-13	

Vessel Name / Fleet Number		
Harvey, Ann	C-4	
Havelstern	IR-3	
Helene	S-8	
Henry, Alexander	MU-16	
Hero	IO-7	
Hiawatha	R-8, S-19	
Highlander Sea	A-2	
Hilal II	IH-7	
Hoey, Carolyn	G-2	
Hoey, Patricia	G-2	
Hoey, Susan	G-2	
Hoey, William	G-2	
Hogan, Joseph J.	J-1	
Holden, John	M-16	
Holiday	S-19	
Holiday Island	N-12	
Holly Ann	H-11	
Hollyhock	U-3	
Hope	IJ-2	
Horizon Montreal	S-9	
Houghton	B-9	
Howe Islander	C-27	
Hudson	C-4	
Huron	U-2	
Huron Belle	L-8	
Huron Lady II	B-12	
Huron Maid	L-8	
Huron	A-13, MU-25	

I

I.V. No. 10	D-10	
I.V. No. 11	D-10	
I.V. No. 13	D-10	
I.V. No. 14	D-10	
I.V. No. 8	D-10	
I.V. No. 9	D-10	
Ian Mac	M-2	
Ida	IO-7	
Ida M.	R-6	
Ida M. II	R-6	
Idaho	G-22	
Iglehart, J.A.W.	I-4	
Ikan Sepat	IP-2	
Ile Des Barques	C-4	
Ile Saint-Ours	C-4	
Illinois	G-22	
Imbeau, Armand	S-17	
Imperial Dartmouth	I-2	
Indian Maiden	M-12	
Indiana	G-22	
Indiana Harbor	A-9	
Inglis, William	C-17	
Inland 2401	I-3	
Inland Seas	I-5	
Integrity	A-11	
Intrepid III	C-23	
Inviken	IV-2	
Invincible	L-17	
Iowa	G-22	
Ira	IC-13	
Irma	IP-4	
Iroquois	I-8, L-6	

To check for vessel changes made after this edition went to press, please visit our website and click on the UPDATES button.

www.knowyourships.com

Cuyahoga taking on a cargo of stone near Port Colborne, Ont. *(Courtesy A. Gindroz)*

Vessel Name / Fleet Number	Vessel Name / Fleet Number	Vessel Name / Fleet Number
Krayney, Khudozhnik IF-2	Louie S.......................................R-7	Marinette IG-3
Kristin M-13	Louisbourg C-4	Marinus Green...........................IB-5
Kristin D. P-8	Louise...T-1	Marion Green IB-5
Krystal...B-3	Louisiana G-22	Mariposa Belle M-10
KTC-115 ....M-13	Louis-Jolliet..............................C-28	Maritime Trader M-13
Kwasind R-8	LST-393 ....MU-9	Mariupol IC-12
Kwintebank IW-2	LT-5 ....MU-10	Marjolaine II C-31
	Lucien L. S-17	Mark-C..IC-5
L	Ludington MU-4	Market, Wm. M-23
	Luedtke, Alan K. L-18	Marquette C-15
L.S.C. 236 ....G-2	Luedtke, Chris E. L-18	Marquette S-28
La Prairie L-12	Luedtke, Erich R.........................L-18	Martin, Rt. Hon. Paul J. C-2
Lac Como M-13	Luedtke, Karl E. L-18	Marysville...................................G-2
Lac Erie M-13	Luedtke, Kurt.............................L-18	Massachusetts G-22
Lac Manitoba M-13	Lykes Energizer IO-3	Matador VI K-3
Lac St-Francois L-12	Lykes Inspirer IO-3	Mather, William G. MU-11
Lac Vancouver M-13	Lykes Raider IO-3	Matthew C-4
Lady Hamilton IS-5	Lykes Runner IO-3	Maumee L-17
Lady Kate....................................B-8	Lykes Winner IO-3	MBT 10 ....M-24
Lady Kim C-26		MBT 20 ....M-24
Lake Erie IF-3	**M**	MBT 33 ....M-24
Lake Eva IB-7		McAllister 132 ....A-1
Lake Explorer U-5	MAC Gagne P-7	McAllister, Daniel.....................MU-1
Lake Express L-4	Macassa Bay E-6	McAsphalt 401..........................M-11
Lake Guardian U-5	MacKay, Tony M-13	McBride, Sam............................C-17
Lake Lisi....................................IO-2	Mackenzie, William Lyon T-10	McCarthy Jr., Walter J...................A-9
Lake Maya IB-7	Mackinac Express A-13	McCauley U-2
Lake Michigan IF-3	Mackinac Islander A-13	McGrath, James E. U-13
Lake Ontario..............................IF-3	Mackinaw U-3	McKee Sons L-17
Lake Superior IC-18, IF-3, MU-13	Mackinaw City............................M-1	McKeil, Doug M-13
Lapointe, Ernest......................MU-1	Madeline M-3	McKeil, Evans M-13
Larsen, Henry C-4	Magnetic.....................................F-4	McKeil, Florence M-13
Larson, Wells F-6	Maid of the Mist IV M-4	McKeil, Jarrett M-13
LaSalle S-28	Maid of the Mist V......................M-4	McKeil, Wyatt M-13
Last Chance C-19	Maid of the Mist VI M-4	McLane MU-9
Laud, Sam....................................A-9	Maid of the Mist VII M-4	McLeary's Spirit M-13
Laurentian U-9	Maine G-22	McLeod, Norman M-11
Lauzier, Louis M.........................C-4	Mainebord IW-2	MCT AlmaK.................................IN-5
LCU 1680 ....N-3	Maisonneuve.............................S-18	MCT Altair..................................IN-5
Le Bateau Mouche L-10	Makeevka IC-12	MCT Arcturus IN-5
Le Draveur................................C-30	Makiri Green IB-5	Mecta Sea..................................IE-1
Le Levant IC-15	Malden P-13	Medemborg IIW-2
Le Survenant III........................C-29	Malte B. IW-1	Menasha G-5, M-17
Le Tareau M-16	Malyovitza IN-2	Menier Consol T-9
Ledastern IR-3	Mandarin IN-1	Menominee L-7, IG-3
Lee, Nancy A. L-13	Manistique M-16	Merweborg IW-2
Leitch, Gordon C. U-13	Manitou Isle M-6	Merwedelta...............................IS-11
Leitch, John D. U-13	Manitou.............................M-5, T-15	Mesabi Miner I-6
Lemos, John G. IP-1	Manitowoc K-1, U-2	Meta IO-7
LeVoyageur...............................S-19	Maple City...................................T-12	Meteor.....................................MU-27
Limnos C-4	Maple Grove O-1	Metis E-18
Linda Jean.................................N-10	Maple MU-6	Michigan K-7, U-2
Linnhurst F-2	Marcey...A-10	Michiganborg IW-2
Lisa E. E-9	Marcoux, Camille S-17	Michipicoten L-17
Lita IO-7	Margaret Ann H-11	Middle Channel..........................C-11
Little Rock MU-2	Margaret M. H-2	Middletown O-3
Livanov, Boris IN-5	Margaretha Green IH-8	Mighty Jake G-8
Lok Maheshwari........................IS-7	Maria Green...............................IH-8	Mighty Jessie..............................G-8
Lok Prakash IS-7	Marie Jeanne..............................IE-2	Mighty Jimmy G-8
Lok Pratap IS-7	Marilis T. IT-2	Mighty John III...........................G-8
Lok Prem....................................IS-7	Marine Star E-10	Miles, Paddy...............................H-14
Lok Rajeshwari IS-7	Marine Supplier H-13	Milin Kamak...............................IN-2
Long, Bert M-13	Marine Trader A-3	

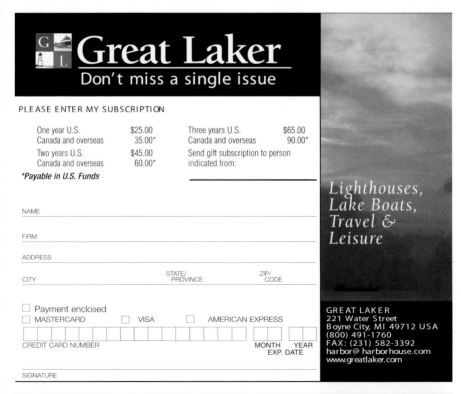

Vessel Name / Fleet Number	Vessel Name / Fleet Number	Vessel Name / Fleet Number
Nordik Express T-14	Ontamich B-13	Pioneer IC-17
Nordik Passeur T-14	Opeongo N-9	Pioneerland G-8
Nordkap IK-4	Oriole S-20	Placentia Hope N-6
Nordon............................IB-2	Orion.............................IS-14	Placentia Pride...............N-6
Norgoma MU-28	Orla IP-4	Placentia Sound R-3
Norisle MU-21	Orna IS-4	Pochard.........................IH-4
Norma B. F-4	Orsula IA-8	Point Chebucto E-2
Norris, James U-13	Osborne, F.M. O-9	Point Halifax E-2
North Carolina............G-22	Osprey P-13, T-12	Point Valiant E-2
North Challenge IY-1	Ostkap IK-4	Point Valour T-7
North Channel..............C-11	Ottawa A-13, W-2	Point Vibert.....................E-2
North Dakota G-22	Outer Island E-8	Point Vigour....................E-2
North Defiance IY-1		Point Viking M-25
Northern Spirit I............S-20	**P**	Point Vim E-2
Northwestern G-24		Pointe Aux Basques E-2
Norton, David Z. O-3	P.M.L. 2501 ....P-13	Pointe Sept-Iles E-2
Nouvelle Orleans C-28	P.M.L. 357 ....P-13	Polaris............................I-11
Nova D. T-14	P.M.L. 9000 ....P-13	Polydefkis P IC-14
Noyes, Hack....................W-7	P.M.L. Alton P-13	Polydefkis......................IS-4
NT Stone Merchant N-11	P.M.L. Salvager P-13	Pomorze Zachodnie IP-4
	Pacific Standard M-13	Pontokratis...................IO-1
O	Palamos IH-4	Pontoporos IO-1
	Palladino, Frank Jr. I-3	Port City Princess..........P-9
Oatka A-3	Palladino, James I-3	Port Mechins................D-10
Ocean Abys L-12	Panam Flota IT-1	Prairieland G-8
Ocean Bravo L-12	Panam Linda IT-1	Presque Isle G-21
Ocean Charlie................L-12	Panam Sol IT-1	Pride of Michigan U-8
Ocean Delta L-12	Panama B-9	Princess of Acadia N-12
Ocean Echo II L-12	Pancaldo IH-4	Princess Wenonah..........B-4
Ocean Foxtrot L-12	Paradise Sound R-3	Princess J-3
Ocean Golf L-12	Parisien, Jean C-2	Prinsenborg IW-2
Ocean Hauler M-13	Parizeau C-4	Progress M-13
Ocean Hercule L-12	Pathfinder I-6	Project Europa IB-6
Ocean Intrepide L-12	Patria II-2, IO-7	Provider S-16
Ocean Jupiter L-12	Patronicola, Calliroe IO-6	Provmar Terminal U-13
Ocean Priti....................IC-9	Paul E. No.1 ....M-13	Provmar Terminal II U-13
Odra IP-4	Paula M. M-16	Provo Wallis C-4
Odyssey II O-2	Peach State....................M-1	PTF-17 ....MU-2
Oglebay Norton O-3	Pearkes, George R. C-4	Puffin.............................IH-4
Oglebay, Earl W. O-3	Peckinpaugh, Day O-3	Pumper...........................N-7
Ohio...............................G-22	Pelee Flyer 1 ....P-1	Purcell, Robert A-11
Oil Queen G-10	Pelee Flyer 2 ....P-1	Purvis, W.I. Scott P-13
Ojibway L-6	Pelee Islander O-10	Purvis, W.J. Ivan P-13
Ojibway...........................M-1	Peninsula G-17	Put-In-Bay.....................M-23
Oklahoma G-22	Pennsylvania G-22	Pytheas..........................IS-4
Okoltchitza....................IN-2	Peonia IS-3	
Old Mission K-8	Pere Marquette 10........E-17	**Q**
Oldendorff, Anna IO-5	Pere Marquette 41 ....P-4	
Oldendorff, Elise..........IO-5	Perelik IN-2	Quebecois.....................U-13
Olderndorff, Bernhard .IO-5	Performance S-24	Queen City....................S-31
Olderndorff, Helena.....IO-5	Perry, John M. C-1	Quinte Loyalist O-5
Olderndorff, Mathilde ..IO-5	Persenk IN-2	
Olderndorff, Regina IO-5	Pete, C. West B-1	**R**
Olderndorff, Rixta IO-5	Petite Forte...................S-26	
Olga IO-7	Pictured Rocks..............P-5	R.C.L. No. II M-16
Olympic Melody IO-6	Pilica IP-4	Racine U-2
Olympic Mentor............IO-6	Pilot 1 ....M-13	Radisson S-17
Olympic Merit...............IO-6	Pine ID-2	Radisson S-28
Olympic Miracle............IO-6	Pineglen C-2	Radisson, Pierre C-4
Omni St-Laurent L-12	Pintail IN-1	Radium Yellowknife A-1
Omni-Atlas L-12	Pioneer II S-27	Randolph, Curtis............D-6
Omni-Richelieu L-12	Pioneer Princess T-11	Ranger III U-7
Ongiara.........................C-17	Pioneer Queen T-11	Rathrowan.....................IG-1
		Raymond, Jean M-13

Vessel Name / Fleet Number	Vessel Name / Fleet Number	Vessel Name / Fleet Number
Rebecca Lynn..............................A-11	Rubin Hawk...................................IK-2	Schwartz, H.J. U-2
Rega IP-4	Rubin Lark.....................................IK-2	Scow 50..A-11
Reiss MU-24	Ruby..B-15	Sea Bear...S-5
Reiss, Richard L-17	Ryerson, Edward L. C-10	Sea Castle..I-7
Reliance P-13	S.M.T.B. No. 7 ....E-1	Sea Chief..B-3
Relief R-10		Sea Colt..S-5
Rennie, Thomas C-17	**S**	Sea Eagle II S-26
Reserve O-3	Sabina...IE-2	Sea Eagle S-5
Rest, William T-12	Sackville....................................MU-31	Sea Fox II.......................................S-4
Rheinstern IR-3	Sacre Bleu S-11	Sea Queen II................................A-12
Rhode Island G-22	Saginaw L-17	Sea-Born..S-1
Richelieu L-14, V-2	Salty Dog. No. 1 ....M-13	Seaflight I G-14
Richter, Arni J. W-3	Salvage Monarch......................H-10	Seaflight II G-14
Richter, C.G. W-3	Salvager M-13	Seaguardian II..............................IT-4
Rickey, James W. D-8	Salvor M-13	Seahound......................................N-1
Ridgeway, Benjamin I-3	Sam II..D-13	Sealink...IT-4
Rio Glory IG-2	Sand Pebble.................................D-3	Segwun.......................................M-30
Risely, Samuel C-4	Sandpiper.....................................H-3	Selvick, Bonnie G. T-1
River Gambler H-6	Sandra Mary M-16	Selvick, Carla Anne......................S-7
Roanoke E-17	Sandviken IV-2	Selvick, John M.............................C-1
Robert John................................G-17	Santiago IB-8	Selvick, Kimberly D-9
Robert W. T-6	Sarah B. G-19	Selvick, Sharon M. S-7
Robin E. E-9	Sarah No. 1 ....T-2	Selvick, William C. S-7
Robin Lynn S-10	Sault au Couchon M-13	Seneca B-9, B-16
Robinson Bay.............................S-24	Sauniere A-5	Serendipity Princess....................P-3
Rochelle Kaye............................R-10	Savard, Felix-Antoine S-17	Seven Sisters H-10
Rocket P-13	Sawmill Explorer S-2	Sevilla Wave.................................IT-2
Roman, Stephen B. E-18	Scan Atlantic IS-2	Shamrock......................................J-4
Rosaire...D-10	Scan Germania IS-2	Shannon......................................G-2
Rosalee D......................................T-6	Scan Hansa IS-2	Shark..C-4
Rosemary....................................M-10	Scan Oceanic IS-2	Sharon Jon..................................S-16
Rouble, J.R. T-2	Scan Polaris IS-2	Sheila Ann...................................IC-17
Royal Pescadores......................IS-6	Scandrett, Fred.........................T-12	Sheila P. P-13
Rubin Halcyon............................IK-2	Schlaeger, Victor L. C-14	Shenehon.....................................G-20

Cason J. Callaway **glides by on a cold but calm Detroit River.** *(Wade P. Streeter)*

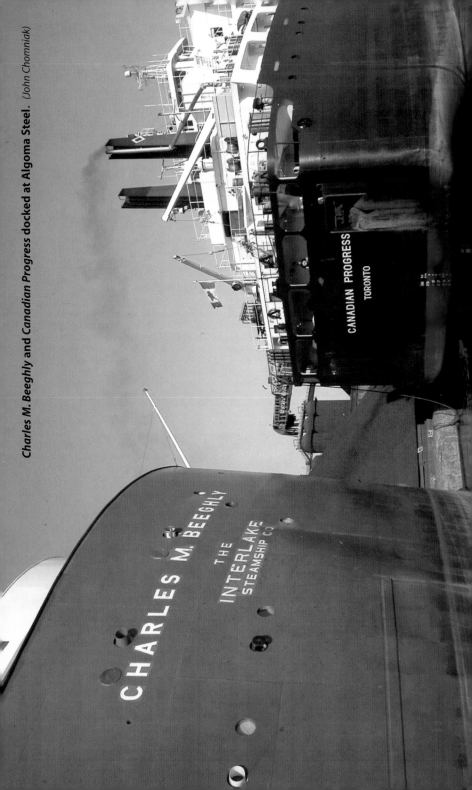

Charles M. Beeghly and Canadian Progress docked at Algoma Steel. (John Chomniak)

Vessel Name / Fleet Number	Vessel Name / Fleet Number	Vessel Name / Fleet Number
Sherwin, John....................I-6	Southdown Challenger H-2	Stella Borealis...........................C-22
Shipka.................................IN-2	Spar Jade IS-12	Stellanova IJ-5
Shipsands..........................T-13	Spar Opal IS-12	Stellaprima IJ-5
Shirley Irene K-4	Spar Ruby IS-12	Still Watch.................................T-5
Shirley Joy.........................L-6	Spartan...L-5	Stokmarnes................................II-1
Shoreline II........................S-15	Speer, Edgar B.........................G-21	Stolt Accord IS-13
Showboat Royal Grace M-10	Spence, John M-13	Stolt Alliance...........................IS-13
Sichem Baltic IC-1	Spencer, Sarah G-27	Stolt Aspiration.......................IS-13
Silversides.........................MU-9	Spirit of Chicago.......................S-21	Stormont M-13
Simcoe Islander........................C-27	Spirit of Ontario 1 ....C-3	Straits Express..........................A-13
Simcoe C-4	Spray...C-4	Straits of Mackinac II A-13
Simonsen U-2	Spring Laker IS-8	Strange Attractor......................IO-3
Simpson, Miss Kim.....................T-13	Spruceglen C-2	Strekalovskiy, Mikhail IM-3
Sir Walter..........................IA-4	Spuds...R-7	Strelkov, Petr.............................IN-4
Siscowet U-4	Spume..C-4	Sturgeon U-4
Skagen IR-2	St Mary IO-2	Sugar Islander II E-3
Skyline Princess..............M-18	St. Clair A-9, M-13	Sullivan, Denis P-6
Skyline Queen M-18	St. John, J.S. O-3	Sundew U-3
Smallwood, Jos. & Clara............M-7	St. Laurent, Louis S......................C-4	Sunliner W-4
Smith, Dean R...................M-9	St. Mary's Cement S-26	Sunny Blossom...........................IL-1
Smith, F.C.G.......................C-4	St. Mary's Cement II..................S-26	Superior G-22
Smith, H.A..........................H-7	St. Mary's Cement III.................S-26	Suriot IV.....................................C-32
Smith, L.L. Jr. U-12	Star of Chicago S-15	Susan E. H-2
Soo River Belle N-10	Star of Saugatuck......................S-29	Susan L. S-7
Sora....................................C-4	State of Michigan......................G-24	Susan Michelle...........................D-2
Soulanges E-14	STC 2004 ....B-18	Susanin, Ivan IM-3
South Bass........................M-23	Ste. Claire MU-29	Swan IB-1
South Carolina.................G-22	Steelhead M-19	Sykes, Wilfred C-10
South Channel..................C-11	Stefania I....................................IF-7	Sylvia..IC-16

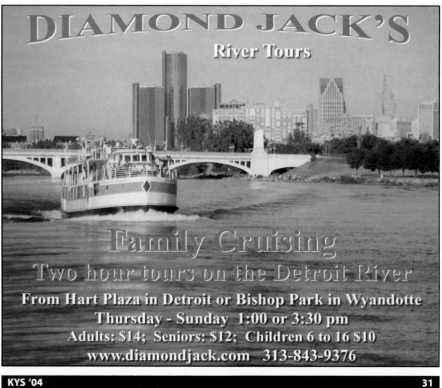

Great Lakes & Seaway Fleets

John J. Boland in the St. Marys River.   *(Roger LeLievre*

GREAT LAKES / SEAWAY FLEETS

Listed after each vessel in order are: Type of Vessel, Year Built, Type of Engine, Maximum Cargo Capacity (at mid-summer draft in long tons) or Gross Tonnage*, Overall Length, Breadth and Depth (from the top of the keel to the top of the upper deck beam) or Draft*. The figures given are as accurate as possible and are given for informational purposes only. Vessels and owners are listed alphabetically as per American Bureau of Shipping and Lloyd's Register of Shipping format. Former names of vessels and years of operation under former names appear beneath the vessel's name. A number in brackets following a vessel's name indicates how many vessels, including the one listed, have carried that name.

KEY TO TYPE OF VESSEL

2B.................................Brigantine	**DR**..Dredge	**ITB** ....Integrated Tug/Barge
2S ....2 Masted Schooner	**DS**....................................Spud Barge	**PA**...........................Passenger Vessel
3S ....3 Masted Schooner	**DV**................................Drilling Vessel	**PB**.......................................Pilot Boat
4S ....4 Masted Schooner	**DW**..Scow	**PF**...........................Passenger Ferry
AC.................................Auto Carrier	**ES**.............................Excursion Ship	**PK**.......................Package Freighter
AT..............................Articulated Tug	**EV**.....................Env. Response Ship	**RR**.........................Roll On/Roll Off
ATB.................Articulated Tug/Barge	**FB**..Fire Boat	**RT**.........................Refueling Tanker
BB...................................Bum Boat	**FD**......................Floating Dry Dock	**RV**........................Research Vessel
BC.................................Bulk Carrier	**FT**.....................................Fishing Tug	**SB**...........................Supply Boat
BK..................Bulk Carrier/Tanker	**GA**................Gambling Casino	**SC**...........................Sand Carrier
BT...................................Buoy Tender	**GC**.............................General Cargo	**SR**...................Search & Rescue
CC..............................Cement Carrier	**GL**.......................................Gate Lifter	**SU**...........................Self-unloader
CF......................................Car Ferry	**GR**...........................Grocery Launch	**SV**...........................Survey Vessel
CO............................Container Vessel	**GU** ....Grain Self Unloader	**TB**..................................Tug Boat
CS...................................Crane Ship	**HL**.....................Heavy Lift Vessel	**TF**..................................Train Ferry
DB...................................Deck Barge	**HY** ....Hydrofoil	**TK**......................................Tanket
DD....................................Destroyer	**IB**....................................Ice Breaker	**TT**.....................Tractor Tug Boat
DH ....Hopper Barge	**IT**.................................Integrated Tug	**TV**...........................Training Vessel

KEY TO PROPULSION

B...Barge	**S** ....Steam - Skinner "Unaflow" Engine
D...Diesel	**T** ....Steam - Turbine Engine
Q.............Steam - Quad Exp. Compound Engine	**U**..............Steam - Uniflow Engine - "Skinner" Design
R.................Steam - Triple Exp. Compound Engine	**W** ....Sailing Vessel (Wind)

Fleet #.	Fleet Name Vessel Name	Type of Vessel	Year Built	Type of Engine	Cargo Cap. or Gross*	Overall Length	Breadth	Depth or Draft*
A-1	**A .B. M. MARINE, THUNDER BAY, ON**							
	McAllister 132	DB	1954	B	7,000	343' 00"	63' 00"	19' 00"
	(Powell No. 1 '54-'61, Alberni Carrier '61-'77, Genmar 132 '77-'79)							
	Radium Yellowknife	TB	1948	D	235*	120' 00"	28' 00"	6' 06"
	W. N. Twolan	TB	1962	D	299*	106' 00"	29' 05"	15' 00"
	(Fleet also includes the 150' derrick barges Radium 603, Radium 604, Radium 607, Radium 610, Radium 611, Radium 617, Radium 623, Radium 625 and Radium 631)							
A-2	**ACHESON VENTURES LLC, PORT HURON, MI**							
	Highlander Sea	ES/2S	1927	W	140*	154' 00"	25' 06"	14' 00"
	(Pilot '27-'76, Star Pilot '76-'98, Caledonia '98-'98)							
A-3	**ACME MARINE SERVICE, DULUTH, MN**							
	Dona	GR	1929	D	10*	35' 00"	9' 00"	4' 06"
	Marine Trader	BB	1939	D	60*	65' 00"	15' 00"	7' 06"
	Oatka	TB	1934	D	10*	40' 00"	10' 00"	4' 06"
A-4	**ALCAN ALUMINUM LTD., PORT ALFRED, QC**							
	Alexis-Simard	TT	1980	D	286*	92' 00"	34' 00"	13' 07"
	Grande Baie	TT	1972	D	194*	86' 06"	30' 00"	12' 00"

Fleet #.	Fleet Name Vessel Name	Type of Vessel	Year Built	Type of Engine	Cargo Cap. or Gross*	Overall Length	Breadth	Depth or Draft*
A-5	**ALGOMA CENTRAL CORP., SAULT STE. MARIE, ON**							
	ALGOMA CENTRAL MARINE GROUP, ST. CATHARINES, ON – DIV. OF ALGOMA CENTRAL CORP.							
	***VESSEL OPERATED BY** SEAWAY MARINE TRANSPORT, ST. CATHARINES, ON., A*							
	PARTNERSHIP BETWEEN ALGOMA CENTRAL CORP. AND UPPER LAKES GROUP, INC.							
	Agawa Canyon*	SU	1970	D	23,400	647' 00"	72' 00"	40' 00"
	Algobay*	SU	1978	D	34,900	730' 00"	75' 10"	46' 06"
	(Algobay '78-'94, Atlantic Trader '94-'97). (Last operated in 2002. Laid up at Toronto, ON.)							
	Algocape* {2}	BC	1967	D	29,950	729' 09"	75' 04"	39' 08"
	(Richelieu {3} '67-'94)							
	Algocen* {2}	BC	1968	D	28,400	730' 00"	75' 03"	39' 08"
	Algoisle*	BC	1963	D	26,700	730' 00"	75' 05"	39' 03"
	(Silver Isle '63-'94) (Last operated in 1999. Laid up at Hamilton, ON.)							
	Algolake*	SU	1977	D	32,150	730' 00"	75' 06"	46' 06"
	Algomarine*	SU	1968	D	27,000	729' 10"	75' 04"	39' 08"
	(Lake Manitoba '68-'87) (Converted to a self-unloader-'89)							
	Algonorth*	BC	1971	D	28,000	729' 11"	75' 02"	42' 11"
	(Temple Bar '71-'76, Lake Nipigon '76-'84, Laketon {2} '84-'86, Lake Nipigon '86-'87)							
	Algontario*	BC	1960	D	29,100	730' 00"	75' 09"	40' 02"
	([Fore Section] Cartiercliffe Hall '76-'88, Winnipeg {2} '88-'94; [Stern Section] Ruhr Ore '60-'76)							
	(Last operated April 13, 1999 – 5 year survey expired July 1999. Laid up at Thunder Bay, ON.)							
	Algoport*	SU	1979	D	32,000	658' 00"	75' 10"	46' 06"
	Algorail* {2}	SU	1968	D	23,750	640' 05"	72' 03"	40' 00"
	Algosoo* {2}	SU	1974	D	31,300	730' 00"	75' 05"	44' 06"
	Algosteel* {2}	SU	1966	D	27,000	729' 11"	75' 04"	39' 08"
	(A. S. Glossbrenner '66-'87, Algogulf {1} '87-'90)							
	Algoville*	SU	1967	D	31,250	730' 00"	77' 11"	39' 08"
	(Senneville '67-'94) (Widened by 3'-'96)							
	Algoway* {2}	SU	1972	D	24,000	650' 00"	72' 00"	40' 00"
	Algowood*	SU	1981	D	31,750	740' 00"	76' 01"	46' 06"
	Capt. Henry Jackman*	SU	1981	D	30,550	730' 00"	76' 01"	42' 00"
	(Lake Wabush '81-'87) (Converted to a self-unloader-'96)							
	John B. Aird*	SU	1983	D	31,300	730' 00"	76' 01"	46' 06"
	Peter R. Cresswell*	SU	1982	D	31,700	730' 00"	76' 01"	42' 00"
	(Algowest '82-'01) (Converted to a self-unloader-'98)							
	SOCIETE QUEBECOISE D' EXPLORATION MINIERE, SAINTE-FOY, QC – CHARTERER							
	Sauniere	SU	1970	D	23,900	642' 10"	74' 10"	42' 00"
	(Bulknes '70-'70, Brooknes '70-'76, Algosea {1} '76-'82)							
	ALGOMA TANKERS LTD., DARTMOUTH, NS – DIVISION OF ALGOMA CENTRAL CORP.							
	Algocatalyst	TK	1972	D	10,560	430' 05"	62' 04"	34' 05"
	(Jon Ramsoy '72-'74, Doan Transport '74-'86, EnerChem Catalyst '86-'99)							
	Algoeast	TK	1977	D	9,657	431' 05"	65' 07"	35' 05"
	(Texaco Brave {2} '77-'86, Le Brave '86-'97, Imperial St. Lawrence {2} '97-'97)							
	(Converted from single-hulled to double-hulled tanker, '00)							
	Algofax	TK	1969	D	13,759	485' 05"	70' 02"	33' 03"
	(Imperial Bedford '69-'97)							
	Algonova	TK	1969	D	6,885	400' 06"	54' 02"	26' 05"
	(Texaco Chief {2} '69-'87, A. G. Farquharson '87-'98)							
	Algosar	TK	1974	D	12,708	435' 00"	74' 00"	32' 00"
	(Imperial St. Clair '74-'97)							
	Algoscotia	TK	2004	D	18,000	488'00"	78'00"	
	CLEVELAND TANKERS (1991), INC., CLEVELAND, OH – CHARTERED BY ALGOMA TANKERS LTD.							
	Gemini	TK	1978	D	5,853*	432' 06"	65' 00"	29' 04"
A-6	**ALLIED SIGNAL, INC., DETROIT, MI**							
	Allied Chemical No. 12	TK	1969	B	801*	200' 01"	35' 01"	8' 06"*
A-7	**ALLOUEZ MARINE SUPPLY, SUPERIOR, WI**							
	Allouez Marine	GR	1948	D	9*	35' 02"	11' 02"	3' 06"

Fleet #.	Fleet Name / Vessel Name	Type of Vessel	Year Built	Type of Engine	Cargo Cap. or Gross*	Overall Length	Breadth	Depth or Draft*
A-8	**AMERICAN MARINE CONSTRUCTION, BENTON HARBOR, MI**							
	Alice E	TB	1944	T	146*	81' 01"	24' 00"	9' 10"
	AMC 100	DB	1979	B	2,273	200' 00"	52' 00"	14' 00"
	AMC 200	DB	1979	B	2,273	200' 00"	36' 00"	11' 08"
	AMC 300	DB	1977	B	1,048	180' 00"	54' 00"	12' 00"
	Defiance	TB	1966	D	26*	44' 08"	18' 00"	6' 00"
A-9	**AMERICAN STEAMSHIP CO., WILLIAMSVILLE, NY**							
	Adam E. Cornelius {4}	SU	1973	D	28,200	680' 00"	78' 00"	42' 00"
	(Roger M. Kyes '73-'89)							
	American Mariner	SU	1980	D	37,200	730' 00"	78' 00"	45' 00"
	(Laid down as Chicago {3})							
	American Republic	SU	1981	D	24,800	634' 10"	68' 00"	40' 00"
	American Spirit	SU	1978	D	59,700	1,004' 00"	105' 00"	50' 00"
	(George A. Stinson '78-'04)							
	Buffalo {3}	SU	1978	D	23,800	634' 10"	68' 00"	40' 00"
	H. Lee White {2}	SU	1974	D	35,200	704' 00"	78' 00"	45' 00"
	Indiana Harbor	SU	1979	D	78,850	1,000' 00"	105' 00"	56' 00"
	John J. Boland {4}	SU	1973	D	33,800	680' 00"	78' 00"	45' 00"
	(Charles E. Wilson '73-'00)							
	Sam Laud	SU	1975	D	23,800	634' 10"	68' 00"	40' 00"
	St. Clair {3}	SU	1976	D	44,000	770' 00"	92' 00"	52' 00"
	Walter J. McCarthy Jr.	SU	1977	D	78,850	1,000' 00"	105' 00"	56' 00"
	(Belle River '77-'90)							
A-10	**AMHERST CONSTRUCTION INC., WILLIAMSVILLE, NY**							
	Burro	TB	1965	D	19*	36' 00"	13' 03"	5' 01"
	Marcey	TB	1966	D	22*	42' 00"	12' 06"	6' 10"
A-11	**ANDRIE, INC., MUSKEGON, MI**							
	A-390	TK	1982	B	2,346*	310' 00"	60' 00"	19' 03"
	(Canonie 40 '82-'92)							
	A-397	TK	1962	B	2,928*	270' 00"	60' 00"	25' 00"
	(Auntie Mame '62-'91, Iron Mike '91-'93)							
	A-410	TK	1955	B	3,793*	335' 00"	54' 00"	26' 06"
	(Methane '55-'63, B-6400 '63-'71, Kelly '71-'86, Canonie 50 '86-'93)							
	Barbara Andrie	TB	1940	D	298*	121' 10"	29' 06"	16' 00"
	(Edmond J. Moran '40-'76)							
	Barbara Rita	TB	1981	D	15*	36' 00"	14' 00"	6' 00"
	Candace Andrie	CS	1958	B	1,000	150' 00"	52' 00"	10' 00"
	(MCD '58-'73, Minnesota '73-'88)							
	Clara Andrie	DR	1930	B	1,000	110' 00"	30' 00"	6' 10"
	John Joseph	TB	1993	D	15*	40' 00"	14' 00"	5' 00"
	Karen Andrie {2}	TB	1965	D	433*	120' 00"	31' 06"	16' 00"
	(Sarah Hays '65-'93)							
	Mari Beth Andrie	TB	1961	D	147*	87' 00"	24' 00"	11' 06"
	(Gladys Bea '61-'73, American Viking '73-'83)							
	Meredith Andrie	DS	1971	B	521*	140' 00"	50' 00"	9' 00"
	(Illinois '71-'02)							
	Rebecca Lynn	TB	1964	D	433*	120' 00"	31' 08"	18' 09"
	(Kathrine Clewis '64-'96)							
	Robert Purcell	TB	1952	D	28*	45' 00"	12' 06"	7' 09"
	Scow 50	DB	1977	B	2,100	180' 00"	54' 00"	12' 00"
	U-738	DB	1981	B	2,100	180' 00"	54' 00"	12' 00"
	LAFARGE CORP., MUSKEGON, MI – VESSELS MANAGED BY ANDRIE, INC.							
	Integrity	CC	1996	B	14,000	460' 00"	70' 00"	37' 00"
	Jacklyn M.	AT	1976	D	198*	140' 02"	40' 01"	22' 03"
	(Andrew Martin '76-'90, Robert L. Torres '90-'94)							
	[ATB Jacklyn M. / Integrity OA dimensions together]					543' 00"	70' 00"	37' 00"

Birchglen makes an April 2003 passage through the Soo Locks. *(JRoger LeLievre)*

Fleet #.	Fleet Name Vessel Name	Type of Vessel	Year Built	Type of Engine	Cargo Cap. or Gross*	Overall Length	Breadth	Depth or Draft*
A-12	**APOSTLE ISLANDS CRUISE SERVICE, BAYFIELD, WI**							
	Eagle Island	ES	1976	D	12*	42' 00"	14' 00"	3' 06"
	(Little Jim '76-'93, Grampa Woo '93-'96)							
	Island Princess {2}	ES	1973	D	63*	65' 07"	20' 05"	7' 03"
	Sea Queen II	ES	1971	D	12*	42' 00"	14' 00"	2' 07"
	Zeeto	ES/3S	1957	W	35*	54' 00"	16' 00"	
A-13	**ARNOLD TRANSIT CO., MACKINAC ISLAND, MI**							
	Algomah	PF/PK	1961	D	125	93' 00"	31' 00"	8' 00"
	Beaver	CF	1952	D	87*	64' 09"	30' 02"	8' 00"
	Chippewa {6}	PF/PK	1962	D	125	93' 00"	31' 00"	8' 00"
	Corsair	CF	1955	D	98*	94' 06"	33' 00"	8' 06"
	Huron {5}	PF/PK	1955	D	80	91' 06"	25' 00"	10' 01"
	Island Express	PC	1988	D	90*	82' 07"	28' 06"	8' 05"
	Mackinac Express	PC	1987	D	90*	82' 07"	28' 06"	8' 05"
	Mackinac Islander	CF	1947	D	99*	84' 00"	30' 00"	8' 03"
	(Drummond Islander '47-'02)							
	Ottawa {2}	PF/PK	1959	D	125	93' 00"	31' 00"	8' 00"
	Straits Express	PC	1995	D	99*	101' 00"	29' 11"	6' 08"
	Straits of Mackinac II	PF/PK	1969	D	89*	89' 11"	27' 00"	8' 08"
A-14	**ATLANTIC TOWING LTD., SAINT JOHN, NB**							
	ATL 2301	DB	1977	B	3,500	230' 00"	60' 00"	14' 00"
	ATL 2302	DB	1977	B	3,500	230' 00"	60' 00"	14' 00"
	ATL 2401	DB	1981	B	4,310	240' 00"	70' 00"	15' 00"
	ATL 2402	DB	1981	B	4,310	240' 00"	70' 00"	15' 00"
	Atlantic Beech	TB	1983	D	294*	104' 02"	30' 03"	13' 02"
	(Irving Beech '83-'98)							
	Atlantic Birch	TB	1967	D	827*	162' 03"	38' 02"	19' 08"
	(Irving Birch '67-'99)							
	Atlantic Eagle	TB	1999	D	3,080*	247' 06"	59' 05"	19' 10"
	Atlantic Elm	TB	1980	D	427*	116' 01"	31' 06"	18' 08"
	(Irving Elm '80-'98)							
	Atlantic Hawk	TB	2000	D	3,080*	247' 06"	59' 05"	19' 10"
	Atlantic Hemlock	TT	1996	D	290*	101' 00"	36' 06"	12' 06"
	Atlantic Hickory	TB	1973	D	886*	153' 06"	38' 10"	22' 00"
	(Irving Miami '73-'95)							
	Atlantic Kingfisher	TB	2002	D	3,453*	239' 08"	59' 00"	26' 02"
	Atlantic Larch	TT	1999	D	392*	101' 01"	36' 07"	17' 01"
	Atlantic Maple	TB	1966	D	487*	125' 08"	32' 04"	17' 06"
	(Irving Maple '66-'98)							
	Atlantic Osprey	TB	2003	D	3,453*	239' 08"	59' 00"	26' 02"
	Atlantic Pine	TB	1976	D	159*	70' 00"	24' 00"	7' 08"
	(Grampa Shorty '76-'76, Irving Pine '76-'98)							
	Atlantic Poplar	TB	1965	D	195*	96' 06"	30' 00"	14' 00"
	(Amherstburg '65-'75, Irving Poplar '75-'96)							
	Atlantic Spruce {2}	TT	1998	D	290*	101' 00"	36' 06"	17' 00"
	Atlantic Teak	TB	1976	D	265*	104' 00"	30' 00"	14' 03"
	(Essar '76-'79, Irving Teak '79-'96)							
	Atlantic Willow	TT	1998	D	360*	101' 00"	36' 06"	17' 00"
	Irving Dolphin	TK/DB	1964	B	1,441	200' 00"	50' 00"	13' 00"
	Irving Juniper	TB	1961	D	247*	110' 00"	27' 02"	13' 03"
	(Thorness '61-'84, Irving Juniper '84-'98, Atlantic Juniper '98-'99)							
B-1	**B & L TUG SERVICE, THESSALON, ON**							
	C. West Pete	TB	1958	D	29*	65' 00"	17' 05"	6' 00"
B-2	**BARGE TRANSPORTATION, INC., DETROIT, MI**							
	Cherokee {2}	DB	1943	B	1,200	155' 00"	50' 00"	13' 06"

Fleet #.	Fleet Name / Vessel Name	Type of Vessel	Year Built	Type of Engine	Cargo Cap. or Gross*	Overall Length	Breadth	Depth or Draft*
B-3	**BASIC TOWING, INC., ESCANABA, MI**							
	BMI-105	DB	1999	B	1,500	200' 00"	42' 06"	10' 00"
	Danicia	TB	1944	D	382*	110' 02"	27' 03"	15' 07"
	(USCGC Chinook [WYT / WYTM-96] '44-'86, Tracie B '86-'98)							
	Erika Kobasic	TB	1939	D	226*	110' 00"	26' 05"	15' 01"
	(USCGC Arundel [WYT / WYTM-90] '39-'84, Karen Andrie {1} '84-'90)							
	Escort	TB	1969	D	26*	50' 00"	13' 00"	7' 00"
	Krystal	TB	1954	D		45' 00"	13' 00"	7' 00"
	(Thunder Bay '54-'02)							
	L. E. Block	BC	1927	T	15,900	621' 00"	64' 00"	33' 00"
	(Last operated Oct. 31, 1981; Laid up at Escanaba, MI.)							
	Mr. Micky	TK	1940	B	664*	195' 00"	35' 00"	10' 00"
	Sea Chief	TB	1952	D	390*	107' 00"	26' 06"	14' 10"
	(U. S. Army LT-1944 .'52-'62, USCOE Washington '62-"00)							
B-4	**BAY CITY BOAT LINE, LLC, BAY CITY, MI**							
	Islander {1}	ES	1946	D	39*	53' 04"	21' 00"	5' 05"
	Princess Wenonah	ES	1954	D	96*	64' 09"	32' 09"	9' 09"
	(William M. Miller '54-'98)							
	West Shore {2}	ES	1947	D	94*	64' 10"	30' 00"	9' 03"
B-5	**BAY SHIPBUILDING CO., STURGEON BAY, WI**							
	Bayship	TB	1943	D	19*	45' 00"	12' 06"	6' 00"
	(Sturshipco)							
B-6	**BAYSAIL, BAY CITY, MI**							
	Appledore IV	2S/ES	1989	W/D	72*	85' 00"	19' 00"	9' 06"
	Appledore V	2S/ES	1992	W/D	34*	65' 00"	16' 00"	8' 06"
B-7	**BEAVER ISLAND BOAT CO., CHARLEVOIX, MI**							
	Beaver Islander	PF/CF	1963	D	95*	96' 03"	27' 05"	9' 09"
	Emerald Isle {2}	PF/CF	1997	D	95*	130' 00"	38' 08"	12' 00"
B-8	**BEST OF ALL TOURS, ERIE, PA**							
	Lady Kate {2}	ES	1952	D	11*	65' 00"	16' 06"	4' 00"
	(G. A. Boeckling II '52-?, Cedar Point III ?-'89, Island Trader '89-'97)							
B-9	**BILLINGTON CONTRACTING, INC., DULUTH, MN**							
	Col. D.D. Gaillard	DB	1916	B		116' 00"	40' 00"	11' 06"
	Coleman	CS	1923	B	502*	153' 06"	40' 06"	10' 06"
	Houghton	TB	1944	D	21*	45' 00"	13' 00"	6' 00"
	Panama	DS	1942	B		210' 01"	44' 01"	10' 01"
	Seneca	TB	1939	D	132*	94' 020"	22' 00"	9' 00"
	(General {1} '39-'39, Raymond Card '39-'40, USS Keshena '40-'47, Mary L. McAllister '47-'81)							
B-10	**BLACK CREEK CONSTRUCTION CO., NANTICOKE, ON**							
	H.H. Misner	TB	1946	D	28*	66' 09"	16' 04"	4' 05"
B-11	**BLUE HERON CO., TOBERMORY, ON**							
	Blue Heron V	ES	1983	D	24*	54' 06"	17' 05"	7' 02"
	Great Blue Heron	ES	1994	D	112*	79' 00"	22' 00"	6' 05"
B-12	**BLUE WATER EXCURSIONS, INC., FORT GRATIOT, MI**							
	Huron Lady II	ES	1993	D	82*	65' 00"	19' 00"	10' 00"
	(Lady Lumina '93-'99)							
B-13	**BLUE WATER FERRY LTD., SOMBRA, ON**							
	Daldean	CF	1951	D	145*	75' 00"	35' 00"	7' 00"
	Ontamich	CF	1939	D	55*	65' 00"	28' 10"	8' 06"
	(Harsens Island '39-'73)							

CHARLES M. BEEGHLY

Vessel Spotlight

The familiar bulk carrier *Charles M. Beeghly* began her career on the Great Lakes in 1958 as the green-hulled *Shenango II* for the Shenango Furnace Co. of Cleveland.

Built at a cost of approximately $8 million by the American Shipbuilding Company of Toledo, the *Shenango II* was the last of three 710-footers to enter service built to similar plans, the other two vessels being *George M. Humphrey* (1954) and *John Sherwin* (1958).

Shenango II in the early 1960s. *(Tom Manse)*

The Beeghly as she looks today. *(Roger LeLievre)*

On May 9, 1962, *Shenango II* established a wheat record for U.S. flagged vessels when she loaded 689,000 bushels at Chicago bound for Trois-Rivieres, Quebec. She set a winter storage cargo record in December 1965 when she loaded 910,340 bushels of oats at Duluth for storage at Buffalo.

Shenango II was sold in 1967 to Pickands-Mather's Interlake Steamship Co. of Cleveland along with her smaller fleet mate *William P. Snyder*. The *Snyder* was immediately chartered back to Shenango Furnace for 1967 and 1968. The *Shenango II* was renamed *Charles M. Beeghly*.

During her 1971/'72 winter lay-up at Fraser Shipyards in Superior, Wis., the *Beeghly* was lengthened 96 feet, increasing her capacity to 31,000 tons. Upon returning to service in 1972, she was the third largest vessel on the Great Lakes. exceeded in length only by the *Roger Blough* (858 feet) and the *Stewart Cort* (1,000 feet). On July 28, 1978, she set a Lorain, Ohio, record, delivering 31,015 tons of iron ore pellets loaded at Taconite Harbor, Minn.

Since it was becoming increasingly expensive and time-consuming to unload cargoes of this size using shore-based equipment, the *Beeghly* was converted to a self-unloader during winter lay-up in 1980/'81 at Fraser Shipyards. The conversion was probably a life-saver, as her sister ship and fleet mate *John Sherwin* was not converted and has not seen service since late 1981. **– George Wharton**

Fleet #.	Fleet Name Vessel Name	Type of Vessel	Year Built	Type of Engine	Cargo Cap. or Gross*	Overall Length	Breadth	Depth or Draft*
B-14	**BUFFALO CHARTERS, INC. / NIAGARA CLIPPER, INC., BUFFALO, NY**							
	Miss Buffalo II	ES	1972	D	88*	86' 00"	24' 00"	6' 00"
	Niagara Clipper	ES	1983	D	65*	112' 00"	29' 00"	6' 06"*
B-15	**BUFFALO INDUSTRIAL DIVING, BUFFALO, NY**							
	Buckeye State	TB	1951	D	21*	45' 00"	12' 04"	6' 06"
	Deep See	TB	1992	D	9*	35' 00"	10' 00"	04' 00"
	J. G. II	TB	1944	D	16*	42' 03"	13' 00"	5' 06"
	West Wind	TB	1941	D	54*	60' 04"	17' 01"	7' 07"
	(West Wind '41-'46, Russell 2 '61-'97)							
	Joanne	TB	1935	D	18*	42' 06"	11' 09"	6' 09"
	(Paul L. Luedtke '94-'98)							
	Ruby	TB	1947	D	93*	68' 09"	20' 00"	8' 00"
	(ST-497 '47-??, Russell 9 '46-'63, Elizabeth McAllister '63-??, Beverly ??-'97, Ruby M. '97-'01)							
B-16	**BUFFALO STATE COLLEGE GREAT LAKES CENTER, BUFFALO, NY**							
	Seneca	RV	2001	D		46' 00"		
B-17	**BUFFALO PUBLIC WORKS DEPT., BUFFALO, NY**							
	Edward M. Cotter	FB	1900	D	208*	118' 00"	24' 00"	11' 06"
	(W. S. Grattan 1900-'53, Firefighter '53-'54)							
B-18	**BUSCH MARINE, INC., CARROLLTON, MI**							
	Gregory J. Busch	TB	1919	D	299*	151' 00"	28' 00"	16' 09"
	(Humaconna '19-'77)							
	STC 2004	DB	1986	B	2,364	240' 00"	50' 00"	9' 05"
C-1	**CALUMET RIVER FLEETING, INC., CHICAGO, IL**							
	Des Plaines	TB	1956	D	175*	98' 00"	28' 00"	8' 04"*
	John M. Perry	TB	1954	D	76*	66' 00"	19' 00"	9' 00"
	(Sanita '54-'77, Soo Chief '77-'81, Susan M. Selvick '81-'96, Nathan S. '96-'02)							
	John M. Selvick	TB	1898	D	256*	118' 00"	24' 00"	12' 07"
	(Illinois {1} 1898-'41, John Roen III '41-'74)							
	Jimmy Wray	TB	1954	D	95*	72' 00"	22' 00"	7' 00"*
	(Sea Wolf '54-'01)							
C-2	**CANADA STEAMSHIP LINES, INC., MONTREAL, QC**							
	Atlantic Erie	SU	1985	D	38,200	736' 07"	75' 10"	50' 00"
	(Hon. Paul Martin '85-'88)							
	Atlantic Huron {2}	SU	1984	D	34,600	736' 07"	78' 01"	46' 06"
	(Prairie Harvest '84-'89, Atlantic Huron {2} '89-'94, Melvin H. Baker II {2} '94-'97)							
	(Converted to a self-unloader, '89; widened by 3' – '03)							
	Atlantic Superior	SU	1982	D	38,900	730' 00"	75' 10"	50' 00"
	(Atlantic Superior '82-'97, M. H. Baker III '97-'03)							
	Birchglen {2}	BC	1983	D	35,315	730' 01"	75' 09"	48' 00"
	(Canada Marquis '83-'91, Federal Richelieu '91-'91, Federal MacKenzie '91-'01, MacKenzie '01-'02)							
	Cedarglen {2}	BC	1959	D	29,100	730' 00"	75' 09"	40' 02"
	(Ems Ore '59-'76, Montcliffe Hall '76-'88, Cartierdoc '88-'02)							
	CSL Laurentien	SU	1977	D	34,938	739' 10"	78' 01"	48' 05"
	(Stern section: Louis R. Desmarais '77-'01) (Rebuilt with new forebody, '01)							
	CSL Niagara	SU	1972	D	34,938	739' 10"	78' 01"	48' 05"
	(Stern section: J. W. McGiffin '72-'99) (Rebuilt with a new forebody, '99)							
	CSL Tadoussac	SU	1969	D	29,700	730' 00"	78' 00"	42' 00"
	(Tadoussac {2} '69-'01) (Rebuilt with new midbody, widened by 3'-'01)							
	Ferbec	BC	1966	D	56,887	732' 06"	104' 02"	57' 09"
	(Fugaku Maru '65-'77)							
	Frontenac {5}	SU	1968	D	27,500	729' 07"	75' 03"	39' 08"
	(Converted to a self-unloader, '73)							
	Halifax	SU	1963	T	30,100	730' 02"	75' 00"	39' 03"
	(Frankcliffe Hall {2} '63-'88; (Converted to a self-unloader, deepened 6'-'80)							
	Jean Parisien	SU	1977	D	33,000	730' 00"	75' 00"	46' 06"

Fleet #.	Fleet Name Vessel Name	Type of Vessel	Year Built	Type of Engine	Cargo Cap. or Gross*	Overall Length	Breadth	Depth or Draft*
	Nanticoke	SU	1980	D	35,100	729' 10"	75' 08"	46' 06"
	Pineglen {2}	BC	1985	D	32,600	736' 07"	75' 10"	42' 00"
	(Paterson '85-'02)							
	Rt. Hon. Paul J. Martin	SU	1973	D	34,938	739' 10"	78' 01"	48' 05"
	(Stern section: H. M. Griffith '73-'00) (Rebuilt with a new forebody, '00)							
	Spruceglen {2}	BC	1983	D	35,315	730' 01"	75' 09"	48' 00"
	(Selkirk Settler '83-'91, Federal St. Louis '91-'91, Federal Fraser {2} '91-2001, Fraser '01-'02)							
	Teakglen	BC	1967	D	17,650	607' 10"	62' 00"	36' 00"
	(Mantadoc '67-'02) (In use as a grain storage vessel at Goderich, ON.)							
C-3	**CANADIAN AMERICAN TRANSPORTATION SYSTEM (CATS) LLC., ROCHESTER, NY**							
	Spirit of Ontario 1	CF	2004	D		284' 00"	78' 00'	
C-4	**CANADIAN COAST GUARD (MINISTER OF FISHERIES AND OCEANS), OTTAWA, ON**							
	CENTRAL AND ARCTIC REGION, SARNIA, ON							
	Advent	RV	1972	D	72*	77' 01"	18' 05"	5' 03"*
	Bittern	SR	1982	D	21*	40' 08"	13' 06"	4' 04"
	Cape Hurd	SR	1982	D	55*	70' 10"	18' 00"	8' 09"
	(CG 126 '82-'85)							
	Caribou Isle	BT	1985	D	92*	75' 06"	19' 08"	7' 04"
	Cove Isle	BT	1980	D	92*	65' 07"	19' 08"	7' 04"
	Griffon	IB	1970	D	2,212*	234' 00"	49' 00"	21' 06"
	Gull Isle	BT	1980	D	80*	65' 07"	19' 08"	7' 04"
	Limnos	RV	1968	D	460*	147' 00"	32' 00"	12' 00"
	Louis M. Lauzier	RV	1976	D	322*	125' 00"	27' 01"	11' 06"
	(Cape Harrison '76-'83)							
	Samuel Risley	IB	1985	D	1,988*	228' 09"	47' 01"	21' 09"
	Shark	RV	1971	D	30*	52' 06"	14' 09"	7' 03"
	Simcoe	BT	1962	D	961*	179' 01"	38' 00"	15' 06"
	Sora	SR	1982	D	21*	41' 00"	14' 01"	4' 04"
	Spray	SR	1994	D	42*	51' 09"	17' 00"	8' 02"

The Interlake fleet's *Kaye E. Barker* and *James R. Barker* pass on the St. Marys River. The two vessels' namesakes are husband and wife. *(Roger LeLievre)*

Fleet #.	Fleet Name Vessel Name	Type of Vessel	Year Built	Type of Engine	Cargo Cap. or Gross*	Overall Length	Breadth	Depth or Draft*
	Spume	SR	1994	D	42*	51' 09"	17' 00"	8' 02"
	Tobermory	SR	1973	D	17*	44' 01"	12' 06"	6' 07"
	Westfort	SR	1973	D	22*	44' 01"	12' 08"	5' 11"
	LAURENTIAN REGION, QUEBEC, QC							
	Amundsen	RV	1978	D	5,910*	295' 09"	63' 09"	31' 04"
	(Sir John Franklin '78-'03)							
	Calanus II	RV	1991	D	138.5*	65' 03"	22' 06"	10' 04"
	Des Groseilliers	IB	1983	D	5,910*	322' 07"	64' 00"	35' 06"
	F. C. G. Smith	SV	1985	D	439*	114' 02"	45' 11"	11' 02"
	Frederick G. Creed	SV	1988	D	151*	66' 11"	32' 00"	11' 10"
	George R. Pearkes	IB	1986	D	3,809*	272' 04"	53' 02"	25' 02"
	Ile Saint-Ours	BT	1986	D	92*	75' 06"	19' 08"	7' 04"
	Isle Rouge	SR	1980	D	57*	70' 10"	18' 01"	8' 09"
	Louisbourg	RV	1977	D	295*	124' 00"	26' 11"	11' 06"
	Martha L. Black	IB	1986	D	3,818*	272' 04"	53' 02"	25' 02"
	Pierre Radisson	IB	1978	D	5,910*	322' 00"	62' 10"	35' 06"
	Tracy	BT	1968	D	963*	181' 01"	38' 00"	16' 00"
	Waban-Aki	AV	1987	D	48*	80' 05"	36' 09"	26' 10"
	MARITIMES REGION, DARTMOUTH, NS							
	Alfred Needler	RV	1982	D	959*	165' 09"	36' 09"	22' 01"
	Cygnus	RV	1982	D	1,211*	205' 01"	40' 00"	15' 05"
	Earl Grey	IB	1986	D	1,971*	230' 00"	46' 02"	22' 01"
	Edward Cornwallis	IB	1986	D	3,727*	272' 04"	53' 02"	24' 06"
	Hudson	RV	1963	D	3,740*	296' 07"	50' 06"	32' 10"
	Ile Des Barques	BT	1985	D	92*	75' 06"	19' 08"	7' 04"
	Louis S. St-Laurent	IB	1969	D	10,908*	392' 06"	80' 00"	53' 06"
	Matthew	RV	1990	D	857*	165' 00"	34' 05"	16' 05"
	Parizeau	RV	1967	D	1,328*	211' 07"	40' 00"	21' 00"
	Provo Wallis	BT	1969	D	1,313*	209' 03"	42' 08"	16' 07"
	Sir William Alexander	IB	1986	D	3,550*	272' 06"	45' 00"	17' 06"
	Terry Fox	IB	1983	D	4,234*	288' 09"	58' 06"	29' 08"
	NEWFOUNDLAND REGION, ST. JOHN'S, NF							
	Ann Harvey	IB	1987	D	3,854*	272' 04"	53' 02"	25' 10"
	Cape Roger	RV	1977	D	1,255*	205' 01"	35' 05"	22' 00"
	Henry Larsen	IB	1988	D	6,172*	327' 05"	64' 08"	35' 09"
	J. E. Bernier	IB	1967	D	2,457*	231' 04"	49' 00"	16' 00"
	Leonard J. Cowley	RV	1984	D	2,243*	236' 03"	46' 07"	24' 03"
	Sir Wilfred Grenfell	SR	1987	D	2,404*	224' 08"	49' 03"	22' 06"
	Teleost	RV	1988	D	2,337*	206' 08"	46' 07"	29' 02"
	(Atlantic Champion '88-'95)							
	Wilfred Templeman	RV	1981	D	925*	166' 00"	36' 09"	22' 01"
C-5	**CANADIAN SAILING EXPEDITIONS INC., HALIFAX, NS**							
	Caledonia	3S	1947	D	958*	245' 00"	30' 01"	15' 04"
	(Akurey '47-'66, Akeroy '66-'68, Petrel '68-'76, Petrel V '76-'00, Cape Harrisson '00-'02)							
	True North	2M	1973	D/W	24*	46' 00"	13' 04"	9' 0"
C-6	**CAPTAIN NORMAC'S RIVERBOAT INN LTD., TORONTO, ON**							
	Jadran		1957	D	2,520*	295' 06"	42' 08"	24' 08"
	(Former Jadranska Plovidba vessel last operated in 1975. Now in use as a floating restaurant.)							
C-7	**CARY McMANUS, DULUTH, MN**							
	Duluth	DR	1962	B	401*	106' 00"	36' 00"	8' 04"
C-8	**CELEST BAY TIMBER & MARINE, DULUTH, MN**							
	Essayons	TB	1908	R	117*	85' 06"	21' 02"	11' 09"
C-9	**CEMBA MOTORSHIPS LTD., PELEE ISLAND, ON**							
	Cemba	TK	1960	D	17*	50' 00"	15' 06"	7' 06"

Fleet #.	Fleet Name / Vessel Name	Type of Vessel	Year Built	Type of Engine	Cargo Cap. or Gross*	Overall Length	Breadth	Depth or Draft*
C-10	**CENTRAL MARINE LOGISTICS, INC., GRIFFITH, IN**							
	Edward L. Ryerson	BC	1960	T	27,500	730' 00"	75' 00"	39' 00"
	(Last operated Dec. 12, 1998 – 5 year survey expired Dec. 2001; Laid up in Sturgeon Bay, WI.)							
	Joseph L. Block	SU	1976	D	37,200	728' 00"	78' 00"	45' 00"
	Wilfred Sykes	SU	1949	T	21,500	678' 00"	70' 00"	37' 00"
	(Converted to a self-unloader, '75)							
C-11	**CHAMPION'S AUTO FERRY, INC., ALGONAC, MI**							
	Champion {1}	CF	1941	D	65*	65' 00"	29' 00"	8' 06"
	Middle Channel	CF	1997	D	97*	79' 00"	31' 00"	8' 03"
	North Channel	CF	1967	D	67*	75' 00"	30' 00"	8' 00"
	South Channel	CF	1973	D	94*	79' 00"	31' 00"	8' 03"
C-12	**CHARLEVOIX COUNTY ROAD COMMISSION, BOYNE CITY, MI**							
	Charlevoix {1}	CF	1926	D	43*	50' 00"	32' 00"	3' 09"
C-13	**CHICAGO CRUISES, INC., CHICAGO, IL**							
	Chicago II	ES	1983	D	42*	123' 03"	28' 06"	7' 00"
	(Star of Sandford '83-'86, Star of Charlevoix {1} '86-'87, Star of Toronto '87-'87, Star of Chicago II '87-'94)							
C-14	**CHICAGO FIRE DEPARTMENT, CHICAGO, IL**							
	Victor L. Schlaeger	FB	1949	D	350*	92' 06"	24' 00"	11' 00"
C-15	**CHICAGO FROM THE LAKE LTD., CHICAGO, IL**							
	Fort Dearborn	ES	1985	D	72*	64' 10"	22' 00"	7' 04"
	Marquette {6}	ES	1957	D	29*	50' 07"	15' 00"	4' 00"
C-16	**CHICAGO WATER PUMPING STATION, CHICAGO, IL**							
	James J. Versluis	TB	1957	D	126*	83' 00"	22' 00"	11' 02"
C-17	**CITY OF TORONTO PARKS & RECREATION DEPARTMENT, TORONTO, ON** **ISLAND FERRY SERVICE**							
	Ongiara	PF	1963	D	180*	78' 00"	36' 00"	9' 09"
	Sam McBride	PF	1939	D	412*	129' 00"	34' 11"	6' 00"
	Thomas Rennie	PF	1950	D	419*	129' 00"	32' 11"	6' 00"
	Trillium	PF	1910	R	611*	150' 00"	30' 00"	8' 04"
	William Inglis	PF	1935	D	238*	99' 00"	24' 10"	6' 00"
	(Shamrock {2} '35-'37)							
C-18	**CITY OF TORONTO PUBLIC WORKS DEPARTMENT, TORONTO, ON**							
	Ned Hanlan II	TB	1966	D	26*	41' 06"	14' 01"	5' 05"
C-19	**CLAYTON FIRE DEPARTMENT, CLAYTON, NY**							
	Last Chance	FB	2003	D		36' 00"	13' 00"	2' 04"
C-20	**CLEVELAND FIRE DEPARTMENT, CLEVELAND, OH**							
	Anthony J. Celebrezze	FB	1961	D	42*	66' 00"	17' 00"	5' 00"
C-21	**CLIFFORD TYNER, BARBEAU, MI**							
	Neebish Islander	CF	1950	D	49*	55' 00"	20' 07"	6' 00"
	(Lillifred '50-'56) (Last operated in 1995; Laid up at Neebish Island, MI.)							
C-22	**CLUB CANAMAC CRUISES, TORONTO, ON**							
	Aurora Borealis	ES	1983	D	277*	101' 00"	24' 00"	6' 00"*
	Carolina Borealis	ES	1943	D	182*	84' 06"	20' 00"	10' 04"
	(HMCS Glenmont [W-27] '43-'45, Glenmont '43-'02) (Rebuilt from a tug, '02)							
	Jaguar II	ES	1968	D	142*	95' 03"	20' 00"	9' 00"
	(Jaguar '68-'86)							
	Stella Borealis	ES	1989	D	356*	118' 00"	26' 00"	7' 00"
C-23	**COCKBURN ISLAND LOGGING INC., SAULT STE. MARIE, ON**							
	Intrepid III	TB	1976	D	39*	66' 00"	17' 00"	7' 06"

Joseph L. Block about to swing to port and enter the ore docks at Two Harbors, Minn. *(Roger LeLievre)*

Fleet #.	Fleet Name Vessel Name	Type of Vessel	Year Built	Type of Engine	Cargo Cap. or Gross*	Overall Length	Breadth	Depth or Draft*
C-24	**COLUMBIA YACHT CLUB, CHICAGO, IL**							
	Abegweit {1}	CF	1947	D	6,694*	372' 06"	61' 00"	24' 09"
	(Abegweit {1} '47 - '81, Abby '81 - '97) (Former CN Marine, Inc. vessel, which last operated in 1981, is now in use as a private, floating clubhouse.)							
C-25	**CONTINENTAL MARINE, INC., LEMONT, IL**							
	Brandon E.	TB	1945	D	19*	42' 01"	12' 10"	5' 02"*
C-26	**COOPER MARINE LTD., SELKIRK, ON**							
	J. W. Cooper	PB	19845	D	25*	48' 00"	14' 07"	5' 00"
	Juleen I	PB	1972	D	23*	46' 00"	14' 01"	4' 05"
	Lady Kim	PB	1974	D	20*	44' 00"	13' 00"	4' 00"
	Mrs. C	PB	1990	D	28*	50' 00"	16' 00"	5' 00"
C-27	**CORPORATION OF THE TOWNSHIP OF FRONTENAC ISLANDS, WOLFE ISLAND, ON**							
	Howe Islander	CF	1946	D	13*	53' 00"	12' 00"	3' 00"
	Simcoe Islander	PF	1964	D	24*	47' 09"	18' 00"	3' 06"
C-28	**CROISIERES AML, INC., QUEBEC, QC**							
	Cavalier des Mers	ES	1974	D	161*	91' 08"1	21' 03"	8' 05"
	(Marine Sprinter '74-'84)							
	Cavalier Grand Fleuve	ES	1987	D	499*	145' 00"	30' 00"	5' 06"
	Cavalier Maxim	ES	1962	D	752*	191' 02"	42' 00"	11' 07"
	(Osborne Castle '62-'78, Le Gobelet D' Argent '78-'88, Gobelet D' Argent '88-'89, Le Maxim '89-'93)							
	Cavalier Royal	ES	1971	D	283*	125' 00"	24' 00"	5' 00"
	Louis-Jolliet	ES	1938	R	2,436*	170' 01"	70' 00"	17' 00"
	Miss Olympia	ES	1972	D	29*	62' 08"	14' 00"	4' 08"
	Nouvelle-Orleans	ES	1989	D	234*	90' 00"	25' 00"	5' 03"
	Tandem	ES	1991	D	102*	66' 00"	22' 00"	2' 02"
	Transit	ES	1992	D	102*	66' 00"	22' 00"	2' 08"
C-29	**CROISIERES DES ILES DE SOREL, INC., SAINTE-ANNE-DE-SOREL, QC**							
	Le Survenant III	ES	1974	D	105*	65' 00"	13' 00"	5' 00"
C-30	**CROISIERES M/S JACQUES-CARTIER, TROIS-RIVIERES, QC**							
	Jacques Cartier	ES	1924	D	441*	135' 00"	35' 00"	10' 00"
	Le Draveur	ES	1992	D	79*	58' 07"	22' 00"	5' 24"
C-31	**CROISIERES MARJOLAINE, INC., CHICOUTIMI, QC**							
	Marjolaine II	ES	1904	D	399*	92' 00"	27' 00"	9' 00"
C-32	**CROISIERES RICHELIEU, INC., SAINT-JEAN-SUR-RICHELIEU, QC**							
	Fort Saint-Jean II	ES	1967	D	109*	62' 09"	19' 10"	
	(Miss Gananoque '67-'77)							
	Suroit IV	ES	1973	D	64*	58' 00"	16' 00"	10' 04"
	(Miss Montreal '73-'99)							
D-1	**DALE T. DEAN – WALPOLE-ALGONAC FERRY LINE, PORT LAMBTON, ON**							
	City of Algonac	CF	1990	D	92*	80' 04"	26' 01"	6' 09"
	Walpole Islander	CF	1986	D	71*	74' 00"	33' 00"	7' 00"
D-2	**DAN MINOR & SONS, INC., PORT COLBORNE, ON**							
	Andrea Marie I	TB	1963	D	87*	75' 02"	24' 07"	7' 03"
	Jeanette M.	TB	1973	D	31*	68' 08"	20' 00"	4' 05"
	Susan Michelle	TB	1995	D	89*	79' 10"	20' 11"	6' 02"
	Welland	TB	1954	D	94*	86' 00"	20' 00"	8' 00"
D-3	**DAWES MARINE TUG & BARGE, INC., NORTH TONAWANDA, NY**							
	Fourth Coast	TB	1957	D	17*	40' 00"	12' 06"	4' 00"
	Sand Pebble	TB	1969	D	30*	48' 00"	15' 00"	8' 00"
	Tommy Ray	TB	1954	D	19*	45' 00"	12' 05"	6' 00"

Fleet #.	Fleet Name Vessel Name	Type of Vessel	Year Built	Type of Engine	Cargo Cap. or Gross*	Overall Length	Breadth	Depth or Draft*
D-4	**DEAN CONSTRUCTION CO. LTD., BELLE RIVER, ON**							
	Americo Dean	TB	1956	D	15*	45' 00"	15' 00"	5' 00"
	Annie M. Dean	TB	1981	D	58*	50' 00"	19' 00"	5' 00"
	Bobby Bowes	TB	1944	D	11*	37' 04"	10' 02"	3' 06"
	Jubilee	DR	1978	D	896*	149' 09"	56' 01"	11' 01"
	Neptune III	TB	1939	D	23*	53' 10"	15' 06"	5' 00"
	Wayne Dean	TB	1946	D	10*	45' 00"	13' 00"	5' 00"
D-5	**DENNIS DOUGHERTY, SAULT STE. MARIE, MI**							
	Gerald D. Neville	TB	1924	D	29*	50' 00"	13' 00"	4' 06"
	(Tobermory '24-'41, Champion {2} '41-'81)							
D-6	**DETROIT CITY FIRE DEPARTMENT, DETROIT, MI**							
	Curtis Randolph	FB	1979	D	85*	77' 10"	21' 06"	9' 03"
D-7	**DIAMOND JACK'S RIVER TOURS, GROSSE ILE, MI**							
	Diamond Belle	ES	1958	D	93*	93' 06"	25' 10"	10' 01"
	(Mackinac Islander {2} '58-'90, Sir Richard '90-'91)							
	Diamond Jack	ES	1955	D	82*	72' 00"	25' 00"	8' 00"
	(Emerald Isle {1} '55-'91)							
	Diamond Queen	ES	1956	D	94*	92' 00"	25' 00"	10' 00"
	(Mohawk '56-'96)							
D-8-	**DISSEN & JUHN CORP., MACEDON, NY**							
	Constructor	TB	1950	D	14*	39' 00"	11' 00"	5' 00"
	James W. Rickey	TB	1935	D	24*	46' 00"	14' 00"	7' 00"
D-9	**DOOR COUNTY CRUISES, LLC., STURGEON BAY, WI**							
	Fred A. Busse	ES	1937	D	99*	92' 00"	22' 04"	11' 00"
	Kimberly Selvick	TB	1975	D	93*	51' 10"	28' 00"	10' 00"
D-10	**DRAGAGE VERREAULT, INC., LES MECHINS, QC**							
	I.V. No. 8	DR	1967	B	348*	96' 03"	36' 00"	
	I.V. No. 9	GC	1936	D	148*	106' 08"	23' 10"	8' 05"
	(A.C.D. '36-'69)							
	I.V. No. 10	GC	1936	D	320*	110' 00"	23' 10"	8' 05"
	(G.T.D. '36-'69)							
	I.V. No. 11	GC	1935	D		106' 08"	24' 00"	8' 00"
	(Donpaco '35-'72)							
	I.V. No. 13	GC	1936	D	148*	106' 08"	24' 00"	8' 00"
	(Newscarrier '36-'72)							
	I.V. No. 14	GC	1937	D	229*	113' 00"	22' 05"	8' 06"
	(Kermic '37-'74)							
	Port Mechins	DR	1949	R	1,321*	200' 00"	40' 02"	18' 00"
	(Haffar '49-'88, Lockeport '88-'92)							
	Rosaire	DR	1952	B	714*	137' 07"	44' 06"	9' 01"
D-11	**DUC d' ORLEANS CRUISE BOAT, CORUNNA, ON**							
	Duc d' Orleans	ES	1943	D	112*	112' 00"	17' 10"	6' 03"
	(HMCS ML-105 '43-'48)							
D-12	**DULUTH TIMBER CO., DULUTH, MN**							
	Faith	DB	1906	B	705*	120'00"	38' 00"	10' 03"
D-13	**DUROCHER MARINE, DIVISION OF KOKOSING CONSTRUCTION CO., CHEBOYGAN, MI**							
	Champion {3}	TB	1974	D	125*	75' 00"	24' 00"	9' 06"
	General {2}	TB	1954	D	119*	71' 00"	19' 06"	9' 06"
	(U. S. Army ST-1999 '54-'61, USCOE Au Sable '61-'84, Challenger {3} '84-'87)							
	Joe Van	TB	1955	D	32*	57' 09"	16' 06"	9' 00"
	Valerie B.	TB	1981	D	101*	65' 00"	24' 06"	10' 00"
	(Mr. Joshua '81-?, Michael Van ?-'03)							

Fleet #.	Fleet Name Vessel Name	Type of Vessel	Year Built	Type of Engine	Cargo Cap. or Gross*	Overall Length	Breadth	Depth or Draft*
	Nancy Anne	TB	1969	D	73*	60' 00"	20' 00"	6' 00"
	Ray Durocher	TB	1943	D	20*	45' 06"	12' 05"	7' 06"
	Sam II	CS	1959	B	700	90' 00"	50' 00"	7' 02"
E-1	**EASTERN CANADA RESPONSE CORP. LTD., OTTAWA, ON**							
	Dover Light	EV	1968	B	7,870	146' 05"	50' 00"	13' 07"
	(Jackson Purchase '68-'83, Eliza S-1877 '83-'86)							
	S.M.T.B. No. 7	EV	1969	B	7,502	150' 00"	33' 00"	14' 00"
E-2	**EASTERN CANADA TOWING LTD., HALIFAX, NS**							
	Point Chebucto	TT	1993	D	412*	110' 00"	33' 00"	17' 00"
	Pointe Aux Basques	TB	1972	D	396*	105' 00"	33' 06"	19' 06"
	Pointe Sept-Iles	TB	1980	D	424*	105' 00"	34' 06"	19' 06"
	Point Halifax	TT	1986	D	417*	110' 00"	36' 00"	19' 00"
	Point Valiant {2}	TT	1998	D	302*	80' 00"	30' 01"	14' 09"
	(Launched as Ocean Jupiter {1})							
	Point Vibert	TB	1961	D	236*	96' 03"	28' 00"	14' 06"
	(Foundation Vibert '61-'73)							
	Point Vigour	TB	1962	D	207*	98' 05"	26' 10"	13' 05"
	(Foundation Vigour '62-'74)							
	Point Vim	TB	1962	D	207*	98' 05"	26' 10"	13' 05"
	(Foundation Vim '62-'74)							
E-3	**EASTERN UPPER PENINSULA TRANSIT AUTHORITY, SAULT STE. MARIE, MI**							
	Drummond Islander III	CF	1989	D	96*	108' 00"	37' 00"	12' 03"
	Drummond Islander IV	CF	2000	D	377*	148' 00"	40' 00"	12' 00"
	Neebish Islander II	CF	1946	D	90*	89' 00"	29' 06"	6' 09"
	(Sugar Islander '46-'95)							
	Sugar Islander II	CF	1995	D	223*	114' 00"	40' 00"	10' 00"

John G. Munson passes a saltwater tanker in the St. Clair River. *(Roger LeLievre)*

Fleet #.	Fleet Name Vessel Name	Type of Vessel	Year Built	Type of Engine	Cargo Cap. or Gross*	Overall Length	Breadth	Depth or Draft*
E-4	**ECOMERTOURS NORD-SUD, INC., RIMOUSKI, QC**							
	Echo Des Mers	PA	1966	D	887*	169' 09"	36' 05"	16' 05"
	(CCGS Nicolet '66-'95, 650 '95-'00)							
E-5	**EDELWEISS CRUISE DINING, MILWAUKEE, WI**							
	Edelweiss I	ES	1988	D	87*	64' 08"	18' 00"	6' 00"
	Edelweiss II	ES	1989	D	89*	73' 08"	20' 00"	7' 00"
E-6	**EDGEWATER BOAT TOURS, SARNIA, ON**							
	Macassa Bay	ES	1986	D	200*	93' 07"	29' 07"	10' 04"
E-7	**EDWARD E. GILLEN CO., MILWAUKEE, WI**							
	Andrew J.	TB	1950	D	25*	47' 00"	15' 07"	8' 00"
	Edith J.	TB	1962	D	19*	45' 03"	13' 00"	8' 00"
	Edward E. Gillen III	TB	1988	D	95*	75' 00"	26' 00"	9' 06"
E-8	**EDWIN M. ERICKSON, BAYFIELD, WI**							
	Outer Island	PK	1942	D	300	112' 00"	32' 00"	8' 06"
	(USS LSM-? '42-'46, Pluswood '46-'53)							
E-9	**EGAN MARINE CORP., LEMONT, IL**							
	Alice E.	TB	1950	D	183*	100' 00"	26' 00"	9' 00"
	(L. L. Wright '50-'55, Martin '55-'74, Mary Ann '74-'77, Judi C. '77-'94)							
	Daniel E.	TB	1967	D	70*	70' 00"	18' 06"	6' 08"
	(Foster M. Ford '67-'84)							
	Denise E.	TB	1912	D	138*	80' 07"	21' 06"	10' 03"
	(Caspian '12-'48, Trojan '48-'81, Cherokee {1} '81-'93)							
	Derek E.	TB	1907	D	85*	72' 06"	20' 01"	10' 06"
	(John Kelderhouse '07-'13, Sachem '13-'90)							
	Lisa E.	TB	1963	D	75*	65' 06"	20' 00"	8' 06"
	(Dixie Scout '63-'90)							
	Robin E.	TB	1889	D	123*	84' 09"	19' 00"	9' 00"
	(Asa W. Hughes 1889-'13, Triton {1} '13-'81, Navajo {2} '81-'92)							
E-10	**EMPIRE CRUISE LINES, U. S. A., ST. THOMAS, ON**							
	Marine Star	PA	1945	T	12,773*	520' 00"	71' 06"	43' 06"
	(USNS Marine Star '45-'55, Aquarama '55-'94) (Last operated in 1962; Laid up at Lackawanna, NY.)							
E-11	**EMPRESS OF CANADA ENTERPRISES LTD., TORONTO, ON**							
	Empress of Canada	ES	1980	D	399*	116' 00"	28' 00"	6' 06"*
	(Island Queen V {2} '80-'89)							
E-12	**EMPRESS RIVER CASINO, JOLIET, IL**							
	Empress	GA	1992	D	1,136*	214' 00"	66' 00"	6' 07"*
	Empress II	GA	1993	D	1,248*	230' 00"	67' 00"	6' 08"*
	Empress III	GA	1994	D	1,126*	288' 00"	76' 00"	10' 07"*
E-13	**ENTERPRISE 2000 CRUISE LINES LTD., TORONTO, ON**							
	Enterprise 2000	ES	1998	D	370*	121' 06"	35' 00"	6' 00"
E-14	**ENTREPRISE MARISSA INC., BEAUPORT, QC**							
	Soulanges	TB	1905	D	72*	77' 00"	17' 00"	8' 00"
	(Dandy '05-'39)							
E-15	**ERIE ISLANDS PETROLEUM, INC., PUT-IN-BAY, OH**							
	Cantankerous	TK	1955	D	323	53' 00"	14' 00"	5' 00"*
E-16	**ERIE-WESTERN PENNSYLVANIA PORT AUTHORITY, ERIE, PA**							
	Canadian Sailor	ES	2001	D	17*	40' 00"	12' 00"	05' 03"
E-17	**ESCANABA & LAKE SUPERIOR RAILROAD CO., WELLS, MI**							
	Roanoke {2}	TF	1930	B	30 rail cars	381' 06"	58' 03"	22' 06"
	(City of Flint 32 '30-'70) (Last operated May 1, 1994; Laid up at Toledo, OH.)							

Crew of the *Joshua A. Hatfield* sometime in the 1930s (above). A haircut Great Lakes-style on the *Hatfield's* fantail (right). *(Photos by Erhardt Peters)*

John A. Holloway makes an icy lockage at the Soo in the late 1950s. *(Tom Manse)*

Fleet #.	Fleet Name Vessel Name	Type of Vessel	Year Built	Type of Engine	Cargo Cap. or Gross*	Overall Length	Breadth	Depth or Draft*
	Pere Marquette 10	TF	1945	B	27 rail cars	400' 00"	53' 00"	22' 00"
	(Last operated Oct. 7, 1994; Laid up at Toledo, OH.)							
	Windsor {2}	TF	1930	B	28 rail cars	370' 05"	65' 00"	21' 06"
	(Last operated May 1, 1994; Laid up at Toledo, OH.)							
E-18	**ESSROC CANADA, INC., NORTH YORK, ON**							
	VESSELS MANAGED BY UPPER LAKES GROUP, INC.							
	Metis	CC	1956	B	5,800	331' 00"	43' 09"	26' 00"
	Stephen B. Roman	CC	1965	D	7,600	488' 09"	56' 00"	35' 06"
	(Fort William '65-'83) (Converted to a self-unloading cement carrier, '83)							
F-1	**FAMILLE DUFOUR CROISIERES, SAINTE-ANNE-DE-BEAUPRE, QC**							
	Famille DuFour	ES	1992	D	451*	132' 00"	29' 00"	11' 00"
	Famille DuFour II	PF	1995	D	465*	127' 06"	34' 09"	10' 06"
F-2	**FAUST CORP., GROSSE POINTE FARMS, MI**							
	Cormorant	TB	1991	D	10*	25' 02"	14' 00"	4' 06"
	Linnhurst	TB	1930	D	11*	37' 06"	10' 06"	4' 08"
F-3	**FEDERAL TERMINALS LTD., PORT CARTIER, QC**							
	Brochu	TT	1973	D	390*	100' 00"	36' 00"	14' 06"
	Vachon	TT	1973	D	390*	100' 00"	36' 00"	14' 06"
F-4	**FERRISS MARINE CONTRACTING CORP., DETROIT, MI**							
	Magnetic	TB	1925	D	30*	55' 00"	14' 00"	6' 06"
	(Col. J.D. Graham '24-'65, Nicholson 65-'83)							
	Norma B.	TB	1940	D	14*	43' 00"	15' 00"	4' 00"
F-5	**FITZ SUSTAINABLE FORESTRY MANAGEMENT LTD., MANITOWANING, ON**							
	Wyn Cooper	TB	1973	D	25*	48' 00"	13' 00"	4' 00"
F-6	**FRASER SHIPYARDS, INC., SUPERIOR, WI**							
	Brenda L.	TB	1941	D	11*	36' 00"	10' 00"	3' 08"
	(Harbour I '41-'58, Su-Joy III '58 -'78)							
	Maxine Thompson	TB	1959	D	30*	47' 04"	13' 00"	6' 06"
	(Susan A. Fraser '59-'78)							
	Murray R.	TB	1946	D	17*	42' 10"	12' 00"	4' 07"
	Phil Milroy	TB	1957	D	41*	47' 11"	16' 08"	8' 04"
	(Merchant of St. Marys '57-'60, Barney B. Barstow '57-'78)							
	Reuben Johnson	TB	1912	D	71*	78' 00"	17' 00"	11' 00"
	(Buffalo {1} '12-'28, USCOE Churchill '28-'48, Buffalo {1} '48-'74, Todd Fraser '74-'78)							
	Todd L.	TB	1965	D	22*	42' 10"	12' 00"	5' 06"
	(Robert W. Fraser '65-'78)							
	Troy L. Johnson	TB	1959	D	24*	42' 08"	12' 00"	5' 05"
	Wally Kendzora	TB	1956	D	24*	43' 00"	12' 00"	5' 06"
	Wells Larson	TB	1953	D	22*	42' 10"	12' 00"	5' 06"
	(E. C. Knudsen '53-'74)							
F-7	**FROST ENGINEERING CO., FRANKFORT, MI**							
	Captain George	TB	1929	D	61*	63' 00"	17' 00"	7' 08"
	(USCOE Captain George '29-'68, Captain George '68-'73, Kurt R. Luetdke '73-'91)							
G-1	**GABRIEL MARINE, ALGONAC, MI**							
	Elmer Dean	TB	1998	D	45*	68' 00"	16' 08"	6' 00"
G-2	**GAELIC TUG BOAT CO., GROSSE ILE, MI**							
	Carolyn Hoey	TB	1951	D	146*	90' 00"	25' 00"	11' 00"
	(Atlas '51-'84 Susan Hoey {1} '84-'85, Atlas '85-'87)							
	G.T.B. No. 2	DH	1968	B	1,600	195' 00"	35' 00"	12' 00"
	L.S.C. 236	TK	1946	B	584*	195' 00"	35' 00"	10' 06"
	Marysville	TK	1973	B	1,136*	200' 00"	50' 00"	12' 06"
	(N.M.S. No. 102 '73-'81)							

	Patricia Hoey {2}	TB	1949	D	146*	88' 06"	25' 00"	11' 00"
	(Propeller '49-'82, Bantry Bay '82-'91)							
	Shannon	TB	1944	D	145*	101' 00"	28' 00"	13' 00"
	(USS Connewango [YT / YTB / YTM-388] '44-'77)							
	Susan Hoey {3}	TB	1950	D	146*	82' 00"	25' 00"	10' 07"
	(Navajo {1} '50-'53, Seaval '53-'64, Mary T. Tracy '64-'69, Yankee '69-'70, Minn '70-'74,							
	William S. Bell '74-'83, Newcastle '83-'93, Laura Lynn '93-'99)							
	William Hoey {2}	TB	1924	D	99*	85' 00"	21' 06"	10' 09"
	(Martha C. '24-'52, Langdon C. Hardwicke '52-'82, Wabash {2} '82-'93, Katie Ann {1} '93-'99)							
G-3	**GALACTICA 001 ENTERPRISE LTD., TORONTO, ON**							
	Galactica 001	ES	1957	D	67*	50' 00"	16' 00"	6' 03"
G-4	**GALCON MARINE LTD., TORONTO, ON**							
	Kenteau	TB	1937	D	15*	54' 07"	16' 04"	4' 02"
G-5	**GALLAGHER MARINE CONSTRUCTION CO., INC., ESCANABA, MI**							
	Bee Jay	TB	1939	D	19*	45' 00"	13' 00"	7' 00"
	Menasha	CS	1926	B	168*	94' 04"	20' 00"	5' 00"
G-6	**GANANOQUE BOAT LINE LTD., GANANOQUE, ON**							
	Thousand Islander	ES	1972	D	200*	96' 11"	22' 01"	5' 05"
	Thousand Islander II	ES	1973	D	200*	99' 00"	22' 01"	5' 00"
	Thousand Islander III	ES	1975	D	376*	118' 00"	28' 00"	6' 00"
	Thousand Islander IV	ES	1976	D	347*	110' 09"	28' 04"	10' 08"
	Thousand Islander V	ES	1979	D	246*	88' 00"	24' 00"	5' 00"
G-7	**GANNON UNIVERSITY, ERIE, PA**							
	Environaut	RV	1950	D	17*	55' 00"	13' 06"	3' 10"*
G-8	**GEO. GRADEL CO., TOLEDO, OH**							
	Amber Jean	TB	1942	D	59*	61' 00"	18' 02"	8' 02"
	Clyde	DB	1922	B	704*	134' 00"	41' 00"	12' 00"
	John Francis	TB	1965	D	99*	75' 00"	22' 00"	9' 00"
	(Dad '65-'98, Creole Eagle '98-'03)							
	Josephine	TB	1957	D	103*	86' 09"	20' 06"	7' 09"
	(Wambrau '57-'87, Sea Diver II '87-'03)							
	Mighty Jake	TB	1969	D	15*	36' 00"	12' 03"	7' 03"
	Mighty Jessie	TB	1954	D	57*	61' 02"	18' 00"	7' 03"
	Mighty Jimmy	TB	1945	D	27*	56' 00"	15' 10"	7' 00"
	Mighty John III	TB	1962	D	24*	45' 00"	15' 00"	5' 10"
	(Niagara Queen '62-'99)							
	Moby Dick	DB	1952	B	835	121' 00"	33' 02"	10' 06"
	Pioneerland	TB	1943	D	45*	59' 06"	17' 00"	7' 06"*
	Prairieland	TB	1955	D	29*	50' 00"	15' 07"	6' 05"*
	Timberland	TB	1946	D	19*	44' 00"	13' 05"	6' 11"*
G-9	**GEORGIAN BAY CRUISE CO. INC., PARRY SOUND, ON**							
	Chippewa III	PA	1954	D	47*	65' 00"	16' 00"	6' 06"
	(Maid of the Mist III '54-'56. Maid of the Mist '56-'92)							
G-10	**GILLESPIE OIL & TRANSIT, INC., ST. JAMES, MI**							
	American Girl	PK	1922	D	40	64' 00"	14' 00"	8' 03"
	Oil Queen	TK	1949	B	50*	65' 00"	16' 00"	6' 00"
G-11	**GODERICH ELEVATORS LTD., GODERICH, ON**							
	Willowglen	BC	1943	R	16,300	620' 06"	60' 00"	35' 00"
	(Launched as Mesabi. Lehigh {3} '43-'81, Joseph X. Robert '81-'82)							
	(Last operated Dec. 21, 1992; In use as a grain storage vessel at Goderich, ON.)							
G-12	**GOODTIME ISLAND CRUISES, INC., SANDUSKY, OH**							
	Goodtime I	ES	1960	D	81*	111' 00"	29' 08"	9' 05"

Fleet #.	Fleet Name Vessel Name	Type of Vessel	Year Built	Type of Engine	Cargo Cap. or Gross*	Overall Length	Breadth	Depth or Draft*
G-13	**GOODTIME TRANSIT BOATS, INC., CLEVELAND, OH**							
	Goodtime III	ES	1990	D	95*	161' 00"	40' 00"	11' 00"
G-14	**GOWESH CANADA INC., TORONTO, ON**							
	Katran-3	HY	1996	D	135*	113' 02"	33' 10"	5' 11"
	Seaflight I	HY	1994	D	135*	113' 02"	33' 10"	5' 11"
	(Katran-1 '94-'98)							
	Seaflight II	HY	1996	D	135*	113' 02"	33' 10"	5' 11"
	(Katran-4 '96-'98)							
G-15	**GRAMPA WOO EXCURSIONS, BEAVER BAY, MN**							
	Grampa Woo III	ES	1978	D	99*	115' 00"	22' 00"	5' 00"*
	(Melissa Briley '78-'98)							
G-16	**GRAND VALLEY STATE UNIVERSITY, ALLENDALE, MI** **ROBERT B. ANNIS WATER RESOURCES INSTITUTE**							
	D. J. Angus	RV	1986	D	14*	45' 00"	14' 00"	4' 00"*
	W. G. Jackson	RV	1996	D	80*	64' 10"	20' 00"	5' 00"*
G-17	**GRAVEL & LAKE SERVICES LTD., THUNDER BAY, ON**							
	Donald Mac	TB	1914	D	69*	71' 00"	17' 00"	10' 00"
	F. A. Johnson	TB	1953	B	439*	150' 00"	32' 00"	10' 00"
	(Capt. Charles T. Parker '52-'54, Rapid Cities '54-'69, S. P. Renolds '69-'70)							
	George N. Carleton	TB	1943	D	97*	82' 00"	21' 00"	11' 00"
	(HMCS Glenlea [W-25] '43-'45, Bansaga '45-'64)							
	Peninsula	TB	1944	D	261*	111' 00"	27' 00"	13' 00"
	(HMCS Norton [W-31] '44-'45, W.A.C. 1 '45-'46)							
	Robert John	TB	1945	D	98*	82' 00"	20' 01"	11' 00"
	(HMCS Gleneagle [W-40] '45-'46, Bansturdy '46-'65)							
	Wolf River	BC	1956	D	5,880	349' 02"	43' 07"	25' 04"
	(Tecumseh {2} '56-'67, New York News {3} '67-'86, Stella Desgagnes '86-'93, Beam Beginner '94-'95)							
G-18	**GREAT LAKES ASSOCIATES, INC., ROCKY RIVER, OH**							
	Joseph H. Frantz	SU	1925	D	13,600	618' 00"	62' 00"	32' 00"
	(Repowered, converted to a self-unloader, '65) Under charter from Oglebay Norton Marine Services.							
	Kinsman Independent {3}	BC	1952	T	18,800	642' 03"	67' 00"	35' 00"
	(Charles L. Hutchinson {3} '52-'62, Ernest R. Breech '62-'88) Last operated Dec. '02. Laid up at Buffalo, NY.							
G-19	**GREAT LAKES DOCK & MATERIALS LLC, MUSKEGON, MI**							
	Fischer Hayden	TB	1967	D	64*	54' 00"	22' 1"	7' 1"
	(Gloria G. Cheramie, Joyce P. Crosby)							
	Duluth	TB	1954	D	82*	70' 00"	20' 00"	9' 08"
	(U. S. Army ST-2015 '54-'62)							
	Sarah B	TB	1953	D	23*	45' 00"	12' 00"	7' 00"
	(ST-2161 '53-'03)							
G-20	**GREAT LAKES ENVIRONMENTAL RESEARCH LABORATORY, MUSKEGON, MI**							
	Shenehon	SV	1952	D	90*	65' 00"	17' 00"	6' 00"
G-21	**GREAT LAKES FLEET, INC., DULUTH, MN** **(At press time, these vessels were scheduled to be sold to the Canadian National Railway** **Co. in mid-2004, pending government approval. If the sale takes place, they will be** **operated by Keystone Great Lakes Inc., fleet No. K-7.)**							
	Arthur M. Anderson	SU	1952	T	25,300	767' 00"	70' 00"	36' 00"
	(Lengthened 120'-'75) (Converted to a self-unloader, '82)							
	Cason J. Callaway	SU	1952	T	25,300	767' 00"	70' 00"	36' 00"
	(Lengthened 120'-'74) (Converted to a self-unloader, '82)							
	Edgar B. Speer	SU	1980	D	73,700	1,004' 00"	105' 00"	56' 00"
	Edwin H. Gott	SU	1979	D	74,100	1,004' 00"	105' 00"	56' 00"
	(Converted from shuttle self-unloader to deck-mounted self-unloader '96)							
	John G. Munson {2}	SU	1952	T	25,550	768' 03"	72' 00"	36' 00"
	(Lengthened 102'-'76)							

Paul H. Townsend passes Agawa Canyon in the Saginaw River. (Todd Shorkey)

	Philip R. Clarke	SU	1952	T	25,300	767' 00"	70' 00"	36' 00"
	(Lengthened 120'-'74) (Converted to a self-unloader, '82)							
	Roger Blough	SU	1972	D	43,900	858' 00"	105' 00"	41' 06"
	GLF GREAT LAKES CORP., DULUTH, MN – DIVISION OF GREAT LAKES FLEET, INC.							
	Presque Isle {2}	IT	1973	D	1,578*	153' 03"	54' 00"	31' 03"
	Presque Isle {2}	SU	1973	B	57,500	974' 06"	104' 07"	46' 06"
	[ITB Presque Isle OA dimensions together]					1,000' 00"	104' 07"	46' 06"
G-22	**THE GREAT LAKES GROUP, CLEVELAND, OH**							
	THE GREAT LAKES TOWING CO., CLEVELAND, OH – DIVISION OF THE GREAT LAKES GROUP							
	Alabama {2}	TB	1916	D	98*	81' 00"	21' 03"	12' 05"
	Arizona	TB	1931	D	98*	84' 04"	20' 00"	12' 06"
	Arkansas {2}	TB	1909	D	98*	81' 00"	21' 03"	12' 05"
	(Yale '09-'48)							
	California	TB	1926	D	98*	81' 00"	20' 00"	12' 06"
	Colorado	TB	1928	D	98*	84' 04"	20' 00"	12' 06"
	Delaware {4}	TB	1924	D	98*	81' 00"	20' 00"	12' 06"
	Florida	TB	1926	D	99*	81' 00"	20' 00"	12' 06"
	(Florida '26-'83, Pinellas '83-'84)							
	Idaho	TB	1931	D	98*	84' 00"	20' 00"	12' 06"
	Illinois {2}	TB	1914	D	99*	81' 00"	20' 00"	12' 06"
	Indiana	TB	1911	D	97*	81' 00"	20' 00"	12' 06"
	Iowa	TB	1915	D	98*	81' 00"	20' 00"	12' 06"
	Kansas	TB	1927	D	98*	81' 00"	20' 00"	12' 06"
	Kentucky {2}	TB	1929	D	98*	84' 04"	20' 00"	12' 06"
	Louisiana	TB	1917	D	98*	81' 00"	20' 00"	12' 06"
	Maine {1}	TB	1921	D	96*	81' 00"	20' 00"	12' 06"
	(Maine {1} '21-'82, Saipan '82-'83, Hillsboro '83-'84)							
	Massachusetts	TB	1928	D	98*	84' 04"	20' 00"	12' 06"
	Milwaukee	DB	1924	B	1,095	172' 00"	40' 00"	11' 06"
	Minnesota {1}	TB	1911	D	98*	81' 00"	20' 00"	12' 06"
	Mississippi	TB	1916	D	98*	81' 00"	20' 00"	12' 06"
	Missouri {2}	TB	1927	D	149*	88' 04"	24' 06"	12' 03"
	(Rogers City {1} '27-'56, Dolomite {1} '56-'81, Chippewa {7} '81-'90)							
	Montana	TB	1929	D	98*	84' 04"	20' 00"	12' 06"
	Nebraska	TB	1929	D	98*	84' 04"	20' 00"	12' 06"
	New Jersey	TB	1924	D	98*	81' 00"	20' 00"	12' 06"
	(New Jersey '24-'52, Petco-21 '52-'53)							
	New York	TB	1913	D	98*	81' 00"	20' 00"	12' 06"
	North Carolina {2}	TB	1952	D	145*	87' 09"	24' 01"	10' 07"
	(Limestone '52-'83, Wicklow '83-'90)							
	North Dakota	TB	1910	D	97*	81' 00"	20' 00"	12' 06"
	(John M. Truby '10-'38)							
	Ohio {3}	TB	1903	D	194*	118' 00"	24' 00"	13' 06"
	(M.F.D. No. 15 '03-'52, Laurence C. Turner '52-'73)							
	Oklahoma	TB	1913	D	97*	81' 00"	20' 00"	12' 06"
	(T. C. Lutz {2} '13-'34)							
	Pennsylvania {3}	TB	1911	D	98*	81' 00"	20' 00"	12' 06"
	Rhode Island	TB	1930	D	98*	84' 04"	20' 00"	12' 06"
	South Carolina	TB	1925	D	102*	86' 00"	21' 00"	11' 00"
	(Welcome {2} '25-'53, Joseph H. Callan '53-'72, South Carolina '72-'82, Tulagi '82-'83)							
	Superior {3}	TB	1912	D	147*	97' 00"	22' 00"	12' 00"
	(Richard Fitzgerald '12-'46)							
	Tennessee	TB	1917	D	98*	81' 00"	20' 00"	12' 06"
	Texas	TB	1916	D	97*	81' 00"	20' 00"	12' 06"
	Vermont	TB	1914	D	98*	81' 00"	20' 00"	12' 06"
	Virginia {2}	TB	1914	D	97*	81' 00"	20' 00"	12' 06"
	Washington {1}	TB	1925	D	97*	81' 00"	20' 00"	12' 06"

Fleet #.	Fleet Name / Vessel Name	Type of Vessel	Year Built	Type of Engine	Cargo Cap. or Gross*	Overall Length	Breadth	Depth or Draft*
	Wisconsin {4}	TB	1897	D	105*	90' 03"	21' 00"	12' 03"
	(America {3} 1897-'82, Midway '82-'83)							
	Wyoming	TB	1929	D	104*	84' 04"	20' 00"	12' 06"
G-23	**GREAT LAKES MARINE ENGINEERING & SALVAGE, INC., ALPENA, MI**							
	Atlas	RV	1941	D	157*	90' 07"	21' 04"	11' 00"
G-24	**GREAT LAKES MARITIME ACADEMY – NORTHWESTERN MICHIGAN COLLEGE, TRAVERSE CITY, MI**							
	Anchor Bay	TV	1953	D	23*	45' 00"	13' 00"	7' 00"*
	(USCOE Anchor Bay '53-?)							
	Northwestern {2}	TV	1969	D	12*	55' 00"	15' 00"	6' 06"
	(USCOE North Central '69-'98)							
	State of Michigan	TV	1986	D	1,914*	224' 00"	43' 00"	20' 00"
	(USS Persistent '86-'98, USCG Persistent '98-'02)							
G-25	**GREAT LAKES SCHOONER CO., TORONTO, ON**							
	Challenge	ES	1980	W	76*	96' 00"	16' 06"	8' 00"
	Kajama	ES	1930	W	263*	128' 09"	22' 09"	11' 08"
G-26	**GREAT LAKES SHIPWRECK HISTORICAL SOCIETY, SAULT STE. MARIE, MI**							
	David Boyd	RV	1982	D	26*	47' 00"	17' 00"	3' 00"*
G-27	**GREAT LAKES TRANSPORT LTD., HALIFAX, NS**							
	Jane Ann IV	TBA	1978	D	954*	137' 06"	42' 08"	21' 04"
	(Ouro Fino '78-'81, Bomare '81-'93, Tignish Sea '93-'98)							
	Sarah Spencer	SU	1959	B	23,200	611" 03"	72' 00"	40' 00"
	(Adam E. Cornelius {3} '59-'89, Capt. Edward V. Smith '89-'91, Sea Barge One '91-'96; (Engine removed, converted to a self-unloading barge, '89)							
	[Jane Ann IV/Sarah Spencer OA dimensions together]					729' 03""	72" 00"	40' 00"
G-28	**GREG RUDNICK, CLEVELAND, OH**							
	Forest City	BB	1934	D	22*	44' 04"	11' 11"	4' 09"
H-1	**HAMILTON PORT AUTHORITY, HAMILTON, ON**							
	Judge McCombs	TB	1948	D	10*	36' 00"	10' 03"	4' 00"
	(Bronte Sue '48-'50)							
H-2	**HANNAH MARINE CORP., LEMONT, IL**							
	Daryl C. Hannah {2}	TB	1956	D	268*	102' 00"	28' 00"	8' 00"
	(Cindy Jo '56-'66, Katherine L. '66-'93)							
	Donald C. Hannah	TB	1962	D	191*	91' 00"	29' 00"	11' 06"
	Hannah 1801	TK	1967	B	1,560*	240' 00"	50' 00"	12' 00"
	(BRI 5 '67-'88, CT-75 '88-'92)							
	Hannah 1802	TK	1967	B	1,560*	240' 00"	50' 00"	12' 00"
	Hannah 2801	TK	1980	B	2,210*	275' 00"	54' 00"	17' 06"
	Hannah 2901	TK	1962	B	1,702*	264' 00"	52' 06"	12' 06"
	Hannah 2902	TK	1962	B	1,702*	264' 00"	52' 06"	12' 06"
	Hannah 2903	TK	1962	B	1,702*	264' 00"	52' 06"	12' 06"
	Hannah 3601	TK	1972	B	2,369*	290' 00"	60' 00"	18' 03"
	Hannah 5101	TK	1978	B	3,356*	360' 00"	60' 00"	22' 06"
	James A. Hannah	TB	1945	D	593*	149' 00"	33' 00"	16' 00"
	(U. S. Army LT-820 '45-'65, Muskegon {1} '65-'71)							
	Kristin Lee Hannah	TB	1953	D	397*	111' 10"	35' 00"	8' 04"
	Margaret M.	TB	1956	D	167*	89' 06"	24' 00"	10' 00"
	(Shuttler '56-'60, Margaret M. Hannah '60-'84)							
	Mark Hannah	TBA	1969	D	191*	127' 05"	32' 01"	14' 03"
	(Lead Horse '69-'73, Gulf Challenger '73-'80, Challenger {2} '80-'93)							
	Mary E. Hannah	TB	1945	D	612*	149' 00"	33' 00"	16' 00"
	(U. S. Army LT-821 '45-'47, Brooklyn '47-'66, Lee Reuben '66-'75)							
	Susan W. Hannah	TBA	1977	D	174*	121' 06"	34' 06"	18' 02"
	(Lady Elda '77-'78, Kings Challenger '78-'78, ITM No. 1 '78-'81, Kings Challenger '81-'86)							

Fleet #.	Fleet Name / Vessel Name	Type of Vessel	Year Built	Type of Engine	Cargo Cap. or Gross*	Overall Length	Breadth	Depth or Draft*
	GENERAL MARINE TOWING, SOUTH CHICAGO, IL – DIVISION OF HANNAH MARINE CORP.							
	Mary Page Hannah {2}	TB	1972	D	99*	59' 08"	24' 01"	10' 03"
	(Kings Squire '72–'78, Juanita D. '78–'79 Katherine L. '79–'93)							
	Hannah D. Hannah	TB	1955	D	134*	86' 00"	24' 00"	10' 00"
	(Harbor Ace '55–'61, Gopher State '61–'71, Betty Gale '71–'93)							
	Peggy D. Hannah	TB	1920	D	145*	108' 00"	25' 00"	14' 00"
	(William A. Whitney '20–'92)							
	Susan E.	TB	1921	D	96*	81' 00"	20' 00"	12' 06"
	(Oregon {1} '21–'78, Ste. Marie I '78–'81, Sioux {2} '81–'91)							
	HMC SHIP MANAGEMENT LTD., LEMONT, IL – AN AFFILIATE OF HANNAH MARINE CORP.							
	Cemex Conquest	CC	1937	B	8,500	437' 06"	55' 00"	28' 00"
	(Red Crown '37–'62, Amoco Indiana '62–'87, Medusa Conquest '87–'99, Southdown Conquest '99–'04)							
	(Converted from a powered tanker to a self-unloading cement barge, '87)							
	C.T.C. No. 1	CC	1943	R	16,300	620' 06"	60' 00"	35' 00"
	(Launched as McIntyre. Frank Purnell {1} '43–'64, Steelton {3} '64–'78, Hull No. 3 '78–'79,							
	Pioneer {4} '79–'82)							
	(Last operated Nov. 12, 1981; In use as a cement storage / transfer vessel in S. Chicago, IL.)							
	Southdown Challenger	CC	1906	S	10,250	552' 01"	56' 00"	31' 00"
	(William P. Snyder '06–'26, Elton Hoyt II {1} '26–'52, Alex D. Chisholm '52–'66, Medusa Challenger '66–'99)							
	(Repowered, '50; Converted to a self-unloading cement carrier, '67)							
	William L. Warner	RT	1973	D	7,500	140' 00"	40' 00"	14' 00"
	(Jos. F. Bigane '73–'04)							
H-3	**HARBOR LIGHT CRUISE LINES, INC., TOLEDO, OH**							
	Sandpiper	ES	1984	D	19*	65' 00"	16' 00"	4' 00"
H-4	**HARBOR TOWN RIVERBOAT CO., INC., ROCHESTER, NY**							
	Harbor Town	ES	1997	D	`71*	64' 05"	24' 00"	5' 05"
H-5	**HARBOUR PRINCESS TOURS, PORT DOVER, ON**							
	Harbour Princess 1	ES		D	252*	100' 00"	22' 00"	4' 05"
	(Johnny B. '56–'89, Garden City '89–'00)							
H-6	**HARLEQUIN CRUISE LINES, TORONTO, ON**							
	River Gambler	ES	1992	D	332*	100' 07"	40' 00"	4' 06"
H-7	**HARRY GAMBLE SHIPYARDS, PORT DOVER, ON**							
	H. A. Smith	TB	1944	D	24*	55' 00"	16' 00"	5' 06"

***Mesabi Miner* downbound at dusk in the St. Marys River.** *(Roger LeLievre)*

Algolake **leaving the Soo Locks last summer.** *(John Chomniak)*

ALGOLAKE

The self-unloading bulk carrier *Algolake* was the first vessel built new for Algoma Central Railway, Sault Ste. Marie, Ont., with wheelhouse and all accommodations aft.

Constructed to the maximum Seaway dimensions of the time by Canadian Shipbuilding and Engineering Ltd. (Collingwood Shipyards) of Collingwood, Ont., *Algolake* was launched Oct. 29, 1976 and christened April 6, 1977. The vessel's rounded bow allowed for maximum cargo-carrying ability for cargoes such as coal, where volume is more of an issue than weight. While the *Algolake* was being built, Algoma won a contract to transport Western and Eastern coal for Ontario Hydro, which meant many coal cargos in *Algolake*'s future.

Algolake set several records early in her career. On July 30, 1977, she carried 27,210 tons of iron ore from Sept Isles, Quebec, to Ashtabula, Ohio. High water on the Great Lakes in the mid-1980s contributed to a record 29,801 tons of coal carried to Nanticoke, Ont., on June 5, 1985, and another record 30,413 tons of western coal July 13, 1986 from Thunder Bay to Nanticoke. On Aug. 19, 2000, the *Algolake*'s crew members distinguished themselves and their vessel by assisting in the rescue of two men who had been drifting on a disabled 18-foot craft in lower Lake Huron for more six hours.

Today, the *Algolake* is owned by Algoma Central Marine of St. Catharines, Ont., and sails under the management of Seaway Marine Transport of St. Catharines, Ont., a partnership of Algoma Central Marine and Upper Lakes Group. Aside from her regular cargoes of coal, the *Algolake* – Capt. Anders Rasmussen on the bridge – has frequently loaded salt, iron ore and potash. **– *George Wharton***

Fleet #.	Fleet Name / Vessel Name	Type of Vessel	Year Built	Type of Engine	Cargo Cap. or Gross*	Overall Length	Breadth	Depth or Draft*
	J. A. Cornett	TB	1937	D	60*	65' 00"	17' 00"	9' 00"
	Jiggs	TB	1911	D	45*	61' 00"	16' 00"	8' 00"
H-8	**HEDDLE MARINE SERVICES INC., HAMILTON, ON**							
	Dalmig	CF	1957	D	538*	175' 10"	40' 01"	11' 10"
	(Pierre de Saurel '57-'87) (Vessel laid up at Hamilton, ON.)							
H-9	**HERITAGE CRUISE LINES, PARRY SOUND, ON**							
	Georgian Clipper	PA	1967	D	170*	78' 08"	12' 06"	6' 00"
H-10	**HERITAGE HARBOR MARINE, GODERICH, ON**							
	Salvage Monarch	TB	1959	D	219*	97' 09"	28' 00"	14' 06"
	Seven Sisters	TB	1954	D	225*	101' 10"	26' 00"	13' 08"
	(Charlie S. '54-'75, Cathy McAllister '75-'02)							
H-11	**HOLLY MARINE TOWING, CHICAGO, IL**							
	Chris Ann	TB	1981	D	45*	51' 09"	17' 00"	6' 01"
	(Captain Robbie '81-'90, Philip M. Pearse '90-'97)							
	Debra Ann	TB	1960	D	36*	46' 02"	15' 02"	6' 03"
	Holly Ann	TB	1926	D	220*	108' 00"	26' 06"	15' 00"
	(Wm. A. Lydon '26-'92)							
	Katie Ann {3}	TB	1962	D	84*	60' 04"	24' 00"	8' 06"
	Margaret Ann	TB	1954	D	131*	82' 00"	24' 06"	11' 06"
	(John A. McGuire '54-'87, William Hoey {1} '87-'94)							
H-12	**HORNE TRANSPORTATION, WOLFE ISLAND, ON**							
	William Darrell	CF	1952	D	66*	66' 00"	28' 00"	6' 00"
H-13	**HOTLINE INDUSTRIES, SUPERIOR, WI**							
	Marine Supplier	GR	1950	D	51*	58' 00"	15' 00"	7' 00"
	(Ted '50-'50, Kaner I '50-'98)							
H-14	**HUFFMAN EQUIPMENT RENTAL AND CONTRACTING, EASTLAKE, OH**							
	Hamp Thomas	TB	1968	D	22*	43' 00"	13' 00"	4' 00"
	Paddy Miles	TB	1934	D	16*	45' 04"	12' 04"	4' 07"
I-1	**ILLINOIS MARINE TOWING, INC., LEMONT, IL**							
	Aggie C	TB	1977	D	89*	81' 00"	26' 00"	6' 10"*
	Albert C	TB	1971	D	47*	61' 02"	18' 00"	5' 08"*
	Eileen C	TB	1982	D	122*	75' 00"	26' 00"	8' 00"*
	William C	TB	1968	D	105*	76' 06"	24' 00"	6' 06"*
I-2	**IMPERIAL OIL LTD. – ESSO PETROLEUM CANADA DIVISION, DARTMOUTH, NS**							
	Imperial Dartmouth	RT	1970	D	1,192*	205' 06"	40' 00"	16' 00"
I-3	**INLAND BULK TRANSFER, CLEVELAND, OH**							
	Benjamin Ridgeway	TB	1969	D	51*	53' 00"	18' 05"	7' 05"
	Frank Palladino Jr.	TB	1980	D	89*	100' 00"	32' 00"	13' 00"
	(Lady Ida '80-'92)							
	Inland 2401	DB	1968	B	2,589	240' 00"	72' 00"	14' 00"
	(OC 240 '68-'77, Martech Enterprise '77-'84, Enterprise '84-'88, Stevens 2401 '88-?)							
	James Palladino	TB	1999	D	392*	109' 11"	34' 01"	16' 01"
	Kellstone 1	SU	1957	B	9,000	396' 00"	71' 00"	22' 06"
	(M-211 '57-'81, Virginia '81-'88, C-11 '88-'93)							
I-4	**INLAND LAKES MANAGEMENT, INC., ALPENA, MI**							
	Alpena {2}	CC	1942	T	15,550	519' 06"	67' 00"	35' 00"
	(Leon Fraser '42-'91 (Shortened 120' and converted to a self-unloading cement carrier, '91)							
	E. M. Ford	CC	1898	Q	7,100	428' 00"	50' 00"	28' 00"
	(Presque Isle {1} 1898-'56)							
	(Converted to a self-unloading cement carrier, '56; Last operated Sept. 16, 1996; In use as a cement storage and transfer vessel at Saginaw, MI.)							

Fleet #.	Fleet Name / Vessel Name	Type of Vessel	Year Built	Type of Engine	Cargo Cap. or Gross*	Overall Length	Breadth	Depth or Draft*
	J. A. W. Iglehart	CC	1936	T	12,500	501' 06"	68' 03"	37' 00"
	(Pan Amoco '36-'55, Amoco '55-'60, H. R. Schemn '60-'65)							
	(Converted from a saltwater tanker to a self-unloading cement carrier, '56)							
	Paul H. Townsend	CC	1945	D	8,400	447' 00"	50' 00"	29' 00"
	(USNS Hickory Coll '45-'46, USNS Coastal Delegate '46-'52)							
	(Converted from a saltwater cargo vessel to a self-unloading cement carrier, '52; Lengthened '58)							
	S. T. Crapo	CC	1927	B	8,900	402' 06"	60' 03"	29' 00"
	(Last operated Sept. 4, 1996; In use as a cement storage / transfer vessel in Green Bay, WI.)							
I-5	**INLAND SEAS EDUCATION ASSOCIATION, SUTTONS BAY, MI**							
	Inland Seas	RV	1994	W	41*	61' 06"	17' 00"	7' 00"
I-6	**THE INTERLAKE STEAMSHIP CO., RICHFIELD, OH**							
	Charles M. Beeghly	SU	1959	T	31,000	806' 00"	75' 00"	37' 06"
	(Shenango II '59-'67) (Lengthened 96'-, '72; Converted to a self-unloader, '81)							
	Herbert C. Jackson	SU	1959	T	24,800	690' 00"	75' 00"	37' 06"
	(Converted to a self-unloader, '75)							
	James R. Barker	SU	1976	D	63,300	1,004' 00"	105' 00"	50' 00"
	Mesabi Miner	SU	1977	D	63,300	1,004' 00"	105' 00"	50' 00"
	Paul R. Tregurtha	SU	1981	D	68,000	1,013' 06"	105' 00"	56' 00"
	(William J. DeLancey '81-'90)							
	INTERLAKE TRANSPORTATION, INC., RICHFIELD, OH – DIV. OF THE INTERLAKE STEAMSHIP CO.							
	Dorothy Ann	AT/TT	1999	D	1,600*	124' 03"	44' 00"	24' 00"
	Pathfinder {3}	SU	1953	B	21,260	606' 02"	70' 00"	36' 00"
	(J. L. Mauthe '53-'98)							
	(Engine removed, converted from a powered bulk carrier to a self-unloading barge, '98)							
	[ATB Dorothy Ann / Pathfinder {3} OA dimensions together]					700' 00"	70' 00"	36' 00"
	LAKES SHIPPING CO., INC., RICHFIELD, OH – DIVISION OF THE INTERLAKE STEAMSHIP CO.							
	John Sherwin {2}	BC	1958	T	31,500	806' 00"	75' 00"	37' 06"
	(Lengthened 96'- '73; Last operated Nov. 16, 1981. In long-term layup at Superior, WI.)							
	Kaye E. Barker	SU	1952	T	25,900	767' 00"	70' 00"	36' 00"
	(Edward B. Greene '52-'85, Benson Ford {3} '85-'89;)							
	(Lengthened 120'- '76; Converted to a self-unloader, '81)							
	Lee A. Tregurtha	SU	1942	T	29,300	826' 00"	75' 00"	39' 00"
	(Laid down as Mobiloil, Launched as Samoset, USS Chiwawa [AO-68] '42-'46, Chiwawa '46-'61,							
	Walter A. Sterling '61-'85, William Clay Ford {2} '85-'89)							
	(Converted from a saltwater tanker to a Great Lakes bulk carrier, '61; Lengthend '96, '76; Converted							
	to a self-unloader, '78)							
I-7	**INTERNATIONAL MARINE SALVAGE CO. LTD., PORT COLBORNE, ON**							
	Canadian Venture	BC	1965	D	28,050	730' 03"	75' 00"	39' 02"
	(Lawrencecliffe Hall {2} '65-'88, David K. Gardiner '88-'94)							
	(Last operated Dec. 12, 2001. Scheduled for scrapping at Port Colborne, ON, in 2004.)							
	Charlie E.	TB	1943	D	32*	63' 00"	16' 06"	7' 06"
	(Kolbe '43-'86, Lois T. '86-'02)							
	Sea Castle	CC	1909	B	2,600	260' 00"	43' 00"	25' 03"
	(Kaministiquia {2} '09-'16, Westoil '16-'23, J. B. John {1} '23-'51, John L. A. Galster '51-'69)							
	(5 year survey expired November, 1983. Laid up in Muskegon, MI.)							
I-8	**INTERNATIONAL MARINE SYSTEMS LTD., MILWAUKEE, WI**							
	Iroquois {1}	ES	1946	D	57*	61' 09"	21' 00"	6' 04"
I-9	**INTERNATIONAL STEEL GROUP – BURNS HARBOR INC., CHESTERTON, IN**							
	Burns Harbor {2}	SU	1980	D	78,850	1,000' 00"	105' 00"	56' 00"
	Stewart J. Cort	SU	1972	D	58,000	1,000' 00"	105' 00"	49' 00"
I-10	**ISLAND EXPRESS BOAT LINES LTD., SANDUSKY, OH**							
	Island Rocket	PF	1997	D	47*	65' 00"	18' 02"	6' 00"
	Island Rocket II	PC	1997	D	32*	64' 07"	19' 02"	6' 05"
	Island Rocket III	PC	1988	D	80*	108' 00"	29' 00"	10' 02"
	(Auk Nu-'02)							

Fleet #.	Fleet Name / Vessel Name	Type of Vessel	Year Built	Type of Engine	Cargo Cap. or Gross*	Overall Length	Breadth	Depth or Draft*
I-11	**ISLAND FERRY SERVICES CORP., CHEBOYGAN, MI**							
	Polaris	PF	1952	D	99*	65' 00"	36' 00"	8' 00"*
I-12	**(THE) ISLE ROYALE LINE, COPPER HARBOR, MI**							
	Isle Royale Queen III	PK	1959	D	88*	85' 00"	18' 04"	9' 05"
J-1	**J. W. WESTCOTT CO., DETROIT, MI**							
	J. W. Westcott II	MB	1949	D	11*	46' 01"	13' 04"	4' 06"
	Joseph J. Hogan	MB	1957	D	16*	40' 00"	12' 06"	5' 00"
	(USCOE Ottawa '57-'95)							
J-2	**JACOBS INVESTMENTS – JRM, INC., CLEVELAND, OH**							
	Nautica Queen	ES	1981	D	95*	124' 00"	31' 02"	8' 10"
	(Bay Queen '81-'85, Arawanna Queen '85-'88, Star of Nautica '88-'92)							
J-3	**JOSEPH G. GAYTON, HARROW, ON**							
	Princess	TB	1903	D	87*	77' 00"	20' 04"	7' 11"
	(Radiant '03-'33, Anna Sheridan '33-'62)							
J-4	**JOSEPH MARTIN, BEAVER ISLAND, MI**							
	Shamrock {1}	TB	1933	D	60*	64' 00"	18' 00"	7' 04"
J-5	**JUBILEE QUEEN CRUISES, TORONTO, ON**							
	Jubilee Queen	ES	1986	D	269*	122' 00"	23' 09"	5' 05"
	(Pioneer Princess III '86-'89)							
J-6	**JULIO CONTRACTING CO., HANCOCK, MI**							
	Winnebago	TB	1945	D	14*	40' 00"	10' 02"	4' 06"
K-1	**K & K WAREHOUSING, MENOMINEE, MI**							
	Manitowoc	DB	1926	B		371' 03"	67' 03"	22' 06"
	Viking I	DB	1925	D		360' 00"	56' 03"	21' 06"
	(Ann Arbor No. 7 '25-'64, Viking {2} '64-'96)							
	(Awaiting possible conversion from a powered carferry to a pulpwood barge at Marinette, WI.)							
	William H. Donner	CS	1914	B	9,400	524' 00"	54' 00"	30' 00"
	(Last operated in 1969; In use as a cargo transfer vessel at Marinette, WI.)							
K-2	**KADINGER MARINE SERVICE, INC., MILWAUKEE, WI**							
	David J. Kadinger	TB	1969	D	98*	65' 06"	22' 00"	8' 06"
	(N. F. Candies ?-?, Connie Guidry ?-'89)							
	Jake M. Kadinger	TB	1984	D	131*	77' 09"	24' oo"	12'00"
	Jason A. Kadinger	TB	1963	D	60*	52' 06"	19'01"	7' 04"
	Kayla D. Kadinger	PA	1958	D	24*	39' 00"	11' 00"	6' 05"
	Kyle D. Kadinger	TB	1962	D	35*	47' 00"	16' 00"	6' 03"
	Ruffy J. Kadinger	TB	1981	D	74*	55' 00"	23' 00"	7' 02"
K-3	**KCBX TERMINALS CO., CHICAGO, IL**							
	Matador VI	TB	1971	D	31*	42' 00"	18' 00"	6' 00"*
K-4	**KELLEYS ISLAND BOAT LINES, MARBLEHEAD, OH**							
	Carlee Emily	PA/CF	1987	D	98*	101' 00"	34' 06"	10' 00"
	(Endeavor '87-'02)							
	Joelle Ann Marie	PA/CF	1960	D	81*	64' 06"	33' 00"	9' 00"
	(Commuter '60-'02)							
	Juliet Alicia	PA/CF	1969	D	95*	100' 00"	34' 03"	8' 00"
	(Kelley Islander '69-'02)							
	Kayla Marie	PA/CF	1975	D	93*	122' 00"	40' 00"	8' 00"
	(R. Bruce Etherige '75-'97)							
	Shirley Irene	PA/CF	1991	D	68*	160' 00"	46' 00"	9' 00"
K-5	**KENT LINE LTD., SAINT JOHN, NB**							
	Irving Canada	TK	1981	D	37,757	628' 06"	90' 02"	48' 03"

Edgar B. Speer gets help from the U.S.C.G. *Mackinaw* during a three-day ice battle in mid-January 2004 in the St. Marys River. *(Paul Hoffmeyer)*

Stewart J. Cort arrives at Milwaukee for an icy winter lay-up on Jan. 24, 2004. *(Andy LaBorde)*

Fleet #.	Fleet Name Vessel Name	Type of Vessel	Year Built	Type of Engine	Cargo Cap. or Gross*	Overall Length	Breadth	Depth or Draft*
	Irving Eskimo	TK	1980	D	38,213	629' 00"	90' 03"	48' 03"
	Kent Carrier	GC	1971	B	8,128	363' 00"	82' 02"	22' 03"
	(Saint John Carrier '71-'79, Nitinat Carrier '79-'84, Irving Carrier '84-'92)							
	Kent Transport	GC	1971	B	7,366	362' 10"	82' 02"	22' 03"
	(Rothesay Carrier '71-'97)							
	Kent Voyageur	GC	1982	D	15,912	488' 10"	78' 01"	42' 00"
	(Reed Voyageur '82-'88, Daishowa Voyageur '88-'96)							
	Wellington Kent {2}	TK	1980	D	11,548	433' 11"	67' 04"	30' 04"
	(Irving Nordic '80-'93)							
K-6	**KEWEENAW EXCURSIONS, INC., HOUGHTON, MI**							
	Keweenaw Star	ES	1981	D	97*	110' 00"	23' 04"	6' 03"
	(Atlantic Star, Privateer, De De Bruce)							
K-7	**KEYSTONE GREAT LAKES, INC., BALA CYNWYD, PA**							
	Great Lakes {2}	TK	1982	B	5,024*	414' 00"	60' 00"	30' 00"
	(Amoco Great Lakes '82-'85)							
	Michigan {10}	AT	1982	D	293*	107' 08"	34' 00"	16' 00"
	(Amoco Michigan '82-'85)							
	[ATB Michigan / Great Lakes {2} OA dimensions together]					454' 00"	60' 00"	30' 00"
K-8	**KINDRA LAKE TOWING LP., DOWNERS GROVE, IL**							
	Buckley	TB	1958	D	94*	95' 00"	26' 00"	11' 00"
	(Linda Brooks '58-'67, Eddie B. {2} '67-'95)							
	Morgan	TB	1974	D	134*	90' 00"	30' 00"	10' 06"
	(Donald O'Toole '74-'86, Bonesey B. '86-'95)							
	Old Mission	TB	1945	D	94*	85' 00"	23' 00"	10' 04"
	(U. S. Army ST-880 '45-'47, USCOE Avondale '47-'64, Adrienne B. '64-'95)							
K-9	**KING COMPANY, INC., HOLLAND, MI**							
	Barry J	TB	1943	D	42*	46' 00"	13' 00"	7' 00"
	Carol Ann	TB	1981	D	115*	68' 00"	24' 00"	8' 08"
	Julie Dee	TB	1903	D	59*	63' 03"	17' 05"	9' 00"
	(Bonita {1} '03-'16, Chicago Harbor No. 4 '16-'60, Eddie B. {1} '60-'69, Seneca Queen '69-'70, Ludington '70 -?)							
	John Henry	TB	1954	D	66*	70' 00"	20' 06"	9' 07"
	(U. S. Army ST-2013 '54-'80)							
	Miss Edna	TB	1935	D	29*	36' 08"	11' 02"	4' 08"
	Muskegon {2}	TB	1973	D	138*	75' 00"	24' 00"	11' 06"
K-10	**KINGSTON 1,000 ISLANDS CRUISES, KINGSTON, ON**							
	Island Belle I	ES	1988	D	150*	65' 00"	22' 00"	8' 00"
	(Spirit of Brockville '88-'91)							
	Island Queen	ES	1975	D	300*	96' 00"	26' 00"	11' 00"
	Island Star	ES	1994	D	220*	97' 00"	30' 00"	10' 00"
	(Le Bateau-Mouche II '94-'98)							
L-1	**L. R. JACKSON FISHIERS LTD., PORT STANLEY, ON**							
	G. W. Jackson	FT	1964	D	109*	70' 02"	23' 08"	4' 00"
	L. R. Jackson	FT	1982	D	146*	63' 00"	21' 00"	6' 00
L-2	**LAFARGE CANADA, INC., MONTREAL, QC** ***MANAGED BY CANADA STEAMSHIP LINES, INC.***							
	English River	CC	1961	D	7,450	404' 03"	60' 00"	36' 06"
	(Converted to a self-unloading cement carrier, '74)							
L-3	**LAFARGE CORP., SOUTHFIELD, MI**							
	J. B. Ford	CC	1904	R	8,000	440' 00"	50' 00"	28' 00"
	(Edwin F. Holmes '04-'16, E. C. Collins '16-'59)							
	(Converted to a self-unloading cement carrier, '59; Last operated Nov. 15, 1985. In use as a cement storage and transfer vessel at Superior WI.)							

Fleet #. Fleet Name Vessel Name	Type of Vessel	Year Built	Type of Engine	Cargo Cap. or Gross*	Overall Length	Breadth	Depth or Draft*
L-4	**LAKE EXPRESS LLC , MILWAUKEE, WI**						
Lake Express	PF	2004	D	500*	192' 00"	57' 00"	
L-5	**LAKE MICHIGAN CARFERRY SERVICE, INC., LUDINGTON, MI**						
Badger [43] {2}	CF	1953	S	4,244*	410' 06"	59' 06"	24' 00"
Spartan [42] {2}	CF	1952	S	4,244*	410' 06"	59' 06"	24' 00"
(Last operated Jan. 20, 1979. In long-term layup at Ludington, MI.)							
L-6	**LAKE MICHIGAN CONTRACTORS, INC., HOLLAND, MI**						
Cherokee {3}	DB	1943	B	1,500	155' 00"	50' 00"	13' 00"
Curly B.	TB	1956	D	131*	84' 00"	26' 00"	9' 02"
(Waverly '56-'74, Brother Collins '74-'80)							
Empire State	TB	1951	D	21*	41' 09"	12' 04"	6' 06"
Iroquois {2}	DS	1950	B	495*	120' 00"	30' 00"	7' 00"
James Harris	TB	1943	D	18*	41' 09"	12' 05"	5' 07
Ojibway {2}	DS	1954	B	517*	120' 00"	50' 00"	10' 00"
Shirley Joy	TB	1978	D	98*	72' 00"	26' 00"	7' 06"
(Douglas B. Mackie '78-'97)							
L-7	**LAKE TOWING, INC., AVON, OH**						
Menominee	TB	1967	D	344*	108' 00"	29' 00"	14' 00"
Upper Canada	CF	1949	D	165*	143' 00"	36' 00"	11' 00"
(Romeo and Annette '49-'66)							
L-8	**LAKES PILOTS ASSOCIATION, PORT HURON, MI**						
Huron Belle	PB	1979	D	21*	50' 00"	16' 00"	7' 09"
Huron Maid	PB	1976	D	26*	46' 00"	16' 00"	3' 05"
L-9	**LARRY C. VANDUSEN, NECEDAH, WI**						
Trinity	TB	1939	D	51*	45' 00"	12' 10"	5' 07"*
(A.H. Camphausen '39-'82)							
L-10	**LE BATEAU-MOUCHE AU VIEUX, MONTREAL, QC**						
Le Bateau-Mouche	ES	1992	D	190*	108' 00"	22' 00"	3' 00"
L-11	**LE GROUPE C.T.M.A. (NAVIGATION MADELEINE INC.), CAP-AUX-MEULES, QC**						
C.T.M.A. Vacancier	PA/RR	1973	D	11,481*	388' 04"	70' 02"	43' 06"
(Aurella '80-'82, Saint Patrick II '82-'98, Egnatia II '98-'00, Ville de Sete '00-'01, City of Cork '01-'02)							
L-12	**LE GROUPE OCEAN, INC., QUEBEC, QC**						
Basse-Cote	DB	1932	B	400	201' 00"	40' 00"	12' 00"
Betsiamites	SU	1969	B	11,600	402' 00"	75' 00"	24' 00"
Coucoucache	TB	1934	D	95*	34' 01"	9' 05"	4' 02"
Jerry G.	TB	1960	D	202*	91' 06"	27' 03"	12' 06"
Lac St-Francois	BC	1979	B	1,200	195' 00"	35' 00"	12' 00"
La Prairie	TB	1975	D	110*	73' 09"	25' 09"	11' 08"
Navcomar #1	DB	1955	B	500	135' 00"	35' 00"	9' 00"
Ocean Abys	DB	1948	B	1,000	140' 00"	40' 00"	9' 00"
Ocean Bravo	TB	1970	D	320*	110' 00"	28' 06"	17' 00"
(Takis V. '70-'80, Donald P '80-'80, Nimue '80-'83, Donald P. '83-'98)							
Ocean Charlie	TB	1973	D	448*	123' 02"	31' 06"	18' 09"
(Leonard W. '73-'98)							
Ocean Delta	TB	1973	D	722*	136' 08"	35' 08"	22' 00"
(Sistella '73-'78, Sandy Cape '78-'80, Captain Ioannis S. '80-'99)							
Ocean Golf	TB	1959	D	159*	103' 00"	25' 10"	11' 09"
(Launched as Stranton. Helen M. McAllister '59-'97)							
Ocean Intrepide	TT	1998	D	302*	80' 00"	30' 01"	14' 09"
Ocean Jupiter {2}	TT	1999	D	302*	80' 00"	30' 00"	13' 04"
Omni-Atlas	CS	1913	B	479*	133' 00"	42' 00"	10' 00"
Omni-Richelieu	TB	1969	D	144*	83' 00"	24' 06"	13' 06"
(Port Alfred II '69-'82)							

Fleet #.	Fleet Name Vessel Name	Type of Vessel	Year Built	Type of Engine	Cargo Cap. or Gross*	Overall Length	Breadth	Depth or Draft*
	Omni St-Laurent	TB	1957	D	161*	99' 02"	24' 09"	12' 06"
	(Diligent '57-'89)							
	Vezina No. 1	TB	1967	D	8.00*	31' 01"	11' 01"	5' 02"
	Windoc {2}	BC	1959	B	29,100	730' 00"	75' 09"	40' 02"
	(Rhine Ore '59-'76, Steelcliffe Hall '76-'88) (Damaged by fire Aug. 11, 2001 after a bridge was lowered on its superstructure. Laid up awaiting conversion to a barge at Montreal.)							

THREE RIVERS BOATMEN LTD. – SUBSIDIARY OF LE GROUPE OCEAN, TROIS-RIVIERES, QC

Fleet #.	Fleet Name Vessel Name	Type of Vessel	Year Built	Type of Engine	Cargo Cap. or Gross*	Overall Length	Breadth	Depth or Draft*
	Andre H.	TB	1963	D	317*	126' 00"	28' 06"	15' 06"
	(Foundation Valiant '63-'73, Point Valiant {1} '73-'95)							
	Avantage	TB	1969	D	367*	116' 10"	32' 09"	16' 03"
	(Sea Lion '69-'97)							
	Duga	TB	1977	D	403*	111' 00"	33' 00"	16' 01"
	Escorte	TT	1964	D	120*	85' 00"	23' 08"	11' 00"*
	(USS Menasha [YTB / YTM-773, YTM-761] '64-'92, Menasha {1} '92-'95)							
	Ocean Echo II	AT	1969	D	438*	104' 08"	35' 05"	18' 00"
	(Atlantic '69-'75, Laval '75-'96)							
	Ocean Foxtrot	TB	1971	D	700*	184' 05"	38' 05"	16' 07"
	(Polor Shore '71-'77, Canmar Supplier VII '77-'95)							
	Ocean Hercule	TB	1976	D	448*	120' 00"	32' 00"	19' 00"
	(Stril Pilot '76-'81, Spirit Sky '81-'86, Ierland '86-'89, Ierlandia '89-'95, Charles Antoine '95-'97)							
	R. F. Grant	TB	1969	D	78*	71' 00"	17' 00"	8' 00"

L-13   LEE MARINE LTD., SOMBRA, ON

Fleet #.	Fleet Name Vessel Name	Type of Vessel	Year Built	Type of Engine	Cargo Cap. or Gross*	Overall Length	Breadth	Depth or Draft*
	Hammond Bay	ES	1992	D	43*	54' 00"	16' 00"	3' 00"
	(Scrimp & Scrounge '92-'95)							
	Nancy A. Lee	TB	1939	D	9*	40' 00"	12' 00"	3' 00"

Algocen unloads at the St. Lawrence Cement dock in Duluth.   (Glenn Blaskiewicz)

Fleet #.	Fleet Name Vessel Name	Type of Vessel	Year Built	Type of Engine	Cargo Cap. or Gross*	Overall Length	Breadth	Depth or Draft*
L-14	**LES BATEAUX BLANCS DU ST. LAURENT**							
	Richelieu	CF	1961	D	882*	200' 00"	70' 06"	10' 00"
	(Trois Rivieres '61-'00)							
L-15	**LES EQUIPMENTS VERREAULT INC., LES MECHINS, QC**							
	Epinette II	TB	1965	D	75*	61' 03"	20' 01"	8' 05"
L-16	**LOCK TOURS CANADA BOAT CRUISES, SAULT STE. MARIE, ON**							
	Chief Shingwauk	ES	1965	D	109*	70' 00"	24' 00"	4' 06"
L-17	**LOWER LAKES TOWING LTD., PORT DOVER, ON**							
	Cuyahoga	SU	1943	D	15,675	620' 00"	60' 00"	35' 00"
	(J. Burton Ayers '43-'95) (Converted to a self-unloader,'74; Repowered,'01)							
	Michipicoten {2}	SU	1952	T	22,300	698' 00"	70' 00"	37' 00"
	(Elton Hoyt 2nd '52-'03) (Lengthened 72'-'57; Converted to a self-unloader,'80)							
	Mississagi	SU	1943	D	15,800	620' 06"	60' 00"	35' 00"
	(Hill Annex '43-'43, George A. Sloan '43-'01) (Converted to a self-unloader,'67; Repowered,'85)							
	Saginaw {3}	SU	1953	T	20,200	639' 03"	72' 00"	36' 00"
	(John J. Boland {3} '53-'99)							
	GRAND RIVER NAVIGATION CO., CLEVELAND, OH – AN AFFILIATE OF LOWER LAKES TOWING							
	Calumet	SU	1929	D	12,450	603' 09"	60' 00"	32' 00"
	(Myron C. Taylor '29-'01) (Converted to a self-unloader, 56; Repowered,'68)							
	Invincible	TBA	1979	D	180*	100' 00"	35' 00"	22' 06"
	(R. W. Sesler '79-'91)							
	Maumee	SU	1929	D	12,650	604' 09"	60' 00"	32' 00"
	(William G. Clyde '29-'61, Calcite II '61-'01) (Converted to a self-unloader,'61; Repowered,"64)							
	Richard Reiss	SU	1943	D	14,900	620' 06"	60' 03"	35' 00"
	(Launched as Adirondack, Richard J. Reiss {2} '43-'86) (Converted to a self-unloader,'64; Repowered,'76)							
	LAKE SERVICE SHIPPING CO. – OWNER; GRAND RIVER NAVIGATION CO. – OPERATOR							
	McKee Sons	SU	1945	B	19,900	579' 02"	71' 06"	38' 06"
	(USNS Marine Angel '45-'52)							
	(Converted from saltwater vessel to a self-unloading Great Lakes bulk carrier,'53; Engine removed and converted to a self-unloading barge,'91)							
L-18	**LUEDTKE ENGINEERING CO., FRANKFORT, MI**							
	Alan K. Luedtke	TB	1944	D	149*	86' 04"	23' 00"	10' 03"
	(U. S. Army ST-527 '44-'55, USCOE Two Rivers '55-'90)							
	Ann Marie	TB	1954	D	119*	71' 00"	19' 06"	9' 06"
	(ST-9684 '54-'80, Lewis Castle '80-'97, Apache '97-'01)							
	Chris E. Luedtke	TB	1936	D	18*	45' 00"	12' 03"	6' 00"
	Erich R. Luedtke	TB	1939	D	18*	45' 00"	12' 03"	6' 00"
	Gretchen B.	TB	1943	D	18*	45' 00"	12' 03"	6' 00"
	Karl E. Luedtke	TB	1928	D	32*	59' 03"	14' 09"	8' 00"
	Kurt Luedtke	TB	1956	D	96*	72' 00"	22' 06"	7' 06"
	(Jere C. '56-'90)							
M-1	**M. C. M. MARINE, INC., SAULT STE. MARIE, MI**							
	Beaver State	TB	1935	D	18*	43' 07"	12' 00"	5' 02"
	Dredge No. 55	DR	1927	B	678*	165' 00"	42' 06"	
	Drummond Islander II	CF	1961	D	97*	65' 00"	36' 00"	9' 00"
	Mackinaw City	TB	1943	D	23*	38' 00"	11' 05"	4' 07"
	Mohawk	TB	1945	D	46*	65' 00"	19' 00"	10' 06"
	Peach State	TB	1961	D	18*	45' 00"	12' 04"	5' 03"
	William C. Gaynor	TB	1956	D	146*	94' 00"	27' 00"	11' 09"
	(William C. Gaynor '56-'88, Captain Barnaby '88-'02)							
	SOO MARINE SUPPLY, SAULT STE. MARIE, MI – A DIVISION OF M.C.M. MARINE							
	Ojibway	SB	1945	D	65*	53' 00"	28' 00"	7' 00"
M-2	**MacDONALD MARINE LTD., GODERICH, ON**							
	Debbie Lyn	TB	1950	D	10*	45' 00"	14' 00"	10' 00"
	(Skipper '50-'60)							

Steamer *Middletown* in winter lay-up at Toledo March 2003. *(Roger LeLievre)*

Fleet #.	Fleet Name / Vessel Name	Type of Vessel	Year Built	Type of Engine	Cargo Cap. or Gross*	Overall Length	Breadth	Depth or Draft*
	Donald Bert	TB	1953	D	11*	45' 00"	14' 00"	10' 00"
	Dover	TB	1931	D	70*	84' 00"	17' 00"	6' 00"
	(Earleejune '31-?, Iveyrose ?-?)							
	Ian Mac	TB	1955	D	12*	45' 00"	14' 00"	10' 00"
M-3	**MADELINE ISLAND FERRY LINE, INC., LaPOINTE, WI**							
	Bayfield {2}	PA/CF	1952	D	83*	120' 00"	43' 00"	10' 00"
	(Charlotte '52-'99)							
	Island Queen {2}	PA/CF	1966	D	90*	75' 00"	34' 09"	10' 00"
	Madeline	PA/CF	1984	D	97*	90' 00"	35' 00"	8' 00"
	Nichevo II	PA/CF	1962	D	89*	65' 00"	32' 00"	8' 09"
M-4	**MAID OF THE MIST STEAMBOAT CO. LTD., NIAGARA FALLS, ON**							
	Maid of the Mist IV	ES	1976	D	74*	72' 00"	16' 00"	7' 00"
	Maid of the Mist V	ES	1983	D	74*	72' 00"	16' 00"	7' 00"
	Maid of the Mist VI	ES	1990	D	155*	78' 09"	29' 06"	7' 00"
	Maid of the Mist VII	ES	1997	D	160*	80' 00"	30' 00"	7' 00"
M-5	**MALCOLM MARINE, ST. CLAIR, MI**							
	Manitou {2}	TB	1943	D	491*	110' 00"	26' 05"	11' 06"
	(USCGC Manitou [WYT-60] '43-'84)							
M-6	**MANITOU ISLAND TRANSIT, LELAND, MI**							
	Manitou Isle	PA/PK	1946	D	39*	52' 00"	14' 00"	8' 00"
	(Namaycush '46-'59)							
	Mishe-Mokwa	PA/CF	1966	D	49*	65' 00"	17' 06"	8' 00"
	(LaSalle '66-'80)							
M-7	**MARINE ATLANTIC, INC., MONCTON, NB**							
	Atlantic Freighter	RR	1978	D	8,661	495' 05"	71' 01"	48' 01"
	(Tor Felicia '78-'78, Merzario Grecia '78-'83, Stena Grecia '83-'86)							
	Caribou	CF	1986	D	27,213*	587' 04"	84' 01"	27' 06"
	Joseph & Clara Smallwood	CF	1989	D	27,614*	587' 03"	84' 01"	22' 02"
	Leif Ericson	CF	1991	D	18,523*	465' 08"	78' 07"	43' 03"
	(Stena Challenger '91-'01)							
M-8	**MARINE MANAGEMENT, INC., CHICAGO, IL**							
	Baldy B.	TB	1932	D	36*	62' 00"	16' 01"	7' 00"
	Nicole S.	TB	1949	D	146*	88' 07"	24' 10"	10' 09"
	(Evening Star '49-'86, Protector '86-'94)							
M-9	**MARINE TECH LLC., DULUTH, MN**							
	Alton Andrew	CS	1958	B		70' 00"	50' 00	6' 00"
	Callie M.	TB	1910	D	51*	64' 03"	16' 09"	8' 06"
	(Chattanooga '10-'79, Howard T. Hagen '79-'94, Nancy Ann '94-2001)							
	Dean R. Smith	DR	1985	B	338*	120' 00"	48' 00"	7' 00"
	(No. 2 '85-'94, B. Yetter '94-'01)							
	Miss Laura	TB	1943	D	146*	81' 01"	24' 00"	9' 10"
	(DPC-3, Fresh Kills, Leopard)							
M-10	**MARIPOSA CRUISE LINE, TORONTO, ON**							
	Captain Matthew Flinders	ES	1982	D	696*	144' 00"	40' 00"	8' 06"
	Mariposa Belle	ES	1970	D	195*	93' 00"	23' 00"	8' 00"
	(Niagara Belle '70-'73)							
	Rosemary	ES	1960	D	52*	68' 00"	15' 06"	6' 08"
	Showboat Royal Grace	ES	1988	D	135*	58' 00"	18' 00"	4' 00"
	Torontonian	ES	1962	D	68*	68' 00"	18' 06"	6' 08"
	(Shiawassie '62-'82)							
M-11	**McASPHALT MARINE TRANSPORTATION LTD., SCARBOROUGH, ON**							
	Everlast	AB	1977	D	1,361*	143' 04"	44' 04"	21' 04"
	(Bilibino '77-'96)							

Canadian Coast Guard cutter *Simcoe* passes under the Blue Water bridges at Port Huron / Point Edward. *(Roger LeLievre)*

McAsphalt 401		TK	1966	B	3,642*	300' 00"	60' 00"	23' 00"
(Pittson 200 '66-'73, Pointe Levy '73-'87)								
Norman McLeod		TK	2001	B	6,809*	379' 02"	71' 06"	30' 02"
[ATB Everlast / Norman McLeod OA dimensions together]					500' 00"	71' 06"	30' 02"	

M-12 McCUE & OTHERS, CEDAR POINT, ON

Indian Maiden	PF	1987	D	128*	74' 00"	23' 00"	8' 00"

M-13 McKEIL WORK BOATS LTD. (McKEIL MARINE LTD.) , HAMILTON, ON

Atomic	TB	1945	D	96*	82' 00"	20' 00"	10' 00"
Beaver D.	TB	1955	D	15*	36' 02"	14' 09"	4' 04"
Bert Long	TB	1974	D	313*	64' 03"	25' 02"	6' 08"
(Miller Surrey, Dorothy Robinson)							
Bonnie B. III	TB	1969	D	308*	100' 03"	32' 00"	17' 00"
(Esso Oranjestad '69-'85, Oranjestad '85-'86, San Nicolas '86-'87, San Nicolas I '87-'88)							
Capt. Ralph Tucker	TK	1966	D	6,491*	440' 00"	60' 00"	31' 00"
(Imperial Acadia '66-'97, Algoscotia '97-'01, Ralph Tucker '01-'01)							
Carrol C I	TB	1969	D	291*	100' 03"	32' 00"	17' 00"
(Launched as Esso Oranjestad II, Esso San Nicolas '69-'86, San Nicolas '86-'87, Carrol C '87-'88)							
Colinette	TB	1943	D	64*	65' 00"	16' 00"	7' 00"
(Ottawa {1} '43-'57, Lac Ottawa '57-'66)							
Doug McKeil {2}	TB	1943	D	196*	130' 00"	30' 00"	15' 01"
(U. S. Army LT-643 '44-'77, Taurus '77-'90, Gaelic Challenge '90-'95, Frankie D. '95-'97, Dawson B. '97-'98)							
Erie West	DB	1951	B	1,800	290' 00"	50' 00"	12' 00"
(Dover Light)							
Evans McKeil	TB	1936	D	284*	110' 07"	25' 06"	11' 06"
(Alhajuela '36-'70, Barbara Ann {2} '70-'89)							
Flo-Mac	TB	1960	D	15*	40' 00"	13' 00"	6' 00"
Florence McKeil	TB	1962	D	207*	98' 05"	26' 00"	9' 07"
(T. 4 '62-?, Foundation Viceroy ?-'72, Feuille D' Erable '72-'97)							
Glenevis	TB	1944	D	91*	80' 06"	20' 00"	9' 07"
(HMCS Glenevis [W-65 / YTM-502] '44-'77)							
Greta V	TB	1951	D	14*	44' 00"	12' 00"	5' 00"
Jarrett McKeil	TB	1956	D	197*	91' 08"	27' 04"	13' 06"
(Robert B. No. 1 '56-'97)							
Jean Raymond	DB	1941	B	6,800	409' 00"	57' 00"	18' 00"
Jerry Newberry	TB	1956	D	244*	98' 00"	28' 02"	14' 04"
(Foundation Victor '56-'73, Point Victor '73-'77, Kay Cole '77-'95)							
John Spence	TB	1972	D	719*	171' 00"	38' 00"	15' 01"
(Mary B. VI '72-'81, Mary B. '81-'82, Mary B. VI '82-'83, Artic Tuktu '83-'94)							
King Fish	TB	1955	D	18*	55' 00"	16' 00"	6' 08"
(Duchess V '55-'00)							
Kristin	TB	1944	D	261*	111' 00"	27' 00"	13' 00"
(HMCS Riverton [W-47 / ATA-528] '44-'79, Techno St-Laurent '79-'02)							
KTC 115	TK	1968	B	6,430*	393' 07"	69' 08"	27' 05"
Lac Como	TB	1944	D	63*	65' 00"	16' 10"	7' 10"
(Tanac 74 '44-'64)							
Lac Erie	TB	1944	D	65*	65' 00"	16' 10"	7' 07"
(Tanmac '44-'74)							
Lac Manitoba	TB	1944	D	65*	65' 00"	16' 10"	7' 07"
(Tanac 75 '44-'52, Manitoba '52-'57)							
Lac Vancouver	TB	1943	D	65*	65' 00"	16' 10"	7' 07"
(Vancouver '43-'74)							
Maritime Trader	DB	1969	B	2,636*	250' 00"	76' 01"	16' 01"
(Barge 252 '69-'82, Genmar 252 '82-'87, McAllister 252 '87-'99)							
McLeary's Spirit	TK	1969	B	6,888*	379' 09"	63' 03"	33' 08"
(LeVent '69-'02)							
Ocean Hauler	TK	1943	B	4,540*	344' 00"	69' 00"	96' 00"
Paul E. No. 1	TB	1945	D	97*	80' 00"	20' 00"	9' 07"
(W.A.C. 4 '45-'46, E. A. Rockett '46-'76)							

Fleet #.	Fleet Name / Vessel Name	Type of Vessel	Year Built	Type of Engine	Cargo Cap. or Gross*	Overall Length	Breadth	Depth or Draft*
	Progress	TB	1948	D	123*	86' 00"	21' 00"	10' 00"
	(P. J. Murer '48-'81, Michael D. Misner '81-'93, Thomas A. Payette '93-'96)							
	Salvager	TB	1961	D	429*	120' 00"	32' 09"	18' 09"
	(M. Moran '61-'70, Port Arthur '70-'72, M. Moran '72-'00)							
	Salty Dog No. 1	TK	1945	B	4,018*	313' 00"	68' 03"	26' 07"
	(Fort Hoskins '45-'66, Ocean Hauler 10 '66-'79, ATC 610 '79-'91)							
	Salvor	TB	1963	D	426*	120' 00"	32' 09"	18' 09"
	(Esther Moran '63-'00)							
	Sault au Couchon	DH	1969	B	10,000	422' 11"	74' 10"	25' 07"
	St. Clair {2}	TF	1927	B	27 rail cars	400' 00"	54' 00"	22' 00"
	(Pere Marquette 12 '27-'70)							
	Stormont	TB	1953	D	108*	80' 00"	20' 00"	9' 07"
	Tony MacKay	TB	1973	D	366*	127' 00"	30' 05"	14' 05"
	(Point Carroll '73-'01)							
	William J. Moore	TB	1970	D	564*	135' 00"	34' 09"	19' 04"
	(Warrawee '70-'76, Seaspan Raider '76-'87, Raider '87-'87, Raider IV '87-'88, Alice A. '88-'02)							
	Wyatt McKeil	TB	1950	D	237*	102' 06"	26' 00"	13' 06"
	(Otis Wack '50-'97)							
	MONTREAL BOATMAN, POINTE AUX TREMBLES, QC – SUBSIDIARY OF McKEIL WORK BOATS							
	Aldo H.	PB	1979	D	37*	56' 04"	15' 04"	6' 02"
	Boatman No. 3	PB	1965	D	13*	33' 08"	11' 00"	6' 00"
	Boatman No. 6	PB	1979	D	39*	56' 07"	18' 07"	6' 03"
	Pilot 1	PB	1994	D	14*	32' 01"	5' 08"	2' 06"
	REMORQUEURS & BARGES MONTREAL LTEE, SALABERRY-DE-VALLEYFIELD, QC A SUBSIDIARY OF McKEIL WORK BOATS							
	Condarrell	CS	1953	D	3,017	259' 00"	43' 06"	21' 00"
	(D. C. Everest '53-'81)							
	Pacific Standard	TB	1967	D	451*	127' 08"	31' 00"	15' 06"
	(Irishman '67-'76, Kwakwani '76-'78, Lorna B. '78-'81)							
	Willmac	TB	1959	D	16*	40' 00"	13' 00"	3' 07"
M-14	**McLEOD BROTHERS MECHANICAL, SAULT STE. MARIE, ON**							
	Kam	TB	1927	D	33*	52' 00"	13' 00"	5' 06"*
	(North Shore Supply '27-'74)							
M-15	**McMULLEN & PITZ CONSTRUCTION CO., MANITOWOC, WI**							
	Dauntless	TB	1937	D	25*	52' 06"	15' 06"	5' 03"
	Erich	TB	1943	D	19*	45' 00"	12' 07"	5' 09"
M-16	**McNALLY MARINE, INC., TORONTO, ON**							
	Bagotville	TB	1964	D	65*	65' 00"	18' 06"	10' 00"
	Canadian	DR	1954	B	1,087*	173' 08"	49' 08"	13' 04"
	Canadian Argosy	DR	1978	B	951*	149' 09"	54' 01"	10' 08"
	Carl M.	TB	1957	D	21*	47' 00"	14' 06"	6' 00"
	Idus Atwell	DR	1962	B	366*	100' 00"	40' 00"	8' 05"
	John Holden	DR	1954	B	148*	89' 08"	30' 01"	6' 02"
	Le Tareau	TB	1985	D	25*	36' 04"	14' 07"	5' 09"
	Manistique	TB	1954	D	16*	38' 00"	12' 01"	3' 02"
	Paula M.	TB	1959	D	12*	46' 06"	16' 01"	4' 10"
	R. C. L. No. II	TB	1958	D	20*	42' 09"	14' 03"	5' 09"
	Sandra Mary	TB	1962	D	97*	80' 00"	21' 00"	10' 09"
	(Flo Cooper '62-'00)							
	Whitby	TB	1978	D	24*	45' 00"	14' 00"	5' 00"
	BEAVER MARINE LTD., A SUBSIDIARY OF McNALLY MARINE INC., HALIFAX, NS							
	Baie Ste. Anne II	TB	1988	D	25*	36' 04"	14' 07"	5' 09"
	Dapper Dan	TB	1948	D	21*	41' 03"	12' 07"	5' 09"
	Mister Joe	TB	1964	D	70*	61' 00"	19' 00"	7' 02"

Fleet #.	Fleet Name / Vessel Name	Type of Vessel	Year Built	Type of Engine	Cargo Cap. or Gross*	Overall Length	Breadth	Depth or Draft*
M-17	**MENASHA TUGBOAT CO., SARNIA, ON**							
	Menasha {2}	TB	1949	D	147*	78' 00"	24' 00"	9' 08"
	(W. C. Harms '49-'54, Hamilton '54-'86, Ruby Casho '86-'88, W. C. Harms '88-'97)							
M-18	**MERCURY CRUISE LINES, PALATINE, IL**							
	Chicago's First Lady	ES	1991	D	62*	96' 00"	22' 00"	9' 00"
	Chicago's Little Lady	ES	1999	D	70*	68' 00"	23' 00"	8' 06"*
	Skyline Princess	ES	1956	D	56*	59' 04"	16' 00"	4' 08"
	Skyline Queen	ES	1959	D	45*	61' 05"	16' 10"	6' 00"
M-19	**MICHIGAN DEPARTMENT OF NATURAL RESOURCES, LANSING, MI**							
	Channel Cat	RV	1968	D	24*	46' 00"	13' 06"	4' 00"
	Chinook	RV	1947	D	26*	50' 00"	12' 00"	5' 00"
	Judy	RV	1950	D	41*	40' 00"	12' 00"	3' 06"
	Steelhead	RV	1967	D	70*	63' 00"	16' 04"	6' 06"
M-20	**MICHIGAN TECHNOLOGICAL UNIVERSITY, HOUGHTON, MI**							
	Agassiz	RV	2002	D	14*	36' 00"	12' 00"	4' 00"
M-21	**MIDDLE BASS BOAT LINE, MIDDLE BASS, OH**							
	Victory	PA/CF	1960	D	14*	63' 07"	15' 03"	4' 08"
M-22	**MIKE SCRUTON, PORT DOVER, ON**							
	Ashtabula	TB	1915	D	66*	68' 07"	17' 00"	11' 00"
	(Ashtabula '15-'55, Tiffin '55-'69, Jenny T. II '69-'02)							
M-23	**MILLER BOAT LINE, INC., PUT-IN-BAY, OH**							
	Islander {3}	PA/CF	1983	D	92*	90' 03"	38' 00"	8' 03"
	Put-In-Bay {3}	PA/CF	1997	D	95*	96' 00"	38' 06"	9' 06"
	South Bass	PA/CF	1989	D	95*	96' 00"	38' 06"	9' 06"
	Wm. Market	PA/CF	1993	D	95*	96' 00"	38' 06"	8' 09"
M-24	**MILWAUKEE BULK TERMINALS, INC., MILWAUKEE, WI**							
	MBT 10	DH	1994	B	1,960	200' 00"	35' 00'	13' 00"
	MBT 20	DH	1994	B	1,960	200' 00"	35' 00'	13' 00"
	MBT 33	DH	1976	B	3,793	240' 00"	52' 06"	14' 06"*
M-25	**MONTREAL SHIPPING, INC., STEPHENVILLE, NF**							
	Point Viking	TB	1962	D	207*	98' 05"	27' 10"	13' 05"
	(Foundation Viking '62-'75)							
M-26	**MORRISH-WALLACE CONSTRUCTION INC, CHEBOYGAN, MI**							
	Amber Mae	TB	1922	D	67*	65' 00"	14' 01"	10' 00"
	(E. W. Sutton '22-'52, Venture '52-'00)							
M-27	**MORTON SALT CO., CHICAGO, IL**							
	Morton Salt 74	DB	1974	B	2,101	195' 00"	35' 00"	12' 00"
M-28	**MURPHY SAILING TOURS LTD., HALIFAX, NS**							
	Theodore Too	ES	2000	D	80*	60' 03"	31' 09"	8' 08"
M-29	**MUSIQUE AQUATIQUE CRUISE LINES, INC., TORONTO, ON**							
	Harbour Star	ES	1978	D	45*	63' 06"	15' 09"	3' 09"
	(K. Wayne Simpson '78-'95)							
M-30	**MUSKOKA LAKES NAVIGATION & HOTEL CO. LTD., GRAVENHURST, ON**							
	Segwun	PA	1887	R	168*	128' 00"	24' 00"	7' 06"
	(Nipissing {2} 1887-'25)							
	Wanda III	PA	1915	R	60*	94' 00"	12' 00"	5' 00"
	Wenonah II	PA	2001	D	470*	127' 00"	28' 00"	6' 00"*
N-1	**NADRO MARINE SERVICES LTD., PORT DOVER, ON**							
	Ecosse	TB	1979	D	146*	91' 00"	26' 01"	8' 06"
	(R & L No. 1 '79-'96)							

Fleet #.	Fleet Name Vessel Name	Type of Vessel	Year Built	Type of Engine	Cargo Cap. or Gross*	Overall Length	Breadth	Depth or Draft*
	Escuminac	TB	1948	D	8.7*	33' 04"	9' 08"	4' 05"
	Miseford	TB	1915	D	116*	85' 00"	20' 00"	10' 06"
	Nadro Clipper	TB	1939	D	64*	70' 00"	23' 00"	6' 06"
	(Stanley Clipper '39-'94)							
	Seahound	TB	1941	D	60*	65' 06"	17' 00"	7' 00"
	([Unnamed] '41-'56, Sea Hound '56-'80, Carolyn Jo '80-'00)							
	Terry S.	TB	1958	D	16*	52' 00"	17' 00"	6' 00"
	Vac	TB	1942	D	37*	65' 00"	21' 00"	6' 06"
	Vigilant 1	TB	1944	D	111*	76' 08"	20' 09"	10' 02"
	(HMCS Glenlivet [W-43] '44-'75, Glenlivet II '75-'77, Canadian Franko '77-'82, Glenlivet II '82-'00)							
N-2	**NAUTICAL ADVENTURES, TORONTO, ON**							
	Empire Sandy	ES/3S	1943	D/W	434*	140' 00"	32' 08"	14' 00"
	(Empire Sandy '43-'48, Ashford '48-'52, Chris M. '52-'79)							
	Wayward Princess	ES	1976	D	325*	92' 00"	26' 00"	10' 00"
	(Cayuga II '76-'82)							
N-3	**NAVY MARINE CORPS RESERVE CENTER, BUFFALO, NY**							
	LCU 1680	TV	1943	D	170*	135' 00"	29' 00"	
N-4	**NELSON CONSTRUCTION CO., LaPOINTE, WI**							
	Eclipse	TB	1937	D	23*	40' 00"	10' 00"	4' 06"
N-5	**NELVANA YACHT CHARTERS, TORONTO, ON**							
	Nelvana {1}	ES	1963	D	61*	55' 10"	16' 00"	5' 00"
N-6	**NEWFOUNDLAND TRANSSHIPMENT LTD., ST. JOHN, NF**							
	Placentia Hope	TT	1998	D	925*	125' 00"	42' 08"	17' 05"
	Placentia Pride	TT	1998	D	925*	125' 00"	42' 08"	17' 05"
N-7	**NIAGARA STEAMSHIP CO., NIAGARA ON THE LAKE, ON**							
	Pumper	ES	1903	R	25*	60' 00"	14' 06"	7' 06"
	(Planet '03-'29, Racey '29-'57, Paul Evans '57-'80, Racey '80-'?)							
N-8	**NICHOLSON TERMINAL & DOCK CO., RIVER ROUGE, MI**							
	Charles E. Jackson	TB	1956	D	12*	35' 00"	10' 06"	5' 01"
	Detroit {1}	TF	1904	B	22 cars	308' 00"	76' 09"	19' 06"
N-9	**NORTH CHANNEL DIVING & MARINE (GARDINER MARINE), RICHARD'S LANDING, ON**							
	Joyce K. Gardiner	TB	1962	D	71*	72' 00"	19' 00"	12' 00"
	(Angus M. '62-'92, Omni Sorel '92-'02)							
	Opeongo	TB	1947	D	21*	50' 00"	13' 00"	6' 00"*
N-10	**NORTHERN MARINE TRANSPORTATION, SAULT STE. MARIE, MI**							
	David Allen	PB	1964	D	32*	56' 04"	13' 03"	6' 00"
	Linda Jean	PB	1950	D	17*	38' 00"	10' 00"	5' 00"
	Soo River Belle	PB	1961	D	25*	40' 00"	14' 00"	6' 00"
N-11	**NORTHERN TRANSPORTATION CO., LTD., EDMONTON, ALBERTA**							
	Keewatin	TB	1974	D	476*	126' 00"	38' 01"	12' 01"
	NT Stone Merchant	DW	1965	B	2,127*	250' 01"	75' 01"	16' 00"
N-12	**NORTHUMBERLAND FERRIES LTD. / BAY FERRIES LTD., CHARLOTTETOWN, PEI**							
	Confederation {2}	CF	1993	D	8,060*	374' 08"	61' 07"	17' 09"
	Holiday Island	CF	1971	D	3,037*	325' 00"	67' 06"	16' 06"
	(Launched as William Pope)							
	Princess of Acadia	CF	1971	D	10,051*	480' 01"	66' 00"	12' 06"
	(Launched as Princess of Nova)							
	The Cat	CF	2002	D	5,400*	318' 02"	85' 03"	14' 09"
N-13	**NORTHWEST MARINE, INC., WAUWATOSA, WI**							
	Islay	TB	1892	D	19*	60' 00"	13' 00"	5' 00"*
	(Islay 1892-'47, Bayfield {1} '47-'83)							

Fleet #.	Fleet Name / Vessel Name	Type of Vessel	Year Built	Type of Engine	Cargo Cap. or Gross*	Overall Length	Breadth	Depth or Draft*

N-14   **NUNAVUT EASTERN ARCTIC SHIPPING INC., (NEAS), VALLEYFIELD, QC**

	Aivik	HL	1980	D	4,860	359' 08"	63' 08"	38' 09"
	(Mont Ventoux '80-'90, Aivik '90-'91, Unilifter '91-'92)							
	Umiavut	GC	1988	D	9,682	371' 02"	63' 01"	37' 00"
	(Completed as Newca, Kapitan Silin '88-'92, Lindengracht '92-'00)							

O-1   **OAK GROVE MARINE AND TRANSPORTATION, INC., CLAYTON, NY**

	Maple Grove	PK	1954	D	55*	75' 00"	21' 00"	5' 06"*

O-2   **ODYSSEY CRUISES, CHICAGO, IL**

	Odyssey II	ES	1993	D	101*	200' 00"	41' 00"	9' 00"*

O-3   **OGLEBAY NORTON MARINE SERVICES CO., CLEVELAND, OH**

(At press time, this company was in Chapter 11 bankruptcy, with vessels reported for sale or lease, possibly to American Steamship Co. or other operators.)

	Armco	SU	1953	T	25,500	767' 00"	70' 00"	36' 00"
	(Lengthened by 120'-'74; Converted to a self-unloader, '82)							
	Buckeye {3}	SU	1952	T	22,300	698' 00"	70' 00"	37' 00"
	(Sparrows Point '52-'90) (Lengthened by 72'-'58; Converted to a self-unloader, '80)							
	Columbia Star	SU	1981	D	78,850	1,000' 00"	105' 00"	56' 00"
	Courtney Burton	SU	1953	T	22,300	690' 00"	70' 00"	37' 00"
	(Ernest T. Weir {2} '53-'78; Converted to a self-unloader, '81).							
	David Z. Norton {3}	SU	1973	D	19,650	630' 00"	68' 00"	36' 11"
	(William R. Roesch '73-'95)							
	Earl W. Oglebay	SU	1973	D	19,650	630' 00"	68' 00"	36' 11"
	(Paul Thayer '73-'95)							
	Fred R. White Jr.	SU	1979	D	23,800	636' 00"	68' 00"	40' 00"
	Middletown	SU	1942	T	26,300	730' 00"	75' 00"	39' 03"
	(Laid down as Marquette. USS Neshanic [AO-71] '42-'47, Gulfoil '47-'61, Pioneer Challenger '61-'62)							
	(Converted from saltwater tanker to Great Lakes bulk carrier, '61; Converted to a self-unloader, '82)							
	Oglebay Norton	SU	1978	D	78,850	1,000' 00"	105' 00"	56' 00"
	Reserve	SU	1953	T	25,500	767' 00"	70' 00"	36' 00"
	(Lengthened 120'-'75; Converted to a self-unloader, '83)							
	Wolverine {4}	SU	1974	D	19,650	630' 00"	68' 00"	36' 11"
	ERIE SAND STEAMSHIP CO., ERIE, PA – A SUBSIDIARY OF OGLEBAY NORTON MARINE							
	J. S. St. John	SC	1945	D	680	174' 00"	32' 02"	15' 00"
	(USS YO-178 '45-'51, Lake Edward '51-'67)							
	Day Peckinpaugh	PA	1921	D	1,490	254' 00"	36' 00"	14' 00"
	(Interwaterways Line Incorporated 101 '21-'32, I.L.I. 101 '32-'36, Richard J. Barnes '36-'58)							
	(Last operated Sept. 9, 1994; Laid up at Erie, PA.)							

O-4   **OLSON DREDGE & DOCK CO., ALGONAC, MI**

	John Michael	TB	1913	D	41*	55' 04"	15' 01"	7' 06"
	(Colonel Ward, Ross Cuddington, Joseph J. Olivieri)							

O-5   **ONTARIO MINISTRY OF TRANSPORTATION & COMMUNICATION, KINGSTON, ON**

	Amherst Islander {2}	PA/CF	1955	D	184*	106' 00"	38' 00"	10' 00"
	Frontenac II	PA/CF	1962	D	666*	181' 00"	45' 00"	10' 00"
	(Charlevoix {2} '62-'92)							
	Glenora	PA/CF	1952	D	209*	127' 00"	33' 00"	9' 00"
	(The St. Joseph Islander '52-'74)							
	Quinte Loyalist	PA/CF	1954	D	209*	127' 00"	32' 00"	8' 00"
	Wolfe Islander III	PA/CF	1975	D	985*	205' 00"	68' 00"	6' 00"

O-6   **ONTARIO POWER GENERATION INC., TORONTO, ON**

	Niagara Queen II	IB	1992	D	57*	56' 01"	18' 00"	6' 08"

O-7   **ONTARIO WATERWAY CRUISES, INC., ORILLIA, ON**

	Kawartha Voyager	PA	1983	D	264*	108' 00"	22' 00"	5' 00"

CATHERINE DESGAGNES

Vessel Spotlight

Although smaller in size compared to most of today's Great Lakes vessels, the *Catherine Desgagnes* is still a frequent visitor to various Great Lakes and Seaway ports. Built by Hall, Russell and Company of Aberdeen, Scotland, this deep-sea bulk and general cargo carrier was launched in 1961 as *Gosforth* for the Burnett Steamship Co. of Newcastle, Great Britain. *Gosforth* sailed under the Burnett banner until 1972, with the years 1970-1972 under Fednav management.

In 1972 the *Gosforth* was purchased by Trico Enterprises, a wholly-owned subsidiary of the Quebec and Ontario Transportation Co. Ltd. (Q&O) of Montreal, which chartered the ship to its parent company. The vessel was renamed *Thorold* (4) and after a refit at Sorel, Quebec, to carry newsprint, departed Baie Comeau, Quebec, July 31, 1972, on her maiden voyage with 4,786 tons of newsprint for Port Canaveral and Port Everglades, Fla.

Originally built with deck cranes, these were removed in 1977. Her tenure with Q&O saw the *Thorold* carry 235 cargoes of which approximately 37 percent were newsprint and 35 percent were grain and wheat products. Other cargoes included steel ingots, zinc, salt, pig iron, phosphates and gypsum.

Q&O ceased operations at the end of 1983, and *Thorold* and her seven remaining fleetmates were acquired by Le Groupe Desgagnes Inc. of Quebec, Quebec. This acquisition marked the formal entry into Great Lakes trading by Desgagnes, whose fleet dates back to the late 1800s.

Thorold was renamed *Catherine Desgagnes* in 1985. Her trade routes on

***Catherine Desgagnes* at Thunder Bay.**   *(Gene Onchulenko)*

the Great Lakes/Seaway continued along with some deep-sea work and the addition of voyages to the Arctic on the resupply run to northern ports. *Catherine Desgagnes* can often be seen on the Great Lakes laden with cargoes such as pig iron or wheat and grain products. **– George Wharton**

Fleet #.	Fleet Name Vessel Name	Type of Vessel	Year Built	Type of Engine	Cargo Cap. or Gross*	Overall Length	Breadth	Depth or Draft*
O-8	**ORILLIA BOAT CRUISES LTD., ORILLIA, ON**							
	Island Princess {1}	ES	1989	D	194*	65' 00"	27' 00"	5' 00"
O-9	**OSBORNE MATERIALS CO., MENTOR, OH**							
	John R. Emery	SC	1905	D	490	140' 00"	33' 00"	14' 00"
	(Trenton {1} '05-'25)							
	Emmet J. Carey	SC	1948	D	900	114' 00"	23' 00"	11' 00"
	(Beatrice Ottinger '48-'63, James B. Lyons '63-'88)							
	F. M. Osborne {2}	SC	1910	D	500	150' 00"	29' 00"	11' 03"
	(Grand Island {1} '10-'58, Lesco '58-'75)							
O-10	**OWEN SOUND TRANSPORTATION CO. LTD., OWEN SOUND, ON**							
	Chi-Cheemaun	PA/CF	1974	D	6,991*	365' 05"	61' 00"	21' 00"
	PELEE ISLAND TRANSPORTATION SERVICES, PELEE ISLAND, ON							
	A DIVISION OF OWEN SOUND TRANSPORTATION CO. LTD.							
	Jiimaan	CF	1992	D	2,830*	176' 09"	42' 03"	13' 06"
	Pelee Islander	CF	1960	D	334*	145' 00"	32' 00"	10' 00"
P-1	**PELEE HYDROFOIL CORP., KINGSVILLE, ON**							
	Pelee Flyer 1	HY	1990	D		90' 07"	20' 04"	6' 07"*
	(Sunrise I '90-'96, Sunrise V '96-'03)							
	Pelee Flyer 2	HY	1990	D		90' 07"	20' 04"	6' 07"*
	(Sunrise II '90-'96, Sunrise VI '96-'03))							
P-2	**PENETANGUISHENE 30,000 ISLAND CRUISES, PENETANGUISHENE, ON**							
	Georgian Queen	ES	1918	D	249*	119' 00"	36' 00"	16' 06"
	(Victoria '18-'18, Murray Stewart '18-'48, David Richard '48-'79)							
P-3	**PENETANGUISHENE MIDLAND COACH LINE 30,000 ISLAND BOAT CRUISES, MIDLAND, ON**							
	Miss Midland	ES	1974	D	119*	68' 07"	19' 04"	6' 04"
	Serendipity Princess	ES	1982	D	93*	69' 00"	23' 00"	4' 03"*
	(Trent Voyageur '82-'87, Serendipity Lady '87-'95)							
P-4	**PERE MARQUETTE SHIPPING CO., LUDINGTON, MI**							
	Pere Marquette 41	SU	1941	B	4,545	403' 00"	58' 00"	23' 06"
	(City of Midland 41 '41-'97; Converted from powered train / carferry to self-unloading barge, '97)							
	Undaunted	AT	1944	D	860*	143' 00"	33' 01"	18' 00"
	(USS Undaunted [ATR-126, ATA-199] '44-'63, USMA Kings Pointer '63-'93, Krystal K. '93-'97)							
	[ATB Undaunted / Pere Marquette 41 OA dimensions together]					493' 06"	58' 00"	23' 06"
P-5	**PICTURED ROCKS CRUISES, INC., MUNISING, MI**							
	Grand Island {2}	ES	1989	D	51*	68' 00"	16' 01"	5' 01"
	Miners Castle	ES	1974	D	72*	68' 00"	17' 00"	5' 00"
	Miss Superior	ES	1984	D	76*	68' 00"	17' 00"	5' 00"
	Pictured Rocks	ES	1972	D	47*	60' 00"	14' 00"	4' 04"
P-6	**PIER WISCONSIN, MILWAUKEE, WI**							
	Denis Sullivan	TV/ES	1994	W	99*	138' 00"	24' 00"	8' 09"
P-7	**PIERRE GAGNE CONTRACTING LTD., THUNDER BAY, ON**							
	M A C Gagne	BC	1964	B	30,500	730' 00"	75' 02"	44' 08"
	(Saguenay {2} '64-'98) (Last operated Nov. 30, 1992. Hull laid up at Thunder Bay, ON.)							
P-8	**PLAUNT TRANSPORTATION CO., INC., CHEBOYGAN, MI**							
	Kristen D.	CF	1988	D	83*	64' 11"	36' 00"	6' 05"
P-9	**PORT CITY PRINCESS CRUISES, INC., MUSKEGON, MI**							
	Port City Princess	ES	1966	D	79*	64' 09"	30' 00"	5' 06"
	(Island Queen {1} '66-'87)							
P-10	**PORT MANSION ENTERTAINMENT GROUP, ST. CATHARINES, ON**							
	Dalhousie Princess	ES	1975	D	281*	106' 00"	24' 00"	8' 02"
	(Island Queen {3} '75-'79, Miss Kingston II '79-'84, M/V Montreal '84-'01)							

Fleet #.	Fleet Name / Vessel Name	Type of Vessel	Year Built	Type of Engine	Cargo Cap. or Gross*	Overall Length	Breadth	Depth or Draft*
P-11	**PORTOFINO ON THE RIVER, WYANDOTTE, MI**							
	Friendship	ES	1968	D	110*	85' 00"	30' 06"	7' 03"
	(Peche Island V '68-'71, Papoose V '71-'82)							
P-12	**PROTEUS CO., CHICAGO, IL.**							
	Atchafalaya	DR	1980	D	760*	196' 08"	40' 06"	16' 04"
	Columbus	DR	1942	D	2,923*	310' 02"	50' 00"	22' 01"
	(USS LST 987 '44-'55, USS Millard County '55-'73, Esperance III '73-'86, Columbus '86-							
P-13	**PURVIS MARINE LTD., SAULT STE. MARIE, ON**							
	Adanac	TB	1913	D	108*	80' 03"	19' 02"	10' 06"
	(Edward C. Whalen '13-'66, John McLean '66-'95)							
	Anglian Lady	TB	1953	D	398*	136' 06"	30' 00"	14' 01"
	(Hamtun '53-'72, Nathalie Letzer '72-'88)							
	Avenger IV	TB	1962	D	293*	120' 00"	30' 05"	17' 05"
	(Avenger '62-'85)							
	Charles W. Johnson	DB	1915	B	1,685	245' 00"	43' 00"	14' 00"
	(Iocolite '15-'47, Imperial Kingston '47-'61)							
	Chief Wawatam	DB	1911	B	4,500	347' 00"	62' 03"	15' 00"
	(Converted from a powered trainferry to a self-unloading barge, '88)							
	G.L.B. No. 1	DB	1953	B	3,215	305' 00"	50' 00"	12' 00"
	(Joe Baugh Jr. '53-'66, ORG 5503 '66-'75)							
	G.L.B. No. 2	DB	1953	B	3,215	305' 02"	50' 00"	12' 00"
	(Jane Newfield '53-'66, ORG 6502 '66-'75)							
	Goki	TB	1940	D	24*	57' 00"	12' 08"	7' 00"
	Lewis G. Harriman	CC	1923	R	5,500	350' 00"	55' 00"	28' 00"
	(John W. Boardman '23-'65)							
	(Last operated April 20,1980. Scheduled to be scrapped in 2004 at Sault Ste. Marie, ON.)							
	Malden	DB	1946	B	1,075	150' 00"	41' 09"	10' 03"
	Martin E. Johnson	TB	1959	D	26*	46' 00"	16' 00"	5' 09"
	Osprey	TB	1944	D	36*	45' 00"	13' 06"	7' 00"
	P.M.L. Alton	DB	1951	B	150	93' 00"	30' 00"	8' 00"
	P.M.L. Salvager	DB	1945	B	5,200	341' 00"	54' 00"	27' 00"
	([Unnamed] '45-'55, Balsambranch '55-'73, M.I.L. Balsam '73-'77, Techno Balsam '77-'77,							
	DDS Salvager '77-'88)							
	P.M.L. 357	DB	1944	B	600	138' 00"	38' 00"	11' 00"
	P.M.L. 2501	TK	1980	B	1,954*	302' 00"	52' 00"	17' 00"
	(CTCO 2505 '80-'96)							
	P.M.L. 9000	TK	1968	B	4,285*	400' 00"	76' 00"	20' 00"
	(Palmer '68-'00)							
	Reliance	TB	1974	D	708*	148' 04"	35' 07"	21' 06"
	(Sinni '74-'81, Irving Cedar '81-'96, Atlantic Cedar '96-'02)							
	Rocket	TB	1901	D	39*	70' 00"	15' 00"	8' 00"
	Sheila P.	TB	1940	D	15*	40' 00"	14' 00"	
	Tecumseh II	DB	1976	B	2,500	180' 00"	54' 00"	12' 00"
	(U-727 '76-'94)							
	Wilfred M. Cohen	TB	1948	D	284*	104' 00"	28' 00"	14' 06"
	(A. T. Lowmaster '48-'75)							
	W. I. Scott Purvis	TB	1938	D	206*	96' 06"	26' 04"	10' 04"
	(Orient Bay '38-'75, Guy M. No. 1 '75-'90)							
	W. J. Ivan Purvis	TB	1938	D	191*	100' 06"	25' 06"	9' 00"
	(Magpie '38-'66, Dana T. Bowen '66-'75)							
	Yankcanuck {2}	CS	1963	D	4,760	324' 03"	49' 00"	26' 00"
P-14	**PUT-IN-BAY BOAT LINE CO., PORT CLINTON, OH**							
	Jet Express	PC	1989	D	93*	92' 08"	28' 06"	8' 04"
	Jet Express II	PC	1992	D	85*	92' 06"	28' 06"	8' 04"
	Jet Express III	PC	2001	D	70*	78' 02"	27' 06"	8' 02"

Fleet #.	Fleet Name Vessel Name	Type of Vessel	Year Built	Type of Engine	Cargo Cap. or Gross*	Overall Length	Breadth	Depth or Draft*
Q-1	**QUEEN CITY YACHT CLUB, TORONTO, ON**							
	Algonquin Queen II	PA	2002	D	36.3*	41' 09"	15' 04"	4' 05"
R-1	**RANDOLPH LEWIS HINTON, BOBCAYGEON, ON**							
	Caravelle II	ES	1975	D	27.5*	41' 03"	13' 04"	3' 09"J5
	Karwartha Spirit	ES	1964	D	88*	64' 10"	23' 05"	7' 04"
	(Miss Muskoka {1} '64-'69, Miss Niagara '69-'72, Miss Buffalo '72-'03)							
R-2	**RANKIN CONSTRUCTION INC., ST. CATHARINES, ON**							
	Judique Flyer	DB	1967	D	67.7*	60' 00"	29' 08"	3' 09"
	(Sweep Scow No. 4 '67-'03)							
R-3	**RAYMOND BURTON BERKSHIRE, PLACENTIA, NF**							
	Paradise Sound	GC	1969	D	430	137' 04"	25' 00"	11' 01"
	(Tower Duchess '69-'84)							
	Placentia Sound	GC	1969	D	713	173' 11"	29' 00"	12' 01"
	(Apollo 1 '69-'80, Arklow River '80-'82, Cynthia June '82-'86, Tora '86-'88, Greeba River '88-'97)							
R-4	**RAYMOND MICHAEL DAVIS, TOBERMORY, ON**							
	Dawn Light	TB	1891	D	64*	75' 00"	24' 00"	12' 00"
	(Le Roy Brooks 1891-'25, Henry Stokes '25-'54, Aburg '54-'81)							
R-5	**RIGEL SHIPPING CANADA, INC., SHEDIAC, NB**							
	Diamond Star	TK	1992	D	10,530	405' 11"	58' 01"	34' 09"
	(Elbestern '92-'93)							
	Emerald Star	TK	1992	D	10,530	405' 11"	58' 01"	34' 09"
	(Emsstern '92-'92)							
	Jade Star	TK	1993	D	10,530	405' 11"	58' 01"	34' 09"
	(Jadestern '93-'94)							
R-6	**ROCKPORT BOAT LINE (1994) LTD., ROCKPORT, ON**							
	Ida M.	ES	1970	D	29*	55' 00"	14' 00"	3' 00"
	Ida M. II	ES	1973	D	116*	63' 02"	22' 02"	5' 00"
R-7	**ROEN SALVAGE CO., STURGEON BAY, WI**							
	Chas Asher	TB	1967	D	10*	50' 00"	18' 00"	8' 00"
	John R. Asher	TB	1943	D	93*	70' 00"	20' 00"	8' 06"
	(U. S. Army ST-71 '43-'46, Russell 8 '46-'64, Reid McAllister '64-'67, Donegal '67-'85)							
	Louie S.	TB	1956	D	43*	37' 00"	12' 00"	5' 00"
	Spuds	TB	1944	D	19*	42' 00"	12' 06"	6' 00"
	Stephan M. Asher	TB	1954	D	60*	65' 00"	19' 01"	5' 04"
	(Captain Bennie '54-'82, Dumar Scout '82-'87)							
	Timmy A.	TB	1953	D	12*	33' 06"	10' 08"	5' 02"
R-8	**ROYAL CANADIAN YACHT CLUB, TORONTO, ON**							
	Elsie D.	PA	1958	D	9*	34' 07"	10' 08"	3' 06"
	Esperanza	PA	1953	D	14*	38' 06"	11' 02"	4' 06"
	Hiawatha	PA	1895	D	46*	56' 01"	14' 04"	6' 02"
	Kwasind	PA	1912	D	47*	70' 08"	15' 09"	5' -5"
R-9	**RUSSELL ISLAND TRANSIT CO., ALGONAC, MI**							
	Islander {2}	CF	1982	D		41' 00"	15' 00"	3' 06"
R-10	**RYBA MARINE CONSTRUCTION CO., CHEBOYGAN, MI**							
	Alcona	TB	1957	D	18*	40' 00"	12' 06"	5' 06"
	Harbor Master	CS	1979	B	100*	70' 00"	27' 00"	4' 00"
	Jarco 1402	CS	1981	B	473*	140' 00"	39' 00"	9' 00"
	Kathy Lynn	TB	1944	D	140*	85' 00"	24' 00"	9' 06"
	(U. S. Army ST-693 '44-'79, Sea Islander '79-'91)							
	Relief	CS	1924	B	1,000	160' 00"	40' 00"	9' 00"
	Rochelle Kaye	TB	1963	D	52*	51' 06"	19' 04"	7' 00"
	(Jaye Anne '63-?, Katanni ?-'97)							
	Tonawanda	CS	1935	B	600	120' 00"	45' 00"	8' 00"

Cedarglen heads into the setting sun on the St. Marys River Aug. 30. 2003.   *(Roger LeLievre)*

Fleet #.	Fleet Name Vessel Name	Type of Vessel	Year Built	Type of Engine	Cargo Cap. or Gross*	Overall Length	Breadth	Depth or Draft*
S-1	**SANKORE MARINE IMMERSION HIGH SCHOOL, DETROIT, MI**							
	Sea-Born	ES	1961	D	55*	65' 00"	17' 00"	5' 00"
	(Falcon '61-'65, Bucky '65-'68, Holiday '68-'72, Speedy IV '72-'74, Capt. Bill Van '74-'76,							
	Pilot II '76-'77, Capt. Eddie B. '77-'94, Huron Lady '94-'01)							
S-2	**SAWMILL CREEK RESORT, HURON, OH**							
	Sawmill Explorer	ES	1953	D	12*	65' 00"	17' 00"	4' 00"
	(Cedar Point II '53-'89, Dispatch '89'-??)							
S-3	**SCOTLUND STIVERS, MARINETTE, WI**							
	Arthur K. Atkinson	PA	1917	D	3,241*	384' 00"	56' 00"	20' 06"
	(Ann Arbor No. 6 '17-'59) (Last operated in April, 1982. Laid up in at DeTour, MI)							
S-4	**SEA FOX THOUSAND ISLANDS BOAT TOURS, KINGSTON, ON**							
	General Brock III	ES	1977	D	56*	50' 05"	15' 04"	
	(Miss Peterborough)							
	Island Heritage	ES	1929	D	21*	63' 09"	9' 08"	4' 09"
	(Miss Ivy Lea No. 1)							
	Sea Fox II	ES	1988	D	55*	39' 08"	20' 00"	2' 00"*
S-5	**SEA SERVICE L. L. C., SUPERIOR, WI**							
	Sea Colt	TB	1984	D	23*	38' 00"	11' 06"	8' 00"
	(Clara '84-'95)							
	Sea Bear	PB	1959	D		45' 00"		
	(Narrows '59-'02)							
	Sea Eagle	PB		D				
S-6	**SEAWAY MARINE TRANSPORT, ST. CATHARINES, ON** *PARTNERSHIP BETWEEN ALGOMA CENTRAL CORP. AND UPPER LAKES GROUP, INC.* *SEE RESPECTIVE FLEETS FOR VESSELS INVOLVED*							
S-7	**SELVICK MARINE TOWING CORP., STURGEON BAY, WI**							
	Carla Anne Selvick	TB	1908	D	191*	96' 00"	23' 00"	11' 02"
	(S.O. Co. No. 19 '08-'16, S.T. Co. No. 19 '16-'18, Socony 19 '18-'47, Esso Tug No. 4 '47-'53,							
	McAllister 44 '53-'55, Roderick McAllister '55-'84)							
	Escort II	TB	1955	D	26*	50' 00"	15' 00"	7' 03"
	Jacquelyn Nicole	TB	1913	D	96*	81' 00"	20' 00"	12' 06"
	(Michigan {4} '13-'78, Ste. Marie II '78-'81, Dakota '81-'92. Ethel E. '92-'02)							
	Jimmy L.	TB	1939	D	148*	110' 00"	25' 00"	13' 00"
	(USCGC Naugatuck [WYT / WYTM-92] '39-'80, Timmy B. '80-'84)							
	Mary Page Hannah {1}	TB	1950	D	461*	143' 00"	33' 01"	14' 06"
	(U. S. Army ATA-230 '49-'72, G. W. Codrington '72-'73, William P. Feeley {2} '73-'73,							
	William W. Stender '73-'78)							
	Sharon M. Selvick	TB	1945	D	28*	45' 06"	13' 00"	7' 01"
	Susan L.	TB	1944	D	163*	86' 00"	23' 00"	10' 04"
	(U. S. Army ST-709 '44-'47, USCOE Stanley '47-'99)							
	William C. Selvick	TB	1944	D	142*	85' 00"	22' 11"	10' 04"
	(U. S. Army ST-500 '44-'49, Sherman H. Serre '49-'77)							
S-8	**SHAMROCK CHARTERING CO., GROSSE POINT, MI**							
	Helene	ES	1927	D	109*	106' 00"	17' 00"	6' 06"*
S-9	**SHELL PRODUCTS CANADA, MONTREAL, QC**							
	Arca	RT	1963		734*	175' 00"	36' 00"	14' 00"
	(Imperial Lachine '63-'03, Josee M. '03-'03)							
	Horizon Montreal	RT	1958	D	2,758*	315' 00"	45' 07"	24' 07"
	(Tyee Shell '58-'69, Arctic Trader '69-'83, Rivershell {4} '83-'95)							
S-10	**SHEPARD MARINE CONSTRUCTION, ST. CLAIR SHORES, MI**							
	Robin Lynn	TB	1952	D	146*	85' 00"	25' 00"	11' 00"
	(Bonita '52-'85, Susan Hoey {2} '85'-'95, Blackie B '95-'97, Susan Hoey {3 }'97-'98)							

Fleet #.	Fleet Name / Vessel Name	Type of Vessel	Year Built	Type of Engine	Cargo Cap. or Gross*	Overall Length	Breadth	Depth or Draft*
S-11	**SHEPLER'S MACKINAC ISLAND FERRY SERVICE, MACKINAW CITY, MI**							
	Capt. Shepler	PF	1986	D	71*	78' 00"	21' 00"	7' 10"
	Felicity	PF	1972	D	84*	65' 00"	18' 01"	8' 03"
	Sacre Bleu	PK	1959	D	92*	94' 10"	31' 00"	9' 09"
	(Put-In-Bay {2} '59-'94)							
	The Hope	PF	1975	D	87*	77' 00"	20' 00"	8' 03"
	The Welcome	PF	1969	D	66*	60' 06"	16' 08"	8' 02"
	Wyandot	PF	1979	D	99*	77' 00"	20' 00"	8' 00"
S-12	**SHIPWRECK TOURS, INC., MUNISING, MI**							
	Miss Munising	ES	1967	D	50*	60' 00"	14' 00"	4' 04"
S-13	**SHORELINE CHARTERS, GILLS ROCK, WI**							
	The Shoreline	ES	1973	D		33' 00"	11' 4"	3' 00"
S-14	**SHORELINE CONTRACTORS INC., CLEVELAND, OH**							
	Eagle	TB	1943	D	31*	57' 09"	14' 05"	6' 10"
S-15	**SHORELINE SIGHTSEEING CO., CHICAGO, IL**							
	Allons-Y	PF	1978	D	25"	40' 00"	12' 00"	8' 00"
	Andiamo	PF	1980	D	25*	40' 00"	12' 00"	8' 00"
	Blue Dog	PF	1981	D	31*	47' 07"	18' 00"	5' 05"
	Cap Streeter	ES	1987	D	28*	63' 06"	24' 04"	7' 07"
	Evening Star	ES	2001	D	93*	83' 00"	23' 00"	7' 00"
	Shoreline II	ES	1987	D	89*	75' 00"	26' 00"	7' 01"
	Star of Chicago {2}	ES	1999	D	73*	64' 10"	22' 08"	7' 05"
S-16	**SIVERTSON'S GRAND PORTAGE – ISLE ROYALE TRANSPORTATION LINES, SUPERIOR, WI**							
	A. E. Clifford	FT	1946	D	33*	45' 00"	15' 00"	7' 00"
	Provider	FT	1959	D	14*	46' 00"	13' 05"	5' 05"
	Sharon Jon	FT	1943	D	17*	32' 04"	11' 06"	5' 00"
	Voyageur II	ES	1970	D	40*	63' 00"	18' 00"	5' 00"
	Wenonah	ES	1960	D	91*	70' 07"	19' 04"	9' 07"
S-17	**SOCIETE DES TRAVERSIERS DU QUEBEC, QUEBEC, QC**							
	Alphonse Desjardins	CF	1971	D	1,741*	214' 00"	71' 06"	20' 00"
	Armand Imbeau	CF	1980	D	1,285*	203' 07"	72' 00"	18' 04"
	Camille Marcoux	CF	1974	D	6,122*	310' 09"	62' 09"	39' 00"
	Catherine-Legardeur	CF	1985	D	1,348*	205' 09"	71' 10"	18' 10"
	Felix-Antoine Savard	CF	1997	D	2,489*	272' 00"	70' 00"	21' 09"
	Grue des Iles	CF	1981	D	447*	155' 10"	41' 01"	12' 06"
	Jos Deschenes	CF	1980	D	1,287*	203' 07"	72' 00"	18' 04"
	Joseph-Savard	CF	1985	D	1,445*	206' 00"	71' 10"	18' 10"
	Lomer Gouin	CF	1971	D	1,741*	214' 00"	71' 06"	20' 00"
	Lucien L.	CF	1967	D	867*	220' 10"	61' 06"	15' 05"
	Radisson {1}	CF	1954	D	1,043*	164' 03"	72' 00"	10' 06"
S-18	**SOCIETE DU PORT DE MONTREAL, MONTREAL, QC**							
	Maisonneuve	TB	1972	D	103*	63' 10"	20' 07"	9' 03"
S-19	**SOO LOCKS BOAT TOURS, SAULT STE. MARIE, MI**							
	Bide-A-Wee {3}	ES	1955	D	99*	64' 07"	23' 00"	7' 11"
	Hiawatha {2}	ES	1959	D	99*	64' 07"	23' 00"	7' 11"
	Holiday	ES	1957	D	99*	64' 07"	23' 00"	7' 11"
	LeVoyageur	ES	1959	D	70*	65' 00"	25' 00"	7' 00"
	Nokomis	ES	1959	D	70*	65' 00"	25' 00"	7' 00"
S- 20	**SPIRIT CRUISE LINE LTD., TORONTO, ON**							
	Northern Spirit I	ES	1983	D	489*	136' 00"	31' 00"	9' 00"
	(New Spirit '83-'89, Pride of Toronto '89-'92)							
	Oriole	ES	1987	D	200*	75' 00"	23' 00"	9' 00"

Fleet #.	Fleet Name / Vessel Name	Type of Vessel	Year Built	Type of Engine	Cargo Cap. or Gross*	Overall Length	Breadth	Depth or Draft*
S- 21	**SPIRIT OF CHICAGO CRUISES, CHICAGO, IL**							
	Spirit of Chicago	ES	1988	D	92*	156' 00"	35' 00"	7' 01"
S-22	**SPIRIT LAKE MARINA, DULUTH, MN**							
	John V. II	TB	1942	D	12*	40' 00"	10' 00"	3' 05"
S-23	**ST. LAWRENCE CRUISE LINES, INC., KINGSTON, ON**							
	Canadian Empress	PA	1981	D	463*	108' 00"	30' 00"	8' 00"
S-24	**ST. LAWRENCE SEAWAY DEVELOPMENT CORP., MASSENA, NY**							
	Robinson Bay	TB	1958	D	213*	103' 00"	26' 10"	14' 06"
	Performance	TB	1997	D		50' 00"		
S-25	**ST. LAWRENCE SEAWAY MANAGEMENT CORP., CORNWALL, ON**							
	VM/S Hercules	GL	1962	D	2,107*	200' 00"	75' 00"	18' 08"
	VM/S Maisonneuve	TB	1974	D	56*	58' 03"	20' 03"	6' 05"
	VM/S St. Lambert	TB	1974	D	20*	30' 08"	13' 01"	6' 05"
S-26	**ST. MARY'S CEMENT CO., TORONTO, ON**							
	Sea Eagle II	TBA	1979	D	560*	132' 00"	35' 00"	19' 00"
	(Sea Eagle '79-'81, Canmar Sea Eagle '81-'91)							
	St. Mary's Cement II	CC	1978	B	19,513	496' 06"	76' 00"	35' 00"
	(Velasco '78-'81, Canmar Shuttle '81-'90)							
	St. Mary's Cement III	CC	1980	B	4,800	335' 00"	76' 08"	17' 09"
	(Bigorange XVI '80-'84, Says '84-'85, Al-Sayb-7 '85-'86, Clarkson Carrier '86-'94)							
	(Last operated Sept. 1, '00; In use as a cement storage barge at Green Bay, WI.)							

GREAT LAKES & INTERNATIONAL TOWING & SALVAGE CO., INC., BURLINGTON, ON
CHARTERED BY ST. MARY'S CEMENT CO.

	Petite Forte	TB	1969	D	368*	127' 00"	32' 00"	14' 06"
	(E. Bronson Ingram '69-'72, Jarmac 42 '72-'73, Scotsman '73-'81, Al Battal '81-'86)							
	St. Mary's Cement	CC	1986	B	9,400	360' 00"	60' 00"	23' 03"
S-27	**STANTON CRUISE LINES, THUNDER BAY, ON**							
	Pioneer II	ES	1959	D	28*	52' 01"	11' 08"	3' 09"
	(Witte-De-With '59-'72, Miss Algonquin Park '72-'74, David H. Simpson '74-'90, London Princess '90-'02)							
S-28	**STAR LINE MACKINAC ISLAND FERRY, ST. IGNACE, MI**							
	Cadillac {5}	PF	1990	D	73*	64' 07"	20' 00"	7' 07"
	Joliet {3}	PF	1993	D	83*	64' 08"	22' 00"	8' 03"
	LaSalle {4}	PF	1983	D	55*	65' 00"	20' 00"	7' 05"
	Marquette {5}	PF	1979	D	55*	62' 03"	22' 00"	7' 01"
	Nicolet {2}	PF	1985	D	51*	65' 00"	20' 00"	7' 05"
	Radisson {2}	PF	1988	D	97*	80' 00"	23' 06"	7' 00"
S-29	**STAR OF SAUGATUCK BOAT CRUISES, SAUGATUCK, MI**							
	Star of Saugatuck	ES	1978	D	12*	57' 00"	14' 00"	2' 04"
S-30	**STATE OF NEW YORK POWER AUTHORITY, LEWISTON, NY**							
	Breaker	TB	1962	D	29*	43' 03"	14' 03"	5' 00"
	Daniel Joncaire	TB	1979	D	25*	43' 03"	15' 00"	5' 00"
S-31	**STEPHEN HUME, DETROIT, MI**							
	Queen City {2}	PA	1911	D	248*	116' 00"	23' 00"	12' 07"
	(Polana '11-'30, Jalobert '30-'54, Macassa {2} '54-'65; Last operated 1982. Laid up at Detroit, MI.)							
S-32	**STEVEN WALLACE, PENETANGUISHENE, ON**							
	Georgian Storm	TB	1931	D	167*	91' 00"	24' 02"	12' 00"
	(Capitaine Simard '31-'57, Renee Simard '57-'86)							
T-1	**T & T DREDGING, INC., GRAND RAPIDS, MI**							
	Bonnie G. Selvick	TB	1928	D	95*	86' 00"	21' 00"	12' 00"
	(E. James Fucik '28-'77)							

TUGS

MCM's workhorse tug *Mohawk* pushes a derrick barge at the Soo. *(Roger LeLievre)*

William J. Moore on the drydock at Hamilton. *(Paul Beesley)*

Magnetic assists a ship at Detroit.
(Ferriss Marine Contracting)

Donald C. Hannah and barge cross Lake St. Clair. *(Roger LeLievre)*

Fleet #.	Fleet Name / Vessel Name	Type of Vessel	Year Built	Type of Engine	Cargo Cap. or Gross*	Overall Length	Breadth	Depth or Draft*
	Louise	DR		B				
	Wolverine	TB	1952	D	22*	42' 05"	14' 00"	7' 00"
T- 2	**TALISMAN ENERGY INC., CALGARY, AL**							
	J.R. Rouble	DV	1958	D	562*	123' 06"	49' 08"	16' 00"
	(Mr. Neil)							
	Miss Libby	DV	1972	B	924*	160' 01"	54' 01"	11' 01"
	Dr. Bob	DV	1973	B	1,022*	160' 01"	54' 01"	11' 01"
	Mr. Chris '73-'03)							
	Sarah No. 1	TB	1969	D	43*	72' 01"	17' 03"	6' 08"
	Timesaver II	DB	1964	B	510*	91' 08"	70' 08"	9' 01"
T-3	**TEE DEE ENTERPRISES, INC., CHICAGO, IL**							
	Anita Dee 1	ES	1972	D	97*	90' 00"	21' 00"	8' 10"
	(M/V Happy Dolphin '72-'84, Spirit of Toledo '84-?)							
	Anita Dee II	ES	1990	D	81*	140' 00"	33' 00"	8' 06"
T-4	**THOMAS A. KOWAL, ROCHESTER, NY**							
	Apalachee	TB	1943	D	224*	104' 03"	26' 04"	15' 01"
	(Apalachee WYTM-71 '43-??)							
T-5	**THOMAS W. MARSHALL, TORONTO, ON**							
	Still Watch	SV	1960	D	390*	134' 02"	28' 00"	13' 09"
	(CCGS Ville Marie '60-'87, Heavenbound '85-'97)							
T-6	**THUNDER BAY MARINE SERVICE LTD., THUNDER BAY, ON**							
	Agoming	CS	1926	B	155*	100' 00"	34' 00"	9' 00"
	Coastal Cruiser	TB	1939	D	29*	65' 00"	18' 00"	12' 00"
	Robert W.	TB	1949	D	48*	60' 00"	16' 00"	8' 06"
	Rosalee D.	TB	1943	D	22*	55' 00"	16' 00"	10' 00"
T-7	**THUNDER BAY TUG SERVICES LTD., THUNDER BAY, ON**							
	Glenada	TB	1943	D	107*	80' 06"	25' 00"	10' 01"
	(HMCS Glenada [W-30] '43-'45)							
	Point Valour	TB	1958	D	246*	97' 08"	28' 02"	13' 10"
	(Foundation Valour '58-'83)							
T-8	**TOM ERHART-TERRACE INN HOTEL, PETOSKEY, MI**							
	Bay Pride	ES	1987	D	27*	42' 00"	14' 00"	7' 00"
T-9	**TORONTO DRY-DOCK CORP., TORONTO, ON**							
	Menier Consol	FD	1962	B	2,575*	304' 07"	49' 06"	25' 06"
T-10	**TORONTO FIRE DEPARTMENT, TORONTO, ON**							
	Wm. Lyon Mackenzie	FB	1964	D	102*	81' 01"	20' 00"	10' 00"
T-11	**TORONTO PADDLEWHEEL CRUISES LTD., NORTH YORK, ON**							
	Pioneer Princess	ES	1984	D	74*	56' 00"	17' 01"	3' 09"
	Pioneer Queen	ES	1968	D	110*	85' 00"	30' 06"	7' 03"
	(Peche Island III '68-'71, Papoose IV '71-'96)							
T-12	**TORONTO PORT AUTHORITY, TORONTO, ON**							
	Fred Scandrett	TB	1963	D	52*	62' 00"	17' 00"	8' 00"
	(C. E."Ted" Smith '63-'70)							
	Maple City	CF	1951	D	135*	70' 06"	36' 04"	5' 11"
	Osprey	TB	1991	D	5*	25' 09"	8' 08"	3' 06"
	William Rest	TB	1961	D	62*	65' 00"	18' 06"	10' 06"
	Windmill Point	CF	1954	D	118*	65' 00"	36' 00"	10' 00"
T-13	**TORONTO TOURS LTD., TORONTO, ON**							
	Miss Kim Simpson	ES	1960	D	33*	90' 02"	13' 04"	3' 09"
	Shipsands	ES	1972	D	23*	58' 03"	12' 01"	4' 09"

Fleet #.	Fleet Name / Vessel Name	Type of Vessel	Year Built	Type of Engine	Cargo Cap. or Gross*	Overall Length	Breadth	Depth or Draft*
T-14	**TRANSPORT DESGAGNES, INC., QUEBEC, QC**							
	CROISIERES NORDIK, INC., QUEBEC, QC-A DIVISION OF TRANSPORT DESGAGNES, INC.							
	Nordik Passeur	RR	1962	D	627	285' 04"	62' 00"	20' 01"
	(Confederation {1} '62-'93, Hull 28 '93-'94) (5 year survey expired 1994 – Laid up in Quebec, QC.)							
	DESGAGNES SHIPPING INT., INC., QUEBEC, QC-A DIV. OF TRANSPORT DESGAGNES, INC.							
	Anna Desgagnes	RR	1986	D	17,850	565' 00"	75' 00"	45' 00"
	(Truskavets '86-'96, Anna Desgagnes '96-'98, PCC Panama '98-'99)							
	DESGAGNES TANKER, INC., QUEBEC, QC-A DIVISION OF TRANSPORT DESGAGNES, INC.							
	Maria Desgagnes	TK	1999	D	95,607	393' 08"	68' 11"	40' 04"
	(Kilchem Asia '99-'99)							
	Petrolia Desgagnes	TK	1975	D	97,725	441' 05"	56' 06"	32' 10"
	(Jorvan '75-'79, Lido '79-'84, Ek-Sky '84-'98)							
	Thalassa Desgagnes	TK	1976	D	104,667	441' 05"	56' 06"	32' 10"
	(Joasla '76-'79, Orinoco '79-'82, Rio Orinoco '82-'93)							
	Vega Desgagnes	TK	1982	D	82,417	461' 11"	69' 08"	35' 01"
	(Shelltrans '82-'94, Acila '94-'99, Bacalan '99-'01)							
	GROUP DESGAGNES, INC., QUEBEC, QC-A DIVISION OF TRANSPORT DESGAGNES, INC.							
	Amelia Desgagnes	GC	1976	D	7,126	355' 00"	49' 00"	30' 06"
	(Soodoc {2} '76-'90)							
	Camilla Desgagnes	GC	1982	D	7,000	436' 03"	68' 05"	22' 06"
	(Camilla '82-'04)							
	Catherine Desgagnes	GC	1962	D	8,350	410' 03"	56' 04"	31' 00"
	(Gosforth '62-'72, Thorold {4} '72-'85)							
	Cecelia Desgagnes	GC	1971	D	7,875	374' 10"	54' 10"	34' 06"
	(Carl Gorthon '71-'81, Federal Pioneer '81-'85)							
	Jacques Desgagnes	GC	1960	D	1,250	208' 10"	36' 00"	14' 00"
	(Loutre Consol '60-'77)							
	Mathilda Desgagnes	GC	1959	D	6,920	360' 00"	51' 00"	30' 02"
	(Eskimo '59-'80)							
	Melissa Desgagnes	GC	1975	D	7,000	355' 00"	49' 00"	30' 06"
	(Ontadoc {2} '75-'90)							
	Nova D.	GC	1961	D	5,039	404' 01"	60' 05"	36' 06"
	(French River '61-'81, Jensen Star '81-'86, Woodland '86-'91, Woodlands '91-'98, Lorena 1 '98-'03)							
	Nordik Express	CF	1974	D	1,697	219' 11"	44' 00"	16' 01"
	(Theriot Offshore IV '74-'77, Scotoil 4 '77-'79, Tartan Sea '79-'87)							
T-15	**TRAVERSE TALL SHIP CO., TRAVERSE CITY, MI**							
	Manitou {1}	ES/2S	1983	W	78*	114' 00"	21' 00"	9' 00"
	Westwind	ES/2S	1992	W	43*	66' 00"	14' 00"	8' 06"
U-1	**UNCLE SAM BOAT TOURS, ALEXANDRIA, NY**							
	Alexandria Belle	ES	1988	D	72*	104' 00"	32' 00"	7' 08"*
	Island Duchess	ES	1988	D	60*	110' 00"	27' 08"	8' 08"*
	Island Wanderer	ES	1971	D	57*	62' 05"	22' 00"	7' 02"
	Uncle Sam 7	ES	1976	D	55*	60' 04"	22' 00"	7' 01"
U-2	**UNITED STATES ARMY CORPS OF ENGINEERS, CHICAGO, IL – GREAT LAKES / OHIO RIVER DIV.**							
	UNITED STATES ARMY CORPS OF ENGINEERS, BUFFALO, NY – BUFFALO DISTRICT							
	Cheraw	TB	1970	D	356*	109' 00"	30' 06"	16' 03"
	(USS Cheraw [YTB-802] '70-'96)							
	Koziol	TB	1973	D	356*	109' 00"	30' 06"	16' 03"
	(USS Chetek [YTB-827] '73-'96, Chetek '96-'00)							
	McCauley	CS	1948	B		112' 00"	52' 00"	3' 00"*
	Simonsen	CS	1954	B		142' 00"	58' 00"	5' 00"*
	Wheeler	DR	1982	B	10,353	384' 00"	78' 00"	39' 00"
	UNITED STATES ARMY CORPS OF ENGINEERS, CHICAGO, IL – CHICAGO DISTRICT							
	Kenosha	TB	1954	D	82*	70' 00"	20' 00"	9' 08"
	(U. S. Army ST-2011 '54-'65)							

Arthur M. Anderson unloads coal at Escanaba. *(Rod Burdick)*

ARTHUR M. ANDERSON

Vessel Spotlight

One of the best-known lake boats is the *Arthur M. Anderson*. Famed for her heroic role involving the loss of the *Edmund Fitzgerald* in 1975, the *Anderson* was the last vessel to have radio contact with the *Fitzgerald* before her sinking on Lake Superior. Built by American Shipbuilding Co. of Lorain, Ohio, the 647-foot bulk carrier was launched Feb. 16, 1952, for the Pittsburgh Steamship Division of the U.S. Steel Corp. She was one of three identical sister ships (given the designation "AAA class") to enter service for Pittsburgh in 1952, the other two being *Philip R. Clarke* and *Cason J. Callaway*.

During 1953, her first full season of sailing, the vessel carried a record 866,885 tons in 46 trips. The year 1962 marked a milestone when the *Anderson* became the first vessel in the Pittsburgh fleet to transit the relatively new St. Lawrence Seaway system. She departed Conneaut, Ohio, on Aug. 14 and arrived at Port Cartier, Quebec, Aug. 17 to load Canadian iron ore for Gary, Ind. She was also a participant in the experimental extensions of the Great Lakes navigation seasons during the winters of 1974/'75 and 1975/'76.

The *Arthur M. Anderson* was lengthened by 120 feet in the spring of 1975 at Fraser Shipyard, Superior, Wis., and converted to a self-unloader during the 1981/'82 winter lay-up at the same location. Further upgrades included the installation of a bowthruster back in 1966 and the installation of a sternthruster in 1989.

Most recently, the *Anderson* sailed as part of the Great Lakes Fleet, Inc. of Duluth, although that could change in 2004 with the pending sale of GLF to Canadian National Railroad. Although the *Anderson* was designed for the iron ore trade, bulk cargoes such as stone products, limestone, salt or coal can now be found in her cargo holds as well. – *George Wharton*

Fleet #.	Fleet Name / Vessel Name	Type of Vessel	Year Built	Type of Engine	Cargo Cap. or Gross*	Overall Length	Breadth	Depth or Draft*
	Manitowoc	CS	1976	B		132' 00"	44' 00"	8' 00"*
	Racine	TB	1931	D	61*	66' 03"	18' 05"	7' 08"

UNITED STATES ARMY CORPS OF ENGINEERS, DETROIT, MI – DETROIT DISTRICT

Fleet #.	Fleet Name / Vessel Name	Type of Vessel	Year Built	Type of Engine	Cargo Cap. or Gross*	Overall Length	Breadth	Depth or Draft*
	B.W. Bufe	SV	2003	Gas		25' 11"	10' 00"	3' 02"
	D. L. Billmaier	TB	1968	D	356*	109' 00"	30' 06"	16' 03"
	(USS Natchitoches [YTB-799] '68-'95)							
	Demolen	TB	1974	D	356*	109' 00"	30' 06"	16' 03"
	(USS Metacom [YTB-829] '74-'01, Metacom '01-'02)							
	Fairchild	TB	1953	D	23*	45' 00"	13' 00"	7' 00"*
	Hammond Bay	TB	1953	D	23*	45' 00"	13' 00"	7' 00"*
	H. J. Schwartz	CS	1995	B		150' 00"	48' 00"	11' 00"
	Huron	CS	1954	B		100' 00"	34' 00"	4' 06"*
	Michigan	CS	1971	B		120' 00"	33' 00"	3' 06"*
	Nicolet	CS	1971	B		120' 00"	42' 00"	5' 00"*
	Owen M. Frederick	TB	1942	D	56*	65' 00"	17' 00"	7' 06"
	Paul Bunyan	GL	1945	B		150' 00"	65' 00"	12' 06"
	Tawas Bay	TB	1953	D	23*	45' 00"	13' 00"	7' 00"*
	Veler	CS	1991	B	613*	150' 00"	46' 00"	10' 06"
	Whitefish Bay	TB	1953	D	23*	45' 00"	13' 00"	7' 00"*

U-3   UNITED STATES COAST GUARD 9TH COAST GUARD DISTRICT, CLEVELAND, OH

Fleet #.	Fleet Name / Vessel Name	Type of Vessel	Year Built	Type of Engine	Cargo Cap. or Gross*	Overall Length	Breadth	Depth or Draft*
	Acacia **[WLB-406]**	BT	1944	D	1,025*	180' 00"	37' 00"	17' 04"
	(Launched as USCGC Thistle [WAGL-406]) (Scheduled to be decommissioned in 2005.)							
	Alder **[WLB-216]**	BT	2004	D	2,000*	225' 09"	46' 00"	19' 08"
	Biscayne Bay **[WTGB-104]**	IB	1979	D	662*	140' 00"	37' 06"	12' 00"*
	Bristol Bay **[WTGB-102]**	IB	1979	D	662*	140' 00"	37' 06"	12' 00"*
	Buckthorn **[WLI-642]**	BT	1963	D	200*	100' 00"	24' 00"	4' 08"*
	CGB-12000	BT	1991	B	700*	120' 00"	50' 00"	6' 00"*
	CGB-12001	BT	1991	B	700*	120' 00"	50' 00"	6' 00"*
	Hollyhock **[WLB-214]**	BT	2003	D	2,000*	225' 09"	46' 00"	19' 08"
	Katmai Bay **[WTGB-101]**	IB	1978	D	662*	140' 00"	37' 06"	12' 00"*
	Mackinaw **[WAGB-83]**	IB	1944	D	5,252*	290' 00"	74' 00"	29' 00"
	(Launched as USCGC Manitowoc [WAG-83]) (Scheduled to be decommissioned in 2006.)							
	Mackinaw **[WLBB-30]**	IB	2005	D	15'06"*	240' 00"	58' 00"	15' 05"*
	(Scheduled to be commissioned in 2005 and stationed at Cheboygan, MI.)							
	Mobile Bay **[WTGB-103]**	IB	1979	D	662*	140' 00"	37' 06"	12' 00"*
	Neah Bay **[WTGB-105]**	IB	1980	D	662*	140' 00"	37' 06"	12' 00"*
	Sundew **[WLB-404]**	BT	1944	D	1,025*	180' 00"	37' 00"	17' 04"
	(Scheduled for decommissioning in 2004, to be replaced at Duluth by Alder.)							

U-4   UNITED STATES DEPARTMENT OF THE INTERIOR, ANN ARBOR, MI
GREAT LAKES SCIENCE CENTER

Fleet #.	Fleet Name / Vessel Name	Type of Vessel	Year Built	Type of Engine	Cargo Cap. or Gross*	Overall Length	Breadth	Depth or Draft*
	Grayling	RV	1977	D	198*	75' 00"	22' 00"	9' 10"
	Kaho	RV	1961	D	83*	64' 10"	17' 10"	9' 00"
	Kiyi	RV	1999	D	290*	107' 00"	27' 00"	12' 02"
	Musky II	RV	1960	D	25*	45' 00"	14' 04"	5' 00"
	Siscowet	RV	1946	D	54*	57' 00"	14' 06"	7' 00"
	Sturgeon	RV	1977	D	325*	100' 00"	25' 05"	10' 00"

U-5   UNITED STATES ENVIRONMENTAL PROTECTION AGENCY, DULUTH, MN. & CHICAGO, IL

Fleet #.	Fleet Name / Vessel Name	Type of Vessel	Year Built	Type of Engine	Cargo Cap. or Gross*	Overall Length	Breadth	Depth or Draft*
	Bluewater	RV	1970	D	22*	50' 00"	14' 00"	3' 0"
	Lake Explorer	RV	1962	D	69*	82' 10"	17' 07"	5' 11"*
	(USCGC Point Roberts [WPB-82332] '62-'92)							
	Lake Guardian	RV	1981	D	282*	180' 00"	40' 00"	11' 00"
	(Marsea Fourteen '81-'90)							
	Mudpuppy	RV	1988	D	6*	32' 00"	8' 00"	2' 00"

Fleet #.	Fleet Name Vessel Name	Type of Vessel	Year Built	Type of Engine	Cargo Cap. or Gross*	Overall Length	Breadth	Depth or Draft*
U-6	**UNITED STATES FISH AND WILDLIFE SERVICE**							
	JORDAN RIVER NATIONAL FISH HATCHERY, ELMIRA, MI							
	Togue	RV	1975	D	95*	73' 00"	22' 00"	10' 00"
U-7	**UNITED STATES NATIONAL PARK SERVICE-ISLE ROYALE NATIONAL PARK, HOUGHTON, MI**							
	Beaver	GC	1952	B	550	110' 00"	32' 00"	6' 05"
	Charlie Mott	PF	1953	D	28*	56' 00"	14' 00"	4' 07"
	Greenstone	TK	1977	B	30	81' 00"	24' 00"	6' 01"
	J. E. Colombe	TB	1953	D	25*	45' 00"	12' 05"	5' 03"
	Ranger III	PK	1958	D	140	165' 00"	34' 00"	15' 03"
U-8	**UNITED STATES NAVAL SEA CADET CORPS – FC SHERMAN DIVISION, PORT HURON, MI**							
	Greyfox **[TWR-825]**	TV	1985	D	213*	120' 00"	25' 00"	12' 00"*
	(USS TWR-825 '85-'97)							
	UNITED STATES NAVAL SEA CADET CORPS – GREAT LAKES DIVISION, MT. CLEMENS, MI							
	Pride of Michigan **[YP-673]** TV		1977	D	70*	80' 06"	17' 08"	5' 03"*
	(USS YP-673 '77-'89)							
U-9	**UNIVERSITY OF MICHIGAN-CENTER FOR GREAT LAKES & AQUATIC SCIENCES, ANN ARBOR, MI**							
	Laurentian	RV	1977	D	129*	80' 00"	21' 06"	11' 00"
U-10	**UNIVERSITY OF MINNESOTA-DULUTH, DULUTH, MN**							
	Blue Heron	RV	1985	D	175*	119' 06"	28' 00"	15' 06"
	(Fairtry '85-'97)							
U-11	**UNIVERSITY OF WISCONSIN – GREAT LAKES WATER INSTITUTE, MILWAUKEE, WI**							
	Neeskay	RV	1952	D	75*	71' 00"	17' 06"	7' 06"*
U-12	**UNIVERSITY OF WISCONSIN, SUPERIOR, WI**							
	L. L. Smith Jr.	RV	1950	D	38*	57' 06"	16' 06"	6' 06"
U-13	**UPPER LAKES GROUP, INC., TORONTO, ON**							

U-13   *INDICATES VESSELS OPERATED BY SEAWAY MARINE TRANSPORT, ST. CATHARINES, ON*
A PARTNERSHIP BETWEEN ALGOMA CENTRAL CORP. AND UPPER LAKES GROUP, INC.

DISTRIBUTION GRANDS LACS/ST-LAURENT LTEE, TROIS RIVIERES, QC – A DIVISION OF UPPER LAKES GROUP, INC.

	Fleet Name Vessel Name	Type of Vessel	Year Built	Type of Engine	Cargo Cap. or Gross*	Overall Length	Breadth	Depth or Draft*
	Barge Laviolette	BC	1965	B	7,573	498' 00"	75' 00"	39' 03"
	(Grain storage barge constructed from bow and cargo section from powered vessel Canadian Explorer, '01.)							
	Canadian Mariner	BC	1963	T	27,700	730' 00"	75' 00"	39' 03"
	(Newbrunswicker '63-'68, Grande Hermine '68-'72) Scheduled to be converted to a barge in 2004.)							
	Canadian Trader	BC	1969	D	28,300	730' 00"	75' 00"	39' 08"
	(Ottercliffe Hall '69-'83, Royalton {2} '83-'85, Ottercliffe Hall '85-'88. Peter Misener '88-'94) Scheduled to be converted to a barge in 2004.)							
	HAMILTON MARINE & ENGINEERING LTD., – A DIVISION OF UPPER LAKES GROUP, INC.							
	James E. McGrath	TB	1963	D	90*	77' 00"	20' 00"	10' 09"
	1168596 ONTARIO INC., – A DIVISION OF UPPER LAKES GROUP							
	Commodore Straits	TB	1966	D	566*	130' 00"	34' 01"	15' -7"
	(Haida Brave)							
	JACKES SHIPPING, INC., TORONTO, ON – A DIVISION OF UPPER LAKES GROUP, INC.							
	Gordon C. Leitch* {2}	BC	1968	D	29,700	730' 00"	75' 00"	42' 00"
	(Ralph Misener '68-'94) (Converted from a self-unloader to a bulk carrier, '77)							
	PROVMAR FUELS, INC., HAMILTON, ON – A DIVISION OF UPPER LAKES GROUP, INC.							
	Hamilton Energy	TK	1965	D	8,622	201' 05"	34' 01"	14' 09"
	(Partington '65-'79, Shell Scientist '79-'81, Metro Sun '81-'85)							
	Provmar Terminal	TK	1959	B	60,000	403' 05"	55' 06"	28' 05"
	(Varangnes '59-'70, Tommy Wiborg '70-'74, Ungava Transport '74-'85)							
	(Last operated in 1984; In use as a fuel storage barge at Hamilton, ON.)							
	Provmar Terminal II	TK	1948	B	73,740	408' 08"	53' 00"	26' 00"
	(Imperial Sarnia {2} '48-'89; Last operated 1986-In use as a fuel storage barge at Hamilton, ON.)							

Fleet #.	Fleet Name Vessel Name	Type of Vessel	Year Built	Type of Engine	Cargo Cap. or Gross*	Overall Length	Breadth	Depth or Draft*
	ULS CORPORATION, TORONTO, ON – A DIVISION OF UPPER LAKES GROUP, INC.							
	Canadian Enterprise*	SU	1979	D	35,100	730' 00"	75' 08"	46' 06"
	Canadian Leader*	BC	1967	T	28,300	730' 00"	75' 00"	39' 08"
	(Feux-Follets '67-'72)							
	Canadian Miner*	BC	1966	D	28,050	730' 00"	75' 00"	39' 01"
	(Maplecliffe Hall '66-'88, Lemoyne {2} '88-'94)							
	Canadian Navigator*	SU	1967	D	30,925	728' 11"	75' 10"	40' 06"
	(Demeterton '67-'75, St. Lawrence Navigator '75-'80)							
	(Coverted from a saltwater bulk carrier '80; Converted to a self-unloader, '97)							
	Canadian Olympic*	SU	1976	D	35,100	730' 00"	75' 00"	46' 06"
	Canadian Progress*	SU	1968	D	32,700	730' 00"	75' 00"	46' 06"
	Canadian Prospector*	BC	1964	D	30,500	730' 00"	75' 10"	40' 06"
	(Carlton '64-'75, Federal Wear '75-'75, St. Lawrence Prospector '75-'79)							
	(Converted from a saltwater bulk carrier, '79)							
	Canadian Provider*	BC	1963	T	27,450	730' 00"	75' 00"	39' 02"
	(Murray Bay {3} '63-'94)							
	Canadian Ranger*	GU	1943/67	D	25,900	729' 10"	75' 00"	39' 03"
	([**Fore Section**] Grande Ronde '43-'48, Kate N. L. '48-'61, Hilda Marjanne '61-'84) (Coverted from a saltwater bulk carrier '61) ([**Stern Section**] Chimo '67-'83)							
	Canadian Ranger was built by joining of the stern section (pilothouse, engine room, machinery) of the former coastal package freighter Chimo with the bow and mid-body of the laker Hilda Marjanne in 1984; Converted to a self- unloader, '88.							
	Canadian Transfer*	SU	1943/65	D	22,204	650' 06"	60' 00"	35' 00"
	([**Fore Section**] J. H. Hillman Jr. '43-'74, Crispin Oglebay {2} '74-'95, Hamilton Transfer '95-'98)							
	(Converted to a self-unloader, '74) [**Stern Section**] Cabot {1} '65-'83, Canadian Explorer '83-'98)							
	Canadian Transfer was built by joining the stern section of Canadian Explorer (engine room, machinery) with the bow and mid-body of the World War II-era laker Hamilton Transfer in 1998.							
	Canadian Transport* {2}	SU	1979	D	35,100	730' 00"	75' 08"	46' 06"
	James Norris*	SU	1952	U	18,600	663' 06"	67' 00"	35' 00"
	(Converted to a self-unloader, '81)							
	John D. Leitch*	SU	1967	D	31,600	730' 00"	78' 00"	45' 00"
	(Canadian Century '67-'02) (Rebuilt with new mid-body, widened by 3'- '02)							
	Montrealais*	BC	1962	T	27,800	730' 00"	75' 00"	39' 00"
	(Launched as Montrealer)							
	Quebecois*	BC	1963	T	27,800	730' 00"	75' 00"	39' 00"
U-14	**UPPER LAKES TOWING, INC., ESCANABA, MI**							
	Joseph H. Thompson	SU	1944	B	21,200	706' 06"	71' 06"	38' 06"
	(USNS Marine Robin '44-'52)							
	Converted from a saltwater vessel to a self-unloading bulk carrier, '52; Engine removed, converted to a self-unloading barge, '91)							
	Joseph H. Thompson Jr.	TBA	1990	D	841*	146' 06"	38' 00"	35' 00"
V-1	**VAN ENKEVORT TUG & BARGE, INC., BARK RIVER, MI**							
	Great Lakes Trader	SU	2000	B	39,600	740' 00"	78' 00"	45' 00"
	Joyce L. Van Enkevort	AT	1998	D	1,179*	135' 04"	50' 00"	26' 00"
	[**ATB Van Enkevort / Trader OA dimensions together**]					844' 10"	78' 00"	45' 00"
	Olive L. Moore	TB	1928	D	301*	125' 00"	27' 01"	13' 09"
	(John F. Cushing '28-'66, James E. Skelly '66-'66)							
V-2	**VERREAULT NAVIGATION INC., LES MECHINS, QC**							
	Nindawayma	CF	1976	D	6,197*	333' 06"	55' 00"	36' 06"
	(Monte Cruceta '76-'76, Monte Castillo '76-'78, Manx Viking '78-'87, Manx '87-'88, , Skudenes '88-'89, Ontario No.1 {2} '89-'89) (Last operated in 1992; Laid up at Montreal, QC.)							
	Richelieu	PA	1962	D	1.097*	191' 06"	69' 05"	15' 04"
V-3	**VIC POWELL WELDING LTD., DUNNVILLE, ON**							
	Toni D	TB	1959	D	15*	50' 00"	16' 00"	5' 00"

Fleet #.	Fleet Name / Vessel Name	Type of Vessel	Year Built	Type of Engine	Cargo Cap. or Gross*	Overall Length	Breadth	Depth or Draft*
V-4	**VISTA FLEET, DULUTH, MN**							
	Vista King	ES	1978	D	60*	78' 00"	28' 00"	5' 02"
	Vista Star	ES	1987	D	95*	91' 00"	24' 09"	7' 08"
	(Island Empress '87-'88)							
V-5	**VOIGHT'S MARINE SERVICES, ELLISON BAY, WI**							
	Bounty	ES	1968	D	23*	40' 00"	14' 00"	3' 03"
	Island Clipper {2}	ES	1987	D	149*	65' 00"	20' 00"	5' 00"
	Yankee Clipper	ES	1971	D	41*	54' 00"	17' 00"	5' 00"
V-6	**VOYAGEUR CRUISES, INC., CHARLEVOIX, MI**							
	Voyageur	ES	1981	D	72*	105' 00"	21' 06"	6' 00"*
W-1	**WAGNER CHARTER CO., INC., CAROL STREAM, IL**							
	Buccaneer	ES	1925	D	98*	100' 00"	23' 00"	14' 06"
	(USCGC Dexter '25-'35, USS Dexter [YP-67] '35-'46, Kingfisher '46-'61, Jamaica II '61-'61, Trinidad {1} '61-'94)							
	Jamaica	ES	1967	D	88*	105' 00"	25' 00"	10' 06"
W- 2	**WALSTROM MARINE, HARBOR SPRINGS, MI**							
	Ottawa	TB	1914	D	74*	57' 04"	17' 09"	6' 00"
	Elizabeth	TB	1945	D	21*	48' 00"	12' 01"	7' 00"
	(Ashland {2} '44-'72, Charles F. Liscomb '72-'94, Jason '94-'01, Lydie Rae '01-'03)							
W-3	**WASHINGTON ISLAND FERRY LINE, INC., WASHINGTON ISLAND, WI**							
	Arni J. Richter	CF	2003	D	92*	104' 00"	38' 06"	10' 11"
	C. G. Richter	CF	1950	D	82*	70' 06"	25' 00"	9' 05"
	Eyrarbakki	CF	1970	D	95*	87' 00"	36' 00"	7' 06"
	Robert Noble	CF	1979	D	97*	90' 04"	36' 00"	8' 03"
	Voyager	CF	1960	D	98*	65' 00"	35' 00"	8' 00"
	Washington {2}	CF	1989	D	93*	100' 00"	37' 00"	9' 00"
W-4	**WENDELLA BOAT TOURS., CHICAGO, IL**							
	Sunliner	ES	1959	D	41*	67' 00"	20' 00"	4' 00"
	Wendella	ES	1961	D	35*	68' 00"	17' 00"	6' 05"
	Wendella LTD	ES	1992	D	66*	68' 00"	20' 00"	4' 09"
W-5	**WILLIAM ROBERT PARR, PARRY SOUND, ON**							
	Mink Isle	TB	1947	D	27*	50' 00"	13' 00"	6' 07"*
W-6	**WINDY OF CHICAGO LTD., CHICAGO, IL**							
	Windy	ES/4S	1996	W	75*	148' 00"	25' 00"	8' 00"
	Windy II	ES/4S	2000	W	99*	150' 00"	25' 00"	8' 05"
W-7	**WISCONSIN DEPARTMENT OF NATURAL RESOURCES, BAYFIELD & STURGEON BAY, WI**							
	Hack Noyes	RV	1947	D	50*	56' 00"		4' 00"
	Barney Devine	RV	1937	D	42*	50' 00"	14' 05"	6' 00"
Y-1	**YANKEE LADY YACHT CHARTERS, TORONTO, ON**							
	Yankee Lady	ES	1965	D	56*	42' 10"	16' 06"	9' 02"
	(Peggy Vee V '65-'88)							
	Yankee Lady II	ES	1980	D	68*	75' 00"	16' 00"	9' 08"
	(Blue Chip II '80-'89)							
	Yankee Lady III	ES	1995	D	292*	99' 07"	26' 09"	11' 08"
Z-1	**ZENITH TUGBOAT CO., DULUTH, MN**							
	Athena	TB	1939	D	119*	82' 00"	22' 06"	11" 04"
	(John E. Matton, USS Tamaque YTM-741, Athena, James A Harper '73-'86)							
	Titan	TB	1909	D	236*	110' 00"	26' 00"	13' 09"
	(P.J.T. Co. No. 8, Empire)							

VESSEL ENGINE DATA

bhp: brake horsepower, a measure of diesel engine output power measured at the crankshaft before entering gear box or any other power take-out device

ihp: indicated horsepower, based on an internal measurement of mean cylinder pressure, piston area, piston stroke and engine speed. Used for reciprocating engines

shp: shaft horsepower, a measure of engine output at the propeller shaft at the output of the reduction gear box. Used for steam and diesel-electric engines

cpp: controllable pitch propeller

Vessel Name	Engine Manufacturer & Model #	Engine Type	Total Engines	Total Cylinders	Rated HP	Total HP	Speed Props	MPH
Adam E. Cornelius	GM - Electro-Motive Div. - 20-645-E7B	Diesel	2	20	7,200 bhp		1 cpp	16.1
Agawa Canyon	Fairbanks Morse - 10-38D8-1/8	Diesel	4	10	6,662 bhp		1 cpp	13.8
Algobay	Pielstick - 10PC2-3V-400	Diesel	2	10	10,699 bhp		1 cpp	13.8
Algocape	Sulzer - 6RND76	Diesel	1	6	9,599 bhp		1	17.3
Algocatalyst	Pielstick - 12PC2-V-400	Diesel	1	12	6,000 bhp		1 cpp	17.3
Algocen	Fairbanks Morse - 10-38D8-1/8	Diesel	4	10	7,999 bhp		1 cpp	13.8
Algoeast	B&W - 6K45GF	Diesel	1	6	5,299 bhp		1 cpp	15.8
Algofax	M.A.N. - K5Z70/120	Diesel	2	5	6,410 bhp		1	15.5
Algoisle	M.A.N. - K6Z78/155	Diesel	1	6	9,000 bhp		1 cpp	19.3
Algolake	Pielstick - 10PC2-2V-400	Diesel	2	10	9,000 bhp		1 cpp	17.3
Algomarine	Sulzer - 6RND76	Diesel	1	6	9,599 bhp		1 cpp	17.0
Algonorth	Werkspoor - 9TM410	Diesel	2	9	11,999 bhp		1 cpp	16.1
Algonova	Fairbanks Morse - 12-38D8-1/8	Diesel	2	12	4,000 bhp		1 cpp	15.0
Algontario	B&W - 7-74VTBF-160	Diesel	1	7	8,750 bhp		1 cpp	14.4
Algoport	Pielstick - 10PC2-3V-400	Diesel	2	10	10,699 bhp		1 cpp	13.8
Algorail	Fairbanks Morse - 10-38D8-1/8	Diesel	4	10	8,065 bhp		1 cpp	13.8
Algosar	M.A.N. - K5Z70/120E	Diesel	1	5	6,500 bhp		1 cpp	17.3
Algosoo	Pielstick - 10PC2-V-400	Diesel	2	10	9,000 bhp		1 cpp	15.0
Algosteel	Sulzer - 6RND76	Diesel	1	6	9,599 bhp		1	17.0
Algoville	M.A.N. - K6Z78/155	Diesel	1	6	9,900 bhp		1 cpp	17.8
Algoway	Fairbanks Morse - 10-38D8-1/8	Diesel	4	10	8,065 bhp		1 cpp	13.8
Algowood	MaK - 6M552AK	Diesel	2	6	10,199 bhp		1 cpp	13.8
Alpena	De Laval Steam Turbine Co.	Turbine	1	**		4,400 shp	1	14.1
Amelia Desgagnes	Allen - 12PVBCS12-F	Diesel	2	12	4,000 bhp		1 cpp	16.1
American Mariner	GM - Electro-Motive Div. - 20-645-E7	Diesel	2	20	7,200 bhp		1 cpp	15.0
American Republic	GM - Electro-Motive Div. - 20-645-E7	Diesel	2	20	7,200 bhp		2 cpp	15.0
American Spirit	Pielstick - 16PC2-2V-400	Diesel	2	16	16,000 bhp		2	17.3
Anna Desgagnes	M.A.N. - K5SZ70/125B	Diesel	1	5	10,332 bhp		1	17.8
Armco	Westinghouse Elec. Corp.	Turbine	1	**		7,700 shp	1	19.0
Arthur K. Atkinson	Nordberg	Diesel	2	12	5,610 bhp		2 cpp	
Arthur M. Anderson	Westinghouse Elec. Corp.	Turbine	1	**		7,700 shp	1	16.1
Atlantic Erie	Sulzer - 6RLB66	Diesel	1	6	11,100 bhp		1 cpp	16.1
Atlantic Huron	Sulzer - 6RLB66	Diesel	1	6	11,094 bhp		1 cpp	17.3
Atlantic Superior	Sulzer - 6RLA66	Diesel	1	6	11,095 bhp		1 cpp	17.3
Badger	Skinner Engine Co.	Steeple Compound Uniflow	2	4	8,000 ihp		2	18.4
Buckeye	Bethlehem Steel Co.	Turbine	1	**		7,700 shp	1	17.3
Buffalo	GM - Electro-Motive Div. - 20-645-E7	Diesel	2	20	7,200 bhp		1 cpp	16.1
Burns Harbor	GM - Electro-Motive Div. - 20-645-E7	Diesel	4	20	14,400 bhp		2 cpp	18.4
Calumet	Nordberg	Diesel	1	16	4,234 bhp		1	12.1
Canadian Century	B&W - 5-74VT2BF-160	Diesel	1	5	7,500 bhp		1 cpp	16.1
Canadian Enterprise	M.A.N. - 7L40/45	Diesel	2	7	8,804 bhp		1 cpp	13.8
Canadian Leader	Canadian General Electric Co. Ltd.	Turbine	1	**		9,900 shp	1	19.0
Canadian Mariner	General Electric Co.	Turbine	1	**		9,900 shp	1	19.0
Canadian Miner	Fairbanks Morse - 12-38D8-1/8	Diesel	4	12	8,000 bhp		1 cpp	15.0
Canadian Navigator	Doxford Engines Ltd. - 76J4	Diesel	1	4	9,680 bhp		1	16.7
Canadian Olympic	M.A.N. - 8L40/54A	Diesel	2	8	10,001 bhp		1 cpp	15.0
Canadian Progress	Caterpillar - 3612-TA	Diesel	2	12	9,000 bhp		1 cpp	15.5

Vessel Name	Engine Manufacturer & Model #	Engine Type	Total Engines	Total Cylinders	Rated / Total HP	Speed Props	MPH
Canadian Prospector	Gotaverken - 760/1500VGS6U	Diesel	1	6	7,500 bhp	1	16.1
Canadian Provider	John Inglis Co. Ltd.	Turbine	1	**	10,000 shp	1	17.3
Canadian Ranger	Sulzer - 5RND68	Diesel	1	5	6,100 shp	1 cpp	19.6
Canadian Transfer	Sulzer - 5RND68	Diesel	1	5	6,100 bhp	1 cpp	18.4
Canadian Transport	M.A.N. - 8L40/45	Diesel	2	8	10,001 bhp	1 cpp	13.8
Capt. Henry Jackman	MaK - 6M552AK	Diesel	2	6	9,465 bhp	1 cpp	17.3
Capt. Ralph Tucker	B&W - 7-50VT2BF-110	Diesel	1	7	5,326 bhp	1	15.5
Cason J. Callaway	Westinghouse Elec. Corp.	Turbine	1	**	7,700 shp	1	16.1
Catherine Desgagnes	Sulzer - 6SAD60	Diesel	1	6	3,841 bhp	1	15.5
Cecelia Desgagnes	B&W - 6S50LU	Diesel	1	6	5,100 bhp	1 cpp	17.3
Cedarglen	B&W - 7-74VTBF-160	Diesel	1	7	8,750 bhp	1 cpp	15.5
Charles M. Beeghly	General Electric Co.	Turbine	1	**	9,350 shp	1	17.8
Chi-Cheemaun	Ruston Paxman Diesels Ltd. - 16RKCM	Diesel	2	16	7,000 bhp	2	18.7
Columbia Star	GM - Electro-Motive Div. - 20-645-E7B	Diesel	4	20	14,400 bhp	2 cpp	17.3
Courtney Burton	General Electric Co.	Turbine	1	**	7,700 shp	1	16.7
CSL Laurentien	Pielstick - 10PC2-2V-400	Diesel	2	10	9,000 bhp	1 cpp	16.1
CSL Niagara	Pielstick - 10PC2-2V-400	Diesel	2	10	9,000 bhp	1 cpp	15.0
CSL Tadoussac	Sulzer - 6RND76	Diesel	1	6	9,599 bhp	1	17.0
Cuyahoga	Caterpillar - 3608	Diesel	1	8	3,000 bhp	1	
David Z. Norton	Alco - 16V251E	Diesel	2	16	5,600 bhp		16.1
Diamond Star	B&W - 6L35MC	Diesel	1	6	5,030 bhp	1 cpp	14.4
Dorothy Ann / Pathfinder (Articulated Tug / Barge)	GM - Electro-Motive Div. - 20-645-E7B	Diesel	2	20	7,200 bhp	2 Ulstein Z Drive	16.1
E. M. Ford	Cleveland Ship Building Co.	Quadruple Expansion	1	4	1,500 ihp	1	11.5
Earl W. Oglebay	Alco - 16V251E	Diesel	2	16	5,600 bhp	1	16.1
Edgar B. Speer	Pielstick - 18PC2-3V-400	Diesel	2	18	19,260 bhp	2 cpp	17.0
Edward L. Ryerson	General Electric Co.	Turbine	1	**	9,900 shp	1	19.0
Edwin H. Gott	Enterprise - DMRV-16-4	Diesel	2	16	19,500 bhp	2 cpp	16.7
Emerald Star	B&W - 6L35MC	Diesel	1	6	5,030 bhp	1 cpp	14.4
Emmet J. Carey	GM - Detroit Diesel Allison Div. - 6-71N	Diesel	2	6	400 bhp	2	
English River	Werkspoor - TMAB-390	Diesel	1	8	1,850 bhp	1 cpp	13.8
Everlast / Norman McLeod (Articulated Tug / Barge)	Daihatsu - 8DSM-32	Diesel	2	8	? bhp	2	16.5
F. M. Osborne	Caterpillar - D334	Diesel	2	6	410 bhp	1	
Ferbec	Sulzer - 6RD90	Diesel	1	6	14,999 bhp	1	17.3
Fred R. White Jr.	GM - Electro-Motive Div. - 20-645-E7	Diesel	2	20	7,200 bhp	1 cpp	16.1
Frontenac	Sulzer - 6RND76	Diesel	1	6	9,599 bhp	1 cpp	17.0
Gemini	Alco - 16V251E	Diesel	2	16	5,150 bhp	2	14.4
Gordon C. Leitch	Sulzer - 6RND76	Diesel	1	6	9,599 bhp	1 cpp	17.3
H. Lee White	GM - Electro-Motive Div. - 20-645-E7B	Diesel	2	20	7,200 bhp	1 cpp	15.0
Halifax	John Inglis Co. Ltd.	Turbine	1	**	10,000 shp	1	19.6
Herbert C. Jackson	General Electric Co.	Turbine	1	**	6,600 shp	1	
Indiana Harbor	GM - Electro-Motive Div. - 20-645-E7	Diesel	4	20	14,400 bhp	2 cpp	16.1
Invincible / McKee Sons (Articulated Tug / Barge)	GM - Electro-Motive Div. - 16-645-E7B	Diesel	2	16	5,750 bhp	2	13.8
J. A. W. Iglehart	De Laval Steam Turbine Co.	Turbine	1	**	4,400 shp	1	15.0
J. B. Ford	American Ship Building Co.	Triple Exp.	1	3	1,500 ihp	1	
J. S. St. John	GM - Electro-Motive Div. - 8-567	Diesel	1	8	850 bhp	1	11.5
Jacklyn M. / Integrity (Articulated Tug / Barge)	Caterpillar - 3608-DITA	Diesel	2	8	6,008 bhp	2	17.3
Jacques Desgagnes	Lister Blackstone Marine Ltd.	Diesel	2	8	1,200 bhp	2	12.1
Jade Star	B&W - 6L35MC	Diesel	1	6	5,030 bhp	1 cpp	14.4
James Norris	Canadian Vickers Ltd.	Uniflow	1	5	4,000 ihp	1	16.1
James R. Barker	Pielstick - 16PC2-2V-400	Diesel	2	16	16,000 bhp	2 cpp	15.5
Jane Ann IV / Sarah Spencer (Articulated Tug / Barge)	Pielstick - 8PC2-2L-400	Diesel	2	8	8,000 bhp	2	15.8
Jean Parisien	Pielstick - 10PC2-2V-400	Diesel	2	10	9,000 bhp	1 cpp	15.0
Jiimaan	Ruston Paxman Diesels Ltd. - 6RK215	Diesel	2	6	2,839 bhp	2 cpp	15.0
John B. Aird	MaK - 6M552AK	Diesel	2	6	9,459 bhp	1 cpp	13.8
John G. Munson	General Electric Co.	Turbine	1	**	7,700 shp	1	17.3
John J. Boland	GM - Electro-Motive Div. - 20-645-E7B	Diesel	2	20	7,200 bhp	1 cpp	15.0
John R. Emery	GM - Detroit Diesel Allison Div. - 6-110	Diesel	2	6	550 bhp	2	
John Sherwin	De Laval Steam Turbine Co.	Turbine	1	**	9,350 shp	1	16..7

Vessel Name	Engine Manufacturer & Model #	Engine Type	Total Engines	Total Cylinders	Rated HP	Total HP	Speed Props	MPH
Joseph H. Frantz	Enterprise - DMRV-12-4	Diesel	1	12		4,000 bhp	1 cpp	13.2
Joseph H. Thompson Jr. / (Articulated *Tug* / *Barge*)								
Joseph H. Thompson	General Electric Co. - 7FDM16	Diesel	3	16		7,500 bhp	1	
Joseph L. Block	GM - Electro-Motive Div. - 20-645-E7	Diesel	2	20		7,200 bhp	1 cpp	17.3
Joyce L. Van Enkevort / (Articulated *Tug* / *Barge*)								
Great Lakes Trader	Caterpillar - 3612	Diesel	2	12		10,200 bhp	2 cpp	
Kaye E. Barker	De Laval Steam Turbine Co.	Turbine	1	**		7,700 shp	1	17.3
Kinsman Independent	Bethlehem Steel Co.	Turbine	1	**		4,400 shp	1	
L. E. Block	Westinghouse Elec. Corp.	Turbine	1	**		4,950 shp	1	
Lee A. Tregurtha	Bethlehem Steel Co.	Turbine	1	**		7,700 shp	1	16.7
Atlantic Superior	Sulzer - 6RLA66	Diesel	1	6		11,095 bhp	1 cpp	17.3
Maria Desgagnes	B&W - 6S42MC	Diesel	1	6		8,361 bhp	1 cpp	16.1
Marine Star	General Electric Co.	Turbine	1	**		10,001 shp	1	21.9
Mathilda Desgagnes	Fairbanks Morse - 10-38D8-1/8	Diesel	2	10		3,200 bhp	2	
Maumee	Nordberg - FS-1312-H5C	Diesel	1	12		3,240 bhp	1	11.5
Melissa Desgagnes	Allen - 12PVBCS12-F	Diesel	2	12		4,000 bhp	1 cpp	13.8
Mesabi Miner	Pielstick - 16PC2-2V-400	Diesel	2	16		16,000 bhp	2 cpp	15.5
Michigan / (Articulated *Tug* / *Barge*)								
Great Lakes	GM - Electro-Motive Div. - 20-645-E6	Diesel	2	16		3,900 bhp	2	13.2
Michipicoten	Bethlehem Steel Co.	Turbine	1	**		7,700 shp	1	17.3
Middletown	Bethlehem Steel Co.	Turbine	1	**		7,700 shp	1	16.1
Mississagi	Caterpillar - 3612-TA	Diesel	1	12		4,500 bhp	1 cpp	
Montrealais	Canadian General Electric Co. Ltd.	Turbine	1	**		9,900 shp	1	19.0
Nanticoke	Pielstick - 10PC2-2V-400	Diesel	2	10		10,699 bhp	1 cpp	13.8
Oglebay Norton	GM - Electro-Motive Div. - 20-645-E7	Diesel	4	20		14,400 bhp	2 cpp	18.4
Paul H. Townsend	Nordberg	Diesel	1	6		2,150 bhp	1	12.1
Paul R. Tregurtha	Pielstick - 16PC2-3V-400	Diesel	2	16		17,120 bhp	2 cpp	15.5
Peter R. Cresswell	MaK - 6M552AK	Diesel	2	6		10,199 bhp	1 cpp	13.8
Petrolia Desgagnes	B&W - 8K42EF	Diesel	1	8		5,000 bhp	1 cpp	16.4
Philip R. Clarke	Westinghouse Elec. Corp.	Turbine	1	**		7,700 shp	1	16.1
Pineglen	MaK - 6M601AK	Diesel	1	6		8,158 bhp	1 cpp	15.5
Presque Isle	Mirrlees Blackstone Ltd. - KVMR-16	Diesel	2	16		14,840 bhp	2 cpp	
Quebecois	Canadian General Electric Co. Ltd.	Turbine	1	**		9,900 shp	1	19.0
Reserve	Westinghouse Elec. Corp.	Turbine	1	**		7,700 shp	1	19.0
Richard Reiss	GM - Electro-Motive Div. - 20-645-E6	Diesel	1	20		2,950 bhp	1	
Roger Blough	Pielstick - 16PC2V-400	Diesel	2	16		14,200 bhp	1 cpp	16.7
Rt. Hon. Paul J. Martin	Pielstick - 10PC2-V-400	Diesel	2	10		9,000 bhp	1 cpp	15.0
S. T. Crapo	GLEW	Triple Exp.	1	3		1,800 ihp	1	13.2
Saginaw	De Laval Steam Turbine Co.	Turbine	1	**		7,700 shp	1	16.1
Sam Laud	GM - Electro-Motive Div. - 20-645-E7	Diesel	2	20		7,200 bhp	1 cpp	16.1
Sauniere	MaK - 6M552AK	Diesel	2	6		8,799 bhp	1 cpp	15.0
Southdown Challenger	Skinner Engine Co.	Uniflow	1	4		3,500 ihp	1	
St. Clair	GM - Electro-Motive Div. - 20-645-E7	Diesel	3	20		10,800 bhp	1 cpp	16.7
Ste. Claire	Toledo Ship Building Co.	Triple Exp.	1	3		1,083 ihp	1	
Stephen B. Roman (Total)		Diesel				5,996 bhp	1 cpp	18.4
Stephen B. Roman (Center)	Fairbanks Morse - 10-38D8-1/8	Diesel	2	10		3,331 bhp		
Stephen B. Roman (Wing)	Fairbanks Morse - 8-38D8-1/8	Diesel	2	8		2,665 bhp		
Stewart J. Cort	GM - Electro-Motive Div. - 20-645-E7	Diesel	4	20		14,400 bhp	2 cpp	18.4
Susan W. Hannah / (Articulated *Tug* / *Barge*)								
Southdown Conquest	GM - Electro-Motive Div. - 12-645-E5	Diesel	2	12		4,320 bhp	2	11.5
Teakglen	Fairbanks Morse - 8-38D8-1/8	Diesel	4	8		5,332 bhp	1 cpp	16.1
Thalassa Desgagnes	B&W - 8K42EF	Diesel	1	8		5,000 bhp	1 cpp	16.4
Undaunted / (Articulated *Tug* / *Barge*)								
Pere Marquette 41	GM - Cleveland Diesel Div. - 12-278A	Diesel	1	12		2,400 bhp	1	11.5
Vega Desgagnes	Wartsila - 9R32	Diesel	2	9		7,559 bhp	1 cpp	16.1
Walter J. McCarthy Jr.	GM - Electro-Motive Div. - 20-645-E7B	Diesel	4	20		14,400 bhp	2 cpp	16.1
Wellington Kent	MaK - 9M552AK	Diesel	1	9		7,504 bhp	1 cpp	
Wilfred Sykes	Westinghouse Elec. Corp.	Turbine	1	**		7,700 shp	1	16.1
Wolf River	Fairbanks Morse - 10-38D8-1/8	Diesel	1	10		1,880 bhp	1	10.4
Wolverine	Alco - 16V251E	Diesel	2	16		5,600 bhp	1	17.8
Yankcanuck	Cooper-Bessemer Corp.	Diesel	1	8		1,860 bhp	1	11.5

Saltwater Fleets

Olympic Mentor in the Welland Canal. *(Matt Miner)*

This list reflects vessels whose primary trade routes are on saltwater, but which also regularly visit Great Lakes and St. Lawrence Seaway ports. It is not meant to be a complete listing of every saltwater vessel that could potentially visit the Great Lakes and St. Lawrence Seaway. To attempt to do so, given the sheer number of world merchant vessels, would be space prohibitive. Fleets listed may operate other vessels worldwide than those included herein.

Fleet #.	Fleet Name Vessel Name	Type of Vessel	Year Built	Type of Engine	Cargo Cap. or Gross*	Overall Length	Breadth	Depth or Draft*
IA-1	**ADRIYATIC GEMI ISLETMECILIGI VE TICARET AS, ISTANBUL, TURKEY**							
	TK Rotterdam	GC	2001	D	8,749	426' 06"	58' 01"	33' 04"
	(Gaiesti '01-'01)							
IA-2	**ADRICO SHIPPING COMPANY, ATHENS, GREECE**							
	Nobility	GC	1981	D	30,900	617' 06"	76' 00"	47' 07"
	(Nosira Lin '81-'89, Dan Bauta '89-'89, Kristianiafjord '89-'93, Federal Vibeke '93-'00, Kalista '00-'02)							
IA-3	**AMERICAN CANADIAN CARIBBEAN LINE, INC., WARREN, RI, USA**							
	Grande Mariner	PA	1998	D	97*	183' 00"	40' 00"	9' 08"
	Niagara Prince	PA	1994	D	99*	175' 00"	40' 00"	14' 00"
IA-4	**ALLROUNDER MARITIME CO., INC., MANILA, PHILIPPINES**							
	Sir Walter	BC	1996	D	18,315	446' 00"	74' 10"	40' 00"
	(Rubin Stork '96-'03)							
IA-5	**ANGLO-EASTERN SHIP MANAGEMENT LTD., HONG KONG, HONG KONG**							
	FOLLOWING VESSEL UNDER CHARTER TO FEDNAV LTD.							
	Federal Asahi {2}	BC	2000	D	36,563	656' 02"	77' 11"	48' 08"
IA-6	**ASUKA KISEN CO. LTD., JAPAN**							
	Navitas Prelude	TK	2003	D	8,509	387' 02"	61' 08"	31' 10"
	Navitas Quest	TK	2003	D	8,509	387' 02"	61' 08"	31' 10"
IA-7	**ATHENA MARINE CO. LTD., LIMASSOL, CYPRUS**							
	Atlantic Patroller	BC	1999	D	17,451	469' 02"	94' 06"	43' 08"
	FOLLOWING VESSELS UNDER CHARTER TO FEDNAV LTD.							
	Federal Elbe	GC	2003	D	35,200	655' 80"	78' 04"	50' 01"
	Federal Ems	BC	2002	D	35,200	655' 80"	78' 04"	50' 01"
	Federal Leda	GC	2003	D	35,200	655' 80"	78' 04"	50' 01"
	Federal Weser	BC	2001	D	37,372	655' 80"	78' 04"	50' 01"
IA-8	**ATLANTSKA PLOVIDBA D.D., DUBROVNIK, CROATIA**							
	Mljet	BC	1982	D	29,643	622' 01"	74' 11"	49' 10"
	FOLLOWING VESSEL CURRENTLY UNDER CHARTER TO FEDNAV LTD.							
	Orsula	BC	1996	D	34,198	656' 02"	77' 01"	48' 11"
	(Federal Calumet {2} '96-'97)							
IA-9	**AURORA SHIPPING, INC., MANILA, PHILIPPINES**							
	Aurora Topaz	BC	1982	D	28,268	639' 09"	75' 10"	46' 11"
	(Launched as Haifu. Sea Fortune '82-'85, Miss Aliki '86-'93)							
IB-1	**B & N MOORMAN B.V., RIDDERKERK, NETHERLANDS**							
	Andromeda	GC	1999	D	6,715	388' 09"	49' 08"	27' 02"
	Capricorn	GC	2000	D	6,715	388' 09"	49' 08"	27' 02"
	Forte	RO	1989	D	4,001	297' 11"	54' 02"	32' 10"
	Swan	GC	1995	D	4,304	297' 03"	44' 06"	23' 06"
IB-2	**B & N NORDSJOFRAKT AB, SKARHAMN, SWEDEN**							
	Nordon	GC	2002	D	17,600	467' 05"	72' 00"	41' 00"
	Tofton	GC	1980	D	14,883	522' 02"	70' 03"	41' 04"
IB-3	**BALTHELLAS CHARTERING S.A., ATHENS, GREECE**							
	Crystal Spirit	GC	1983	D	6,130	344' 06"	57' 05"	29' 07"

Fleet #.	Fleet Name / Vessel Name	Type of Vessel	Year Built	Type of Engine	Cargo Cap. or Gross*	Overall Length	Breadth	Depth or Draft*
IB-4	**BARU DELTA MARITIME INCORPORATED, PIRAEUS, GREECE**							
	Doxa D	BC	1984	D	30,820	617' 05"	76' 01"	47' 06"
	(Alberta '84-'93, Nea Doxa '93-'02)							
IB-5	**BELUGA GENCHART B.V., ROTTERDAM, THE NETHERLANDS**							
	Makiri Green	GC	1999	D	17,539	468' 07"	70' 07"	43' 08"
	Marinus Green	GC	2000	D	16,000	468' 07"	70' 07"	43' 08"
	Marion Green	GC	1999	D	17,538	468' 07"	70' 07"	43' 08"
IB-6	**BIGLIFT SHIPPING BV, ROOSENDAAL, NETHERLANDS**							
	Enchanter	HL	1998	D	16,069	452' 09"	74' 10"	31' 03"
	Happy Ranger	HL	1998	D	15,065	452' 09"	74' 10"	31' 03"
	Happy River	HL	1998	D	15,700	452' 09"	74' 10"	31' 03"
	Happy Rover	HL	1997	D	15,700	452' 09"	74' 10"	31' 03"
	Project Europa	HL	1983	D	13,493	456' 02"	75' 02"	42' 08"
	Tracer	HL	2000	D	8,874	329' 09"	73' 06"	26' 11"
	Tramper	HL	2000	D	8,874	329' 09"	73' 06"	26' 11"
	Transporter	HL	1999	D	8,874	329' 09"	73' 06"	26' 11"
	Traveller	HL	2000	D	8,874	329' 09"	73' 06"	26' 11"
IB-7	**BLYSTAD TANKERS INC., OSLO, NORWAY**							
	Lake Eva	TK	1989	D	17,485	496' 01"	73' 05"	39' 10"
	(Jakov Sverdlov '89-'03)							
	Lake Maya	TK	1988	D	17,400	496' 01"	73' 05"	41' 01"
	(Kapitan Rudnev '88-'03)							
IB-8	**BRIESE SCHIFFAHRTS GMBH & CO. KG, LEER, GERMANY**							
	Bavaria	GC	1996	D	3,500	288' 09"	42' 00"	23' 04"
	BBC Brazil	GC	1997	D	4,900	330' 01"	54' 06"	26' 07"
	(Launched as Torum. Industrial Harmony '97-'00)							
	BBC Canada	GC	1999	D	4,798	330' 01"	54' 06"	26' 07"
	BBC Denmark	GC	1999	D	4,806	330' 01"	54' 06"	26' 07"
	BBC Finland	GC	2000	D	8,760	353' 06"	59' 09"	33' 02"
	BBC Holland	GC	2002	D	4,303	330' 00"	54' 06"	26' 07"
	BBC Iceland	GC	1999	D	4,806	330' 01"	54' 06"	26' 07"
	(Industrial Accord '99-'02)							
	BBC Japan	GC	2001	D	4,900	330' 01"	54' 06"	26' 07"
	(Juister Riff '01-'01)							
	BBC Norway	GC	2000	D	7,800	353' 06"	59' 09"	33' 02"
	BBC Peru	GC	2001	D	8,760	351' 01"	59' 09"	33'02"
	(Atlantic Progress '02-'03)							
	BBC Scotland	GC	2002	D	4,713	330' 01"	54' 06"	26' 07"
	BBC Texas	GC	1992	D	7,520	351' 01"	62' 04"	34' 09"
	(Paula '92-'00, Tina '00-'00)							
	BBC Venezuala	GC	1999	D	5,240	324' 10"	51' 11"	26' 07"
	(Fockeburg '99-'00, Global Africa '00-'01)							
	BBC Shanghai	GC	2001	D	4,900	330' 01"	54' 06"	26' 07"
	Frigga	GC	1987	D	3,938	328' 01"	45' 11"	24' 05"
	Santiago	GC	1997	D	3,525	280' 10"	42' 00"	23' 04"
	Westerland	GC	1996	D	4,251	296' 09"	43' 04"	23' 11"
	(Swallow '96-'03)							
IB-9	**BRIESE SHIPPING B.V., MIDWOLDA, NETHERLANDS**							
	Aramis	GC	2001	D	3,171	269' 00"	40' 06"	21' 09"
IC-1	**CAMILLO EITZEN & CO. AS, LYSAKER, NORWAY**							
	Sichem Baltic	TK	1985	D	7,177	347' 09"	59' 09"	26' 07"
	(Golden Arrow '85-'87, Dansborg '87-'90, Kilchem Baltic '90-'01)							

<table>
Fleet #.	Fleet Name Vessel Name	Type of Vessel	Year Built	Type of Engine	Cargo Cap. or Gross*	Overall Length	Breadth	Depth or Draft*
IC-2	**CANADA MARITIME LTD., HAMILTON, BERMUDA**							
	CanMar Bravery	CO	1978	D	33,027	715' 02"	104' 00"	54' 02"
	CanMar Endurance	CO	1983	D	32,424	727' 02"	105' 08"	49' 03"
</table>

(Tokyo Maru '83-'90, Alligator Joy '90-'95, CanMar Endeavour '96-'98, Contship Endeavour '98-'99, Cast Performance '99-03))

<table>
	CanMar Glory	CO	1979	D	18,964	580' 10"	88' 09"	44' 04"
</table>

(Seatrain Saratoga '79-'80, TFL Jefferson '80-'87, Asian Senator '87-'90, CMB Mover '90-'90, CMB Monarch '90-'91, Sea Falcon '91-'94)

<table>
	CanMar Honour	CO	1998	D	40,879	803' 10"	105' 08"	35' 05"
	CanMar Pride	CO	1998	D	40,879	803' 10"	105' 08"	35' 05"*
	CanMan Spirit							
	CanMar Triumph	CO	1978	D	18,606	580' 10"	88' 10"	44' 04"
</table>

(Seatrain Independence '78-'81, Dart Americana '81-'87, American Senator '87-'89, CMB Marque '89-'90)

<table>
	CanMar Valour	CO	1979	D	18,800	580' 07"	88' 09"	44' 04"
</table>

(Seatrain Oriskany '79-'81, Dart Britain '81-'87, Taiwan Senator '87-'90, OOCL Assurance '90-'97)

<table>
	CanMar Venture	CO	2003	D	Under Construction			
	CanMar Victory	CO	1979	D	18,381	580' 09"	88' 10"	44' 04"
</table>

(Seatrain Chesapeake '79-'81, Dart Atlantica '81-'87, Singapore Senator '87-'89, American Senator '89-'90)

<table>
	Cast Prominence	CO	1996	D	34,330	709' 01"	105' 10"	62' 04"
</table>

(CanMar Courage '96-'03)

<table>
	Cast Prospect	CO	1995	D	34,330	709' 01"	105' 10"	62' 04"
</table>

(CanMar Fortune '95-'03)

<table>
	Montreal Senator	CO	1982	D	32,207	738' 01"	105' 08"	61'07"
</table>

(America Maru '82-'90, Alligator Excellence '90-'95, CanMar Success '98-98, Contship Success '98-'99, Cast Power '99-'03)

IC-3   **CANADIAN FOREST NAVIGATION (CANFORNAV) LTD., MONTREAL, QC, CANADA**

At press time, Canadian Forest Navigation Co., Ltd. had the following vessels under long or short-term charter. Please consult their respective fleets for details:
Bluewing, Cinnamon, Goldeneye, Greenwing, Milo, Pintail, Orna, Peonia, Pochard, Puffin, Pytheas, Toro, Woody

IC-4   **CANSHIP LTD., ST. JOHN'S, NFLD, CANADA**

<table>
	Astron	RR	1971	D	1,910	278' 08"	45' 03"	21' 03"
</table>

(Atlantic Bermudian '71-'75, Londis '75-'76, Merzario Sardinia '76-'78)

German-flag *Frida* on her 2003 maiden voyage into the Great Lakes. *(John Chomniak)*

Panam Flota at Sarnia. (Matt Miner)

Fleet #.	Fleet Name Vessel Name	Type of Vessel	Year Built	Type of Engine	Cargo Cap. or Gross*	Overall Length	Breadth	Depth or Draft*
IC-5	**CARISBROOKE SHIPPING PLC, COWES, ISLE OF WIGHT, UNITED KINGDOM**							
	Catharina-C	GC	1999	D	5,057	312' 00"	49' 07"	23' 02"
	Cheryl-C	GC	1982	D	2,367	230' 01"	42' 11"	19' 09"
	(Norbrit Hope '82-'85, Norbrit Rijn '85-'87, Catarina Caldas '87-'91)							
	Emily-C	GC	1996	D	4,650	294' 07"	43' 02"	23' 05"
	Johanna-C	GC	1998	D	4,570	294' 11"	43' 04"	23' 06"
	Mark-C	GC	1996	D	4,620	294' 11"	43' 04"	23' 06"
IC-6	**CATSAMBIS SHIPPING LTD., PIRAEUS, GREECE**							
	Adimon	BC	1977	D	30,880	644' 11"	75' 04"	47' 06"
	(Hercegovonia '77-'98)							
IC-7	**CHARTWORLD SHIPPING CORP., ATHENS, GREECE**							
	Chem Bothnia	TK	1985	D	6,730	351' 01"	55' 10"	27' 11"
	(Ace '85-'85, Ace Chemi '85-'91, Kilchem Bothnia '91-'99)							
IC-8	**CHEKKA SHIPPING S.A., ATHENS, GREECE**							
	Alexander K.	BC	1978	D	30,353	622' 07"	76' 05"	47' 05"
	(Federal Saguenay {1} '78-'95, Federal Calliope '95-'99, Calliope '99-'00)							
	Antoine	BC	1995	D	18,315	447' 10"	74' 10"	40' 00"
	(Rubin Eagle '95-'03)							
	Beauty K.	BC	1996	D	18,315	446' 00"	74' 10"	40' 00"
	(Rubin Falcon '96-'03)							
IC-9	**CHINA OCEAN SHIPPING CO. (COSCO), BEIJING, PEOPLE'S REPUBLIC OF CHINA**							
	Ocean Priti	BC	1982	D	27,019	599' 05"	75' 04"	46' 08"
	Yick Hua	BC	1984	D	28,086	584' 08"	75' 11"	48' 05"
IC-10	**CLIPPER CRUISE LINE, ST. LOUIS, MISSOURI, USA**							
	Nantucket Clipper	PA	1984	D	96*	207' 00"	37' 00"	11' 06"
IC-11	**CLIPPER ELITE CARRIERS A/S, COPENHAGEN, DENMARK**							
	CEC Crusader	GC	2000	D	8,880	328' 01"	66' 11"	36' 05"
	CEC Faith	GC	1994	D	7,225	331' 08"	63' 00"	30' 06"
	(Arktis Faith '94-'00)							
	CEC Fighter	GC	1994	D	7,225	331' 08"	63' 00"	30' 06"
	(Arktis Fighter '94-'94, Ville de Rodae '94-'96, Arktis Fighter '96-'02)							
	CEC Future	GC	1994	D	7,225	331' 08"	63' 00"	30' 06"
	(Arktis Future '01-'01)							
	CEC Hunter	GC	1995	D	5,401	319' 07"	53' 08"	27' 11"
	(Arktis Hunter '95-'00)							
	CEC Mirage	GC	1998	D	8,973	328' 01"	66' 11"	36' 05"
	(Arktis Mirage '98-'99, Nancy Delmas '99-'00)							
IC-12	**COMMERCIAL FLEET OF DONBASS LLC, DONETSK, UKRAINE**							
	Avdeevka	BC	1977	D	26,398	570' 11"	75' 03"	47' 07"
	(Goldensari '77-'80, Bogasari Tiga '80-'86)							
	General Blazhevich	GC	1981	D	7,805	399' 09"	67' 00"	27' 03"
	Dobrush	BC	1982	D	28,160	644' 06"	75' 10"	46' 11"
	(World Goodwill '82-'85)							
	Makeevka	BC	1982	D	28,136	644' 06"	75' 07"	46' 11"
	(World Shanghai '82-'85)							
	Mariupol	BC	1977	D	27,559	584' 04"	75' 02"	48' 03"
	(Arctic Skou '77-'85, Zdhanov '85-'89)							
IC-13	**COMMERCIAL TRADING & DISCOUNT CO. LTD., ATHENS, GREECE**							
	Ira	BC	1979	D	26,697	591' 02"	75' 10"	45' 08"
	Ivi	BC	1979	D	26,697	591' 04"	75' 10"	45' 08"
IC-14	**COMMON PROGRESS COMPANIA NAVIERA S.A., PIRAEUS, GREECE**							
	Kastor P	BC	1983	D	22,713	528' 03"	75' 07"	45' 07"
	(Sea Augusta '83-'85, Jovian Lily '85-'91)							

Fleet #.	Fleet Name / Vessel Name	Type of Vessel	Year Built	Type of Engine	Cargo Cap. or Gross*	Overall Length	Breadth	Depth or Draft*
	Polydefkis P	BC	1982	D	22,713	528' 03"	75' 07"	45' 07"
	(Sea Astrea '82-'85, Jovian Luzon '85-'91)							
IC-15	**COMPAGNIE DES ILES DU PONANT, NANTES, FRANCE**							
	Le Levant	PA	1998	D	3,504*	326' 09"	45' 11"	11' 06"*
IC-16	**CORNER SHIPPING CO. LTD., PIRAEUS, GREECE**							
	Sylvia	BC	1981	D	22,525	539' 02"	75' 02"	44' 06"
	(Chimo '81-'89, Bergen Pride '89-'93, China Power '93-'96)							
IC-17	**CSL INTERNATIONAL, INC., BEVERLY, MASSACHUSETTS, USA**							
	CSL Asia	BC	1999	D	45,729	609' 05"	99' 09"	54' 02"
	CSL Atlas	SU	1990	D	67,308	746' 01"	105' 02"	63' 00"
	CSL Cabo	SU	1971	D	31,364	596' 02"	84' 04"	49' 10"
	CSL Spirit	SU	2000	D	70,037	737' 10"	105' 07"	64' 00"
	CSL Trailblazer	SU	1978	D	26,608	583' 11"	85' 02"	46' 03"
	Shelia Ann	SU	1999	D	70,037	737' 10"	105' 07"	64' 00"
	MARBULK SHIPPING, INC. – MANAGED BY CSL INTERNATIONAL, INC. **PARTNERSHIP BETWEEN CSL INTERNATIONAL, INC. AND ALGOMA CENTRAL CORP.**							
	Ambassador	SU	1983	D	37,263	730' 00"	75' 10"	50' 00"
	(Canadian Ambassador '83-'85, Ambassador '85-'00, Algosea {2} '00-'00)							
	Pioneer	SU	1981	D	37,448	730' 00"	75' 10"	50' 00"
	(Canadian Pioneer '81-'86)							
IC-18	**CYPRUS MARITIME CO. LTD., ATHENS GREECE**							
	Lake Superior	BC	1982	D	30,670	617' 04"	76' 00"	47' 07"
	(Broompark '82-'99, Millenum Raptor '99-'02, Cardinal '02-'02)							
ID-1	**DENSAN SHIPPING CO. LTD., ISTANBUL, TURKEY**							
	Gunay A	BC	1981	D	30,900	617' 04"	76' 00"	47' 07"
	(Nosira Sharon '81-'89, Berta Dan '89-'93)							
ID-2	**DIANA SHIPPING AGENCIES S.A., PIRAEUS, GREECE**							
	Elm	BC	1984	D	21,978	509' 02"	75' 01"	44' 07"
	(Polarqueen '85-'96)							
	Pine	BC	2002	D	24,765	576' 02"	76' 01"	44' 25
IE-1	**ELMIRA SHIPPING & TRADING S.A., ATHENS, GREECE** *FOLLOWING VESSELS UNDER CHARTER TO FEDNAV LTD.*							
	Aegean Sea	BC	1983	D	31,431	598' 09"	77' 06"	50' 06"
	(Southern Pacific '83-'91, Consensus Pacific '91-'94, Aegean Clipper '94-'98)							
	Mecta Sea	BC	1984	D	28,166	584' 08"	75' 11"	48' 05"
	(Socrates '84-'92, Union '92-'97)							
	Tecam Sea	BC	1984	D	28,166	584' 08"	75' 11"	48' 05"
	(Rich Alliance '84-'89, Monte Bonita '89-'93,University '93-'95, Alam University '95-'97)							
IE-2	**ENZIAN SHIPPING AG, BERNE, SWITZERLAND**							
	Alessia	GC	1999	D	5,647	311' 03"	42' 09"	23' 02"
	Celene	GC	2001	D	8,600	424' 05"	52' 000"	31 09"
	Claudia	GC	1999	D	5,647	311' 06"	42' 09"	23 02"
	Kathrin	GC	1999	D	2,999	311' 00"	42' 09"	23 02"
	Marie Jeanne	GC	1999	D	5,049	311' 11"	43' 04"	23' 05"
	Sabina	GC	2000	D	9,231	419' 06"	52' 05"	32' 00"
IE-3	**ER DENIZCILIK SANAYI NAKLIYAT VE TICARET A.S., ISTANBUL, TURKEY**							
	Balaban I	BC	1979	D	24,747	562' 06"	75' 00"	46' 00"
	(Ocean Glory '79-'83, Serafim '83-'91)							
IF-1	**FAIRFIELD-MAXWELL LTD., ROSELAND, NEW JERSEY, USA**							
	Fairchem Vanguard	TK	1999	D	16,408	436' 04"	74' 06"	39' 08"

Puffin **transits the Welland Canal on her maiden voyage.** *(Courtesy A. Gindroz)*

***Pilic*a upbound in the East Outer Channel below Amherstburg.** *(Courtesy A. Gindroz)*

Fleet #.	Fleet Name Vessel Name	Type of Vessel	Year Built	Type of Engine	Cargo Cap. or Gross*	Overall Length	Breadth	Depth or Draft*
IF-2	**FAR-EASTERN SHIPPING CO. (FESCO), VLADIVOSTOK, RUSSIA**							
	Grigoriy Aleksandrov	BC	1986	D	24,105	603' 06"	74' 08"	45' 09"
	Khudozhnik Kraynev	BC	1986	D	24,105	605' 00"	75' 01"	46' 03"
IF-3	**FEDNAV LTD., MONTREAL, QUEBEC, CANADA**							
	CANARCTIC SHIPPING CO. LTD. - A DIVISION OF FEDNAV LTD.							
	Arctic	BC	1978	D	26,440	692' 04"	75' 05"	49' 05"
	Federal Baffin	BC	1995	D	43,732	623' 04"	100' 00"	54' 06"
	Federal Franklin	BC	1995	D	43,706	623' 04"	100' 00"	54' 06"
	FEDNAV INTERNATIONAL LTD. - A DIVISION OF FEDNAV LTD.							
	Federal Hudson {3}	BC	2000	D	35,750	656' 02"	77' 11"	48' 08"
	Federal Hunter {2}	BC	2001	D	36,563	656' 02"	77' 11"	48' 08"
	Federal Kivalina	BC	2000	D	36,563	656' 02"	77' 11"	48' 08"
	Federal Maas {2}	BC	1997	D	34,372	656' 02"	77' 11"	48' 08"
	Federal Oshima	BC	1999	D	35,700	656' 02"	77' 11"	48' 08"
	Federal Progress (Northern Progress '89-'02)	BC	1989	D	38,130	580' 07"	86' 07"	48' 08"
	Federal Rhine {2}	BC	1997	D	34,372	656' 02"	77' 11"	48' 08"
	Federal Rideau	BC	2000	D	36,563	656' 02"	77' 11"	48' 08"
	Federal Saguenay {2}	BC	1996	D	34,372	656' 02"	77' 11"	48' 08"
	Federal Schelde {3}	BC	1997	D	34,372	656' 02"	77' 11"	48' 08"
	Federal St. Laurent {3}	BC	1996	D	34,372	656' 02"	77' 11"	48' 08"
	Federal Venture (Northern Venture '89-'02)	BC	1989	D	38,130	580' 07"	86' 07"	48' 08"
	Federal Welland	BC	2000	D	35,750	656' 02"	77' 11"	48' 08"
	Federal Yukon	BC	2000	D	35,750	656' 02"	77' 11"	48' 08"
	Lake Erie (Federal Ottawa '80-'95)	BC	1980	D	35,630	737' 06"	76' 02"	47' 01"
	Lake Michigan (Federal Maas {1} '81- 95)	BC	1981	D	38,294	729' 11"	76' 03"	47' 01"
	Lake Ontario (Federal Danube '80 95)	BC	1980	D	35,630	729' 11"	76' 03"	47' 01"
	Lake Superior (Federal Thames '81- 95)	BC	1981	D	35,630	729' 11"	76' 03"	47' 01"

At press time, FedNav Ltd. also had the following vessels under charter. Please consult their respective fleets for details: Aegean Sea, Daviken, Federal Agno, Calliroe Patronicola, Federal Asahi, Federal Elbe, Federal Ems, Federal Fuji, Federal Kumano, Federal Leda, Federal Polaris, Federal Shimanto, Federal Sumida, Federal Weser, Federal Yoshino, Goviken, Helena Oldendorff, Inviken, Lake Carling, Lake Charles, Lake Erie, Lake Michigan, Lake Ontario, Lake Superior, Mecta Sea, Olympic Melody, Olimpic Miracle, Orsula, Regina Oldendorff, Rixta Oldendorff, Sandviken, Spar Garnet, Spar Jade, Spar Opal, Spar Ruby, Tecam Sea, Utviken and Yarmouth

FedNav Ltd. also had the following vessels under construction, for delivery in 2004 and 2005: Federal Danube, Federal Mackinac, Federal Manitou, Federal Margaree, Federal Matane and Federal Seto

Fleet #.	Fleet Name Vessel Name	Type of Vessel	Year Built	Type of Engine	Cargo Cap. or Gross*	Overall Length	Breadth	Depth or Draft*
IF-4	**FINBETA S.P.A., SAVONA, ITALY**							
	Turchese	TK	1999	D	12,000	446' 02"	67' 00"	33' 10"
IF-5	**FLINTER GRONINGEN B.V. (ANCORA AFS MGRS.), GRONINGEN, THE NETHERLANDS**							
	Flinterbaltica	GC	2004	D	3,400	270' 06"	41' 03"	21' 06"
	Flinterbelt	GC	2004	D	3,400	270' 06"	41' 03"	21' 06"
	Flinterbjorn	GC	2004	D	3,400	270' 06"	41' 03"	21' 06"
	Flinterborg	GC	2004	D	3,400	270' 06"	41' 03"	21' 06"
	Fliterbothnia	GC	2004	D	3,480	270' 06"	41' 03"	21' 06"
	Flinterdam	GC	1996	D	4,506	325' 07"	44' 06"	23' 06"
	Flinterdijk	GC	2000	D	6,250	366' 07"	48' 08"	26' 09"
	Flinterduin	GC	2000	D	6,359	364' 01"	49' 02"	26' 09"

Fleet #.	Fleet Name / Vessel Name	Type of Vessel	Year Built	Type of Engine	Cargo Cap. or Gross*	Overall Length	Breadth	Depth or Draft*
	Flintereems	GC	2000	D	6,200	366' 07"	48' 08"	26' 09"
	Flinterhaven	GC	1997	D	6,067	366' 07"	48' 08"	26' 09"
	Flinterland	GC	1995	D	4,216	300' 01"	44' 08"	23' 07"
	Flintermaas	GC	2000	D	6,200	366' 07"	48' 08"	26' 09"
	Flintersky	GC	2001	D	9,200	424' 06"	55' 05"	32' 10"
	Flinterspirit	GC	2001	D	6,358	366' 07"	48' 08"	26' 09"
	Flinterstar	GC	2002	D	9,200	424' 06"	55' 05"	32' 10"
	Flinterzee	GC	1997	D	6,075	366' 07"	48' 08"	26' 09"
	Flinterzijl	GC	1996	D	4,540	325' 09"	44' 09"	23' 07"
IF-6	**FORTUM OIL AND GAS OY, FORTUM, FINLAND**							
	Kihu	TK	1984	D	22,717	527' 11"	76' 00"	46' 08"
	Tavi	TK	1985	D	22,717	527' 11"	76' 00"	58' 05"
	Tuvaq	TK	1977	D	15,955	539' 08"	72' 10"	39' 04"
IF-7	**FRANCO COMPANIA NAVIERA S.A., ATHENS, GREECE**							
	Stefania I	BC	1985	D	28,269	584' 08"	75' 11"	48' 05"
	(Astral Ocean '85-'95, Sea Crystal '95-'97)							
IF-8	**FUKUJIN KISEN CO. LTD., OCHI EHIME, JAPAN**							
	FOLLOWING VESSELS UNDER CHARTER TO FEDNAV LTD.							
	Federal Shimanto	BC	2001	D	32,787	624' 08"	77' 05"	49' 10"
	Federal Yoshino	BC	2001	D	32,787	624' 08"	77' 05"	49' 10"
IG-1	**GEARBULK HOLDING LTD., HAMILTON, BERMUDA**							
	Alouette Arrow	GC	1980	D	14,241	522' 04"	70' 03"	36' 10"
	(Finnarctis '80-'91, Chimo '91-'94)							
	Rathrowan	TK	1991	D	4,059	315' 00"	47' 08"	27' 03'
IG-2	**GENESIS SEATRADING CORP., PIRAEUS, GREECE**							
	Rio Glory	BC	1981	D	30,900	617' 04"	76' 00"	47' 07"
	(Darya Kamal '81-'01)							
IG-3	**GREAT LAKES EUROPEAN SHIPPING AS, ORNSKOLDSVIK, SWEDEN**							
	WILSON SHIP MANAGEMENT, MGR.							
	Marinette	GC	1967	D	12,497	503' 03"	66' 07"	36' 09"
	(Tunadal '75-'97, Abitibi John Cabot '97-'98)							
	Menominee	GC	1967	D	12,497	503' 03"	66' 07"	36' 09"
	(Holmsund '67-'97)							
IH-1	**HALFDAN DITLEV-SIMONSEN & CO. AS, BILLINGSTAD, NORWAY**							
	Viscaya	TK	1982	D	26,328	569' 00"	75' 00"	46' 07"
	(Lake Anina '82-'90, Jo Breid '90-'99)							
IH-2	**HAPAG-LLOYD SEETOURISTIK (CRUISES) GMBH, HAMBURG, GERMANY**							
	C. Columbus	PA	1997	D	14,903*	475' 09"	70' 06"	43' 06"
IH-3	**HARBOR SHIPPING & TRADING CO. S.A., CHIOS, GREECE**							
	Chios Charity	BC	1981	D	29,002	589' 11"	76' 01"	47' 07"
	(Violetta '81-'86, Capetan Yiannis '86-'88, Federal Nord '88-'96, Nordic Moor '96-'98)							
	Chios Harmony	BC	1977	D	29,337	594' 01"	75' 11"	47' 07"
	(Golden Dolphin '77-'90, Romanee '90-'91)							
	Chios Pride	BC	1981	D	28,500	627' 07"	75' 03"	44' 04"
	(Regent Palm '81-'87, Protoporos III '87-'89, Crystal B . '89-'95, Ocean Leader '95-'97)							
	Chios Sailor	BC	1984	D	30,850	617' 04"	75' 11"	47' 07"
	(Radnik '77-'96, Grant Carrier '96-'01)							
IH-4	**HARREN & PARTNER SCHIFFAHRTS GMBH, BREMEN, GERMANY**							
	Fret Meuse	RR	1997	D	5,085	331' 00"	61' 00"	31' 10"
	(Scan Partner '97-'03)							
	Palamos	RR	1997	D	5,085	331' 00"	61' 00"	31' 10"
	(Scan Pacific '97-'01, Palamos '01-'02, Fret Marne '02-'03)							

Fleet #.	Fleet Name / Vessel Name	Type of Vessel	Year Built	Type of Engine	Cargo Cap. or Gross*	Overall Length	Breadth	Depth or Draft*
	Pancaldo	HL	2000	D	7,000	387' 01"	64' 03"	30' 08"
	FOLLOWING VESSELS UNDER CHARTER TO CANADIAN FOREST NAVIGATION LTD.							
	Pochard	BC	2003	D	35,200	629' 09"	77' 05"	50' 00"
	Puffin	BC	2003	D	35,200	629' 09"	77' 05"	50' 00"
IH-5	**HELIKON SHIPPING ENTERPRISES LTD., LONDON, ENGLAND, UNITED KINGDOM**							
	Elikon	BC	1980	D	16,106	582' 00"	75' 02"	44' 04"
	(Bailey '80-'89)							
IH-6	**HERNING SHIPPING A.S., HERNING DENMARK**							
	Ditte Theresa	TK	1977	D	4,501	301' 10"	47' 07"	29' 10"
	(Bravado '77-'96)							
IH-7	**HILAL SHIPPING TRADING & INDUSTRY CO., ISTANBUL, TURKEY**							
	Hilal II	BC	1981	D	25,845	585' 00"	75' 09"	45' 11"
	(Yin Kim '81-'94)							
IH-8	**HOLLAND SHIP SERVICE B.V., ROTTERDAM, NETHERLANDS**							
	Margaretha Green	GC	1999	D	17,539	468' 07"	70' 07"	43' 08"
	Maria Green	GC	1998	D	17,539	468' 07"	70' 07"	43' 08"
II -1	**INDOCHINA SHIPMANAGEMENT LTD., HONG KONG, HONG KONG**							
	Cashin	BC	1984	D	28,791	606' 11"	75' 11"	48' 01"
	(LT Argosy '84-'98, Millenium Hawk ' 98-'02)							
	Giant	BC	1981	D	27,048	627' 07"	75' 03"	44' 03"
	(Oak Star '81-'82, Soren Toubro '82-'98, Millenium Falcon '02)							
	Kent	BC	1984	D	28,786	606' 11"	75' 11"	48' 01"
	(LT Odyssey '84-'98, Millenium Osprey '98-'02)							
	Stokmarnes	BC	1983	D	28,788	606' 11"	75' 11"	48' 01"
	(Mangal Desai '83-'98, Millenium Eagle '98-'02)							

Persenk waits to load at Sarnia. *(Courtesy A. Gindroz)*

Fleet #.	Fleet Name Vessel Name	Type of Vessel	Year Built	Type of Engine	Cargo Cap. or Gross*	Overall Length	Breadth	Depth or Draft*
II-2	**INTERSCAN SCHIFFAHRTSGESELLSCHAFT MBH, HAMBURG, GERMANY**							
	Patria	GC	1996	D	3,519	270' 03"	41' 02"	23' 07"
II-3	**INTERSEE SCHIFFAHRTS-GESELLSCHAFT MBH & CO. , HAREN-EMS, GERMANY**							
	Carola	GC	2000	D	8,600	424' 05"	51' 08"	31' 08"
	Jana	GC	2002	D	8,930	433' 00"	51' 09"	31' 00'
	Thelka	GC	2002	D	8,930	433' 00"	51' 09"	31' 00'
	Winona	GC	2003	D	9,600	433' 09"	52' 01"	31' 07"
	(Vermontborg '03-'03)							
II-4	**INTERSHIP NAVIGATION CO. LTD., LIMASSOL, CYPRUS**							
	BBC Russia	GC	2002	D	17,471	469' 00"	74' 08"	43' 06"
IJ-1	**J. G. GOUMAS (SHIPPING) CO. S.A., PIRAEUS, GREECE**							
	Alaska Rainbow	BC	1985	D	22,782	515' 11"	75' 07"	44' 08"
	Washington Rainbow II	BC	1984	D	22,828	515' 11"	75' 07"	44' 08"
IJ-2	**JADROPLOV DD, SPLIT, CROATIA**							
	Hope	BC	1982	D	30,900	617' 03"	76' 00"	47' 07"
	(Nosira Madeleine '82-'89, Bella Dan '89-'93, Hope 1 '93-'02)							
IJ-3	**JO TANKERS B.V., SPIJKENISSE, NETHERLANDS**							
	Jo Spirit	TK	1998	D	6,248	352' 02"	52' 02"	30' 02"
IJ-4	**JSM SHIPPING GMBH & CO., JORK, GERMANY**							
	Frida	GC	2003	D	10,300	465' 08"	59' 0"	23' 09"
IJ-5	**JUMBO SHIPPING CO. S.A., ROTTERDAM, NETHERLANDS**							
	Daniella	HL	1989	D	7,600	322' 09"	68' 06"	37' 02"
	(Stellaprima '89-'90)							
	Fairlane	HL	2000	D	7,300	361' 03"	68' 05"	44' 02"
	Fairlift	HL	1990	D	7,780	329' 02"	68' 10"	43' 08"
	Fairload	HL	1995	D	7,500	313' 11"	60' 03"	37' 02"
	Jumbo Challenger	HL	1983	D	6,375	360' 11"	63' 00"	34' 05"
	Jumbo Spirit	HL	1995	D	5,200	313' 11"	60' 03"	37' 02"
	Jumbo Vision	HL	2000	D	7,300	361' 03"	68' 05"	44' 02"
	Stellanova	HL	1996	D	5,198	313' 08"	60' 03"	37' 02"
	Stellaprima	HL	1991	D	7,600	329' 02"	68' 10"	43' 08"
IK-1	**K.C. MARITIME LTD., HONG KONG, PEOPLE'S REPUBLIC OF CHINA**							
	Darya Devi	BC	1985	D	28,019	584' 08"	75' 11"	48' 05"
	(Astral Mariner '85-'90, Lake Challenge '90-'97, Manila Angus '97-'98)							
IK-2	**KEISHIN KAIUN K.K., HAKATA, JAPAN**							
	Rubin Halcyon	BC	1997	D	18,315	486' 03"	74' 10"	40' 00"
	Rubin Hawk	BC	1995	D	18,233	486' 03"	74' 10"	40' 00"
	Rubin Lark	BC	1997	D	18,315	486' 01"	74' 10"	40' 00"
IK-3	**KNUTSEN O.A.S. SHIPPING A/S, HAUGESUND, NORWAY**							
	Ellen Knutsen	TK	1992	D	17,071	464' 03"	75' 07"	38' 09"
	Sidsel Knutsen	TK	1993	D	22,625	533' 02"	75' 05"	48' 07"
	Synnove Knutsen	TK	1992	D	17,071	464' 03"	75' 07"	38' 09"
	Torill Knutsen	TK	1990	D	14,910	464' 08"	75' 07"	38' 09"
	Turid Knutsen	TK	1993	D	22,000	533' 03"	75' 07"	48' 07"
IK-4	**KREY SCHIFFAHRTS GMBH & CO. KG, SIMONSWOLDE, GERMANY**							
	Falderntor	GC	1996	D	5,027	314' 11"	51' 11"	25' 11"
	(Ivaran Primero '96-'97, Delmas Mahury '97-'99, Falderntor '99-'01, Boyne River '01-'02, Huon Gulf '02-'03)							
	Nordkap	GC	2000	D	8,760	353' 06"	59' 09"	33' 02"
	Ostkap	GC	2000	D	8,760	353' 06"	59' 09"	33' 02"
IL-1	**LAURIN MARITIME (AMERICA), INC., HOUSTON, TEXAS, USA**							
	Mountain Blossom	TK	1986	D	19,993	527' 07"	74' 11"	39' 04"

Fleet #.	Fleet Name / Vessel Name	Type of Vessel	Year Built	Type of Engine	Cargo Cap. or Gross*	Overall Length	Breadth	Depth or Draft*
	Nordic Blossom	TK	1981	D	19,954	505' 03"	74' 07"	45' 04"
	(Nordic Sun '81-'89, Nordic '89 -'94)							
	Sunny Blossom	TK	1986	D	19,995	527' 07"	74' 11"	39' 05"
IL-2	**LIETUVOS JURU LAIVININKYSTE (LITHUANIAN SHIPPING CO.), KLAIPEDA, LITHUANIA**							
	Kapitonas A. Lucka	BC	1980	D	14,550	479' 08"	67' 09"	42' 04"
	(Ivan Nesterov '80 -'91)							
	Kapitonas Andzejauskas	BC	1978	D	14,550	479' 08"	67' 09"	42' 04"
	(Kapitan Meshcheryakove '78 -'92, Kapitonas Mesceriakov '92-'96)							
	Kapitonas Domeika	BC	1979	D	14,550	479' 08"	67' 09"	42' 04"
	(Kapitan Valvilov '79 -'92, Kapitonas Valvilov '92-'95)							
	Kapitonas Kaminskas	BC	1978	D	14,550	479' 08"	67' 09"	42' 04"
	(Kapitan Gudin '78-'92, Kapitonas Gudin '92-'95)							
	Kapitonas Marcinkus	BC	1977	D	14,550	479' 08"	67' 09"	42' 04"
	(Kapitan Ismiakov '77-'92, Kapitonas Ismiakov 92-'96)							
	Kapitonas Serafinas	BC	1980	D	14,550	479' 08"	67' 09"	42' 04"
	(Kapitan Stulov '80-'91, Kapitonas Stulov '91-'97)							
	Kapitonas Stulpinas	BC	1981	D	14,550	479' 08"	67' 09"	42' 04"
	(Yustas Paleckis '81-'92)							
IL-3	**LYDIA MAR SHIPPING CO. S.A., ATHENS, GREECE**							
	Dorothea	BC	1984	D	22,025	508' 05"	74' 08"	44' 06"
	(Garnet Star '84-'94)							
IM-1	**MALAYSIA INTERNATIONAL SHIPPING CORP., SELANGOR, SINGAPORE**							
	Federal Bergen	BC	1984	D	29,159	593' 00"	76' 00"	47' 00"
	(High Peak '84 -'90, Federal Bergen '90 -'92, Thunder Bay '92-'93)							
IM-2	**MAYFLOWER SHIP MANAGEMENT CO., PIRAUES, GREECE**							
	Yellowknife	BC	1984	D	29,651	622' 00"	74' 08"	49' 08"
	(Bihac '84-'93, La Boheme '93-'95, Lindsey M. '98-'99, Med Pride '99-'01)							
	FOLLOWING VESSEL CURRENTLY UNDER CHARTER TO FEDNAV LTD.							
	Yarmouth	BC	1985	D	29,462	601' 00"	76' 00"	48' 11"
	(Paolo Pittaluga '85-'91, Federal Oslo '91-'00)							
IM-3	**MURMANSK SHIPPING CO., MURMANSK, RUSSIA**							
	Admiral Ushakov	BC	1979	D	19,885	531' 07"	75' 01"	44' 05"
	Aleksandr Nevskiy	BC	1978	D	19,590	532' 02"	75' 02"	44' 05"
	Ivan Susanin	BC	1981	D	19,885	531' 10"	75' 02"	44' 05"
	Kapitan Chukhchin	BC	1981	D	19,240	531' 10"	75' 02"	44' 05"
	Kolguev	BC	1987	D	28,358	590' 07"	75' 10"	48' 07"
	(Great Laker '87-'02)							
	Mikhail Strekalovskiy	BC	1981	D	19,252	531' 10"	75' 02"	44' 05"
	Pavel Vavilov	BC	1981	D	19,252	531' 10"	75' 02"	44' 05"
IN-1	**NAVARONE S.A. MARINE ENTERPRISES, LIMASSOL, CYPRUS**							
	FOLLOWING VESSELS UNDER CHARTER TO CANADIAN FOREST NAVIGATION LTD.							
	Pintail	BC	1983	D	25,035	647' 08"	75' 10"	46' 11"
	(Punica '83-'95)							
	Bluewing	BC	2002	D	26,747	581' 00"	77' 07"	31' 08"
	Cinnamon	BC	2002	D	26,737	581' 00"	77' 07"	31' 08"
	Greenwing	BC	2002	D	26,722	581' 00"	77' 07"	31' 08"
	Kakawli	BC	2004	D	27,000	581' 00"	77' 07"	31' 08"
	Mandarin	BC	2003	D	26,700	581' 00"	77' 07"	31' 08"
	White Knight	BC	2004	D	27,000	581' 00"	77' 07"	31' 08"
IN-2	**NAVIGATION MARITIME BULGARE LTD., VARNA, BULGARIA**							
	Bogdan	BC	1997	D	14,011	466' 02"	72' 08"	36' 04"
	Kamenitza	BC	1980	D	24,150	605' 08"	75' 00"	46' 05"
	Kapitan Georgi Georgiev	BC	1980	D	24,150	605' 08"	75' 00"	46' 05"
	Kom	BC	1997	D	13,971	466' 02"	72' 10"	36' 05"

Federal Agno passes Gros Cap Light west of the Soo Locks. *(JRoger LeLievre)*

Fleet #.	Fleet Name / Vessel Name	Type of Vessel	Year Built	Type of Engine	Cargo Cap. or Gross*	Overall Length	Breadth	Depth or Draft*
	Koznitsa	BC	1984	D	24,100	605' 08"	75' 02"	46' 07"
	Malyovitza	BC	1983	D	24,456	605' 00"	75' 05"	46' 06"
	Milin Kamak	BC	1979	D	25,857	607' 07"	75' 02"	46' 07"
	Okoltchitza	BC	1982	D	24,148	605' 08"	75' 05"	46' 06"
	Perelik	BC	1998	D	13,887	466' 02"	72' 10"	36' 05"
	Persenk	BC	1998	D	13,900	466' 02"	72' 08"	36' 04"
	Shipka	BC	1978	D	24,385	607' 07"	75' 02"	46' 07"
IN-3	**NB TWO SHIPPING LTD., LIMASSOL, CYPRUS**							
	Kapitan Bochek	BC	1982	D	19,252	531' 10"	75' 02"	44' 03"
	Kapitan Kudlay	BC	1983	D	19,252	531' 10"	75' 02"	44' 03"
	Kapitan Nazarev	BC	1984	D	19,252	531' 10"	75' 02"	44' 03"
	Kapitan Vakula	BC	1982	D	19,240	531' 10"	75' 00"	44' 00"
	Kapitan Vodenko	BC	1982	D	19,240	531' 10"	75' 00"	44' 00"
IN-4	**NORTHERN SHIPPING CO., ARKHANGELSK, RUSSIA**							
	Petr Strelkov	BC	1977	D	14,200	498' 00"	68' 11"	38' 01"
IN-5	**NOVOROSSIYSK SHIPPING CO. (NOVOSHIP), NOVOROSSIYSK, RUSSIA**							
	Alioth	TK	1999	D	19,996	489' 10"	77' 11"	41' 06"
	Boris Livanov	BC	1986	D	23,940	605' 09"	75' 00"	46' 05"
	Khirurg Vishnevskiy	TK	1988	D	16,970	497' 01"	73' 07"	39' 10"
	Leonid Utesov	TK	1989	D	16,970	497' 01"	73' 07"	39' 10"
	MCT Almak	TK	1999	D	17,561	489' 10"	77' 11"	41' 06"
	MCT Altair	TK	2000	D	19,996	489' 10"	77' 11"	41' 06"
	MCT Arcturus	TK	2000	D	17,553	489' 10"	77' 11"	41' 06"
	Vladimir Vysotskiy	TK	1988	D	16,970	497' 01"	73' 07"	39' 10"
IO-1	**OCEAN FREIGHTERS LTD., PIRAEUS, GREECE**							
	Pontokratis	BC	1981	D	28,738	590' 02"	75' 11"	47' 07"
	Pontoporos	BC	1984	D	29,155	590' 02"	75' 11"	47' 07"
IO-2	**OCEAN SHIPPING CO., TBILISI, REPUBLIC OF GEORGIA**							
	Aiet	TK	1981	D	22,622	505' 02"	74' 06"	45' 02"
	(Iver Taurus '81–'82, Northern Tiger '82–'87, Poti '87–'00)							
	Lake Lisi	TK	1985	D	16,421	496' 05"	73' 07"	39' 10"
	(David Bakradze '85-'94, Bakradze '94-'00)							
	St Mary	TK	1988	D	16,421	496' 05"	73' 07"	39' 10"
	(Akademik Uznadze '88-'94, Uznadze '94-'00)							
IO-3	**OCEANBULK MARITIME S.A., ATHENS, GREECE**							
	Lykes Energizer	RR	1992	D	17,510	569' 03"	75' 07"	45' 01"
	(Kovrov '92-'97, Elan Vital '97-'97, Thorsriver '97-'00)							
	Lykes Inspirer	GC	1990	D	17,565	569' 03"	75' 11"	45' 01"
	(Krasnodon '00-'96, Elena K. '96-'98, Res Cogitans '98-'99, Thorslake '99-'00)							
	Lykes Raider	GC	1990	D	17,420	569' 02"	75' 04"	44.09"
	(Kislovodsk '90-'96, Barbara L. '96-'97, Bremer Voyager '97-'98, Nordana Successor '98-'99, Seaboard Venezuela '99-'00, Global Brasil '00-'01)							
	Lykes Runner	RR	1991	D	17,420	569' 02"	75' 04"	44.09"
	(Krasnograd '91-'92, Beloostrov '92-'98, Nordana Kitale '98-'98, Nordana Kigoma '98-'99, Nordana Surveyor '99-'01)							
	Lykes Winner	RR	1990	D	17,565	569' 02"	75' 09"	45' 01"
	(Evgeniy Mravinskiy '90-'96, Alioth Star '96-'97, Global Hawk '97-'98, Nordana Kampala '98-'99, Cobra '99-'99, Thorshope '99-'00)							
	Strange Attractor	BC	1978	D	28,873	593' 02"	76' 00"	47' 07"
	(Launched as Graiglwyd. Lantau Trader '79-'95)							
IO-4	**OCEANEX INC., MONTREAL, QUEBEC, CANADA**							
	ASL Sanderling	RR	1977	D	15,195	364' 01"	88' 05"	57' 07"
	(Rauenfels '77-'80, Essen '80-'81, Kongsfjord '81-'83. Onno '83-'87)							
	Cabot {2}	RR	1979	D	7,132	564' 09"	73' 11"	45' 09"

Fleet #.	Fleet Name Vessel Name	Type of Vessel	Year Built	Type of Engine	Cargo Cap. or Gross*	Overall Length	Breadth	Depth or Draft*
	Cicero	RR	1978	D	6,985	482' 10"	73' 11"	45' 09"
IO-5	**OLDENDORFF CARRIERS GMBH & CO., LUBECK, GERMANY**							
	Anna Oldendorff	BC	1994	D	18,297	604' 07"	74' 09"	40' 00"
	Bernhard Oldendorff	BC	1991	D	77,499	803' 08"	65' 09"	65' 09"
	Elise Oldendorff	BC	1998	D	20,142	488' 10"	75' 09"	44' 03"
	Mathilde Oldendorff	BC	1999	D	20,427	488' 10"	75' 11"	44' 03"
	FOLLOWING VESSELS UNDER CHARTER TO FEDNAV LTD.							
	Helena Oldendorff	BC	1984	D	28,354	644' 06"	75' 10"	46' 11"
	(Noble River '84-'86)							
	Regina Oldendorff	BC	1986	D	28,031	639' 09"	75' 10"	46' 11"
	Rixta Oldendorff	BC	1986	D	28,031	639' 09"	75' 10"	46' 11"
IO-6	**OLYMPIC SHIPPING AND MANAGEMENT S.A., MONTE CARLO, MONACO**							
	Olympic Mentor	BC	1984	D	29,693	599' 09"	75' 11"	48' 07"
	(Calliroe Patronicola '84-'84, Patricia-R. '84-'88)							
	Olympic Merit	BC	1985	D	29,611	599' 09"	75' 11"	48' 07"
	FOLLOWING VESSELS UNDER CHARTER TO FEDNAV LTD.							
	Calliroe Patronicola	BC	1985	D	29,608	599' 09"	75' 11"	48' 07"
	Olympic Melody	BC	1984	D	29,640	599' 09"	75' 11"	48' 07"
	Olympic Miracle	BC	1984	D	29,670	599' 09"	75' 11"	48' 07"
IO-7	**ORION SCHIFFAHRTS-GESELLSCHAFT REITH & CO., HAMBURG, GERMANY**							
	Caro	BC	1984	D	11,356	485' 11"	75' 09"	41' 08"
	Crio	BC	1984	D	11,356	485' 11"	75' 09"	41' 08"
	Hero	BC	1984	D	11,356	485' 11"	75' 09"	41' 08"
	(Mount Fuji '84-'90)							
	Ida	BC	1995	D	18,172	486' 01"	74' 10"	40' 00"
	Lita	BC	1995	D	18,173	486' 01"	74' 10"	40' 00"
	Meta	BC	1987	D	18,612	477' 04"	75' 11"	40' 08"
	Olga	BC	1996	D	18,319	486' 01"	74' 10"	40' 00"
	Patria	GC	1985	D	8,880	377' 11"	61' 01"	32' 02"
IP-1	**PACIFIC & ATLANTIC CORPORATION, ATHENS, GREECE**							
	John G. Lemos	BC	1986	D	17,832	472' 04"	75' 04"	40' 00"
	(Cinchona ' 86-'91, Centa Dan '91-'93, Tropic Confidence '93-'01)							
	Express Progress	BC	1986	D	17,247	477' 04"	69' 03"	43' 00"
	(Sifnos Island '86-'89, Clipper Mandarin '89-'00)							
IP-2	**PACIFIC CARRIERS LTD., SINGAPORE, SINGAPORE**							
	Alam Sejahtera	BC	1985	D	29,692	599' 09"	75' 10"	48' 07"
	(Olympic Dignity '85-'92)							
	Alam Sempurna	BC	1984	D	28,094	584' 08"	75' 11"	48' 05"
	Alam Senang	BC	1984	D	28,098	584' 08"	75' 11"	48' 05"
	(Golden Alliance '84-'88, Atlantic '88-'93)							
	Ikan Sepat	BC	1984	D	28,503	590' 03"	75' 04"	47' 07"
	(Trident Venture '84-'90)							
IP-3	**PAN OCEAN SHIPPING CO. LTD., SEOUL, REPUBLIC OF KOREA**							
	Bum Dong	TK	1980	D	17,823	442' 11"	75' 06"	39' 09"
IP-4	**POLISH STEAMSHIP CO., SZCZECIN, POLAND**							
	Clipper Eagle	BC	1994	D	16,900	490' 04"	76' 00"	39' 08"
	Clipper Falcon	BC	1994	D	16,900	490' 04"	76' 00"	39' 08"
	Irma	BC	2000	D	34,948	655' 10"	77' 05"	50' 02"
	Iryda	BC	1999	D	34,946	655' 10"	77' 07"	50' 02"
	Isa	BC	1999	D	34,939	655' 10"	77' 07"	50' 02"
	Isadora	BC	1999	D	34,948	655' 10"	77' 05"	50' 02"
	Isolda	BC	1999	D	34,949	655' 10"	77' 07"	50' 02"
	Kopalnia Halemba	BC	1990	D	11,715	471' 01"	63' 08"	36' 05"

Fleet #.	Fleet Name Vessel Name	Type of Vessel	Year Built	Type of Engine	Cargo Cap. or Gross*	Overall Length	Breadth	Depth or Draft*
	Kopalnia Borynia	BC	1989	D	11.898	471' 07"	63' 06"	36' 04"
	Nogat	BC	1999	D	11,542	498' 01"	75' 04"	40' 01"
	Odra	BC	1992	D	13,790	471' 05"	68' 08"	37' 02"
	(Odranes '92-'99)							
	Orla	BC	1999	D	17,064	490' 02"	76' 00"	39' 08"
	Pilica	BC	1999	D	17,064	490' 02"	76' 00"	39' 08"
	Pomorze Zachodnie	BC	1985	D	26,696	591' 04"	75' 11"	45' 08"
	Rega	BC	1995	D	16,880	490' 03"	76' 00"	39' 08"
	(Fossnes '95-'02)							
	Warta	BC	1992	D	13,790	471' 05"	68' 08"	37' 02"
	(Wartanes '92-'99)							
	Wisla	BC	1992	D	13,770	471' 05"	68' 08"	37' 02"
	(Wislanes '92-'99)							
	Ziemia Chelminska	BC	1984	D	26,700	591' 04"	75' 11"	45' 08"
	Ziemia Cieszynska	BC	1993	D	26,264	591' 01"	75' 09"	45' 07"
	(Ziemia Cieszynska '93-'93, Lake Carling '93-'03)							
	Ziemia Gnieznienska	BC	1985	D	26,696	591' 04"	75' 11"	45' 08"
	Ziemia Gornoslaska	BC	1990	D	26,209	591' 01"	75' 09"	45' 07"
	(Ziemia Gornoslaska '88- 91, Lake Charles '91-'03)							
	Ziemia Lodzka	BC	1992	D	26,264	591' 01"	75' 09"	45' 07"
	(Ziemia Lodzka '92-'92, Lake Champlain '92-'03)							
	Ziemia Suwalska	BC	1984	D	26,706	591' 04"	75' 11"	45' 08"
	Ziemia Tarnowska	BC	1985	D	26,700	591' 04"	75' 11"	45' 08"
	(Launched as Pomorze Zachodnie)							
	Ziemia Zamojska	BC	1984	D	26,600	591' 04"	75' 11"	45' 08"
IP-5	**PRECIOUS SHIPPING LINES, BANGKOK, THAILAND**							
	Wana Naree	BC	1980	D	26,977	566' 00"	75' 11"	48' 05"
IP-6	**PRIMAL SHIPMANAGEMENT, INC., ATHENS, GREECE**							
	Arizona Dream	BC	1980	D	27,311	627' 07"	75' 03	44' 00"
	(El General '83-'83, Protector '83-'88, Loretta V '88-'91, G. Dost '91-'95, Mina Cebi '95-'01)							
IR-1	**REEDEREI ALNWICK HARMSTORF GMBH & CO., HAMBURG, GERMANY**							
	BBC America	GC	1999	D	4,806	328' 00"	54' 04"	26' 05"
IR-2	**REEDEREI HANS-PETER ECKHOFF GMBH CO. HG, JORK, GERMANY**							
	Kamilla	GC	1985	D	2,785	322' 06"	44' 07"	23' 00"
	Skagen	GC	1999	D	3,490	283' 04"	41' 09"	23' 02"
IR-3	**RIGEL SCHIFFAHRTS GMBH, BREMEN, GERMANY**							
	Alsterstern	TK	1994	D	16,700	529' 05"	75' 05"	38' 05"
	Havelstern	TK	1994	D	17,080	529' 05"	75' 05"	38' 05"
	Isarstern	TK	1995	D	17,078	528' 03"	75' 06"	38' 05"
	Ledastern	TK	1993	D	10,500	405' 11"	58' 01"	34' 09"
	Rheinstern	TK	1993	D	17,080	529' 05"	75' 05"	38' 05"
	Travestern	TK	1993	D	17,080	529' 05"	75' 05"	38' 05"
IS-1	**SCANDIA SHIPPING HELLAS, INC., ATHENS, GREECE**							
	Armonikos	BC	1979	D	30,689	674' 03"	75' 08"	47' 07"
	(Docegulf '79-'98)							
	Taxideftis	BC	1984	D	28,503	590' 03"	75' 04"	47' 07"
	(Trident Mariner '84-'01)							
IS-2	**SCANSCOT SHIPPING SERVICES (DEUTSCHLAND) GMBH, HAMBURG, GERMANY**							
	Scan Atlantic	RR	1999	D	7,100	416' 02"	67' 07"	37' 09"
	Scan Germania	RR	2000	D	7,172	415' 01"	65' 07"	37' 09"
	Scan Hansa	RR	1999	D	7,228	416' 02"	67' 07"	37' 09"
	Scan Oceanic	RR	1997	D	5,085	331' 00"	61' 00"	31' 10"
	Scan Polaris	RR	1996	D	5,100	331' 00"	61' 00"	31' 10"

Netherlands-registered *Flintermaas* **in the St. Marys River.** *(Roger LeLievre)*

Fleet #.	Fleet Name / Vessel Name	Type of Vessel	Year Built	Type of Engine	Cargo Cap. or Gross*	Overall Length	Breadth	Depth or Draft*
IS-3	**SEAARLAND SHIPPING MANAGEMENT, VILLACH, AUSTRIA**							
	THE FOLLWING VESSEL UNDER CHARTER TO CANADIAN FOREST NAVIGATION LTD.							
	Peonia	BC`	1983	D	27,995	647' 06"	75' 07"	46' 09"
IS-4	**SEASTAR NAVIGATION CO. LTD., ATHENS, GREECE**							
	Polydefkis	BC	1976	D	30,244	621' 06"	75' 00"	47' 11"
	(Peter '76-'81, Philippe L.D. '81-'85, La Richardais '85-'93)							
	THE FOLLWING VESSELS UNDER CHARTER TO CANADIAN FOREST NAVIGATION LTD.							
	Goldeneye	BC	1986	D	26,706	591' 06"	75' 10"	48' 07"
	(Sun Ocean '86-'93, Luna Verde '93-'00)							
	Milo	BC	1984	D	17,065	584' 00"	75' 08"	48' 02"
	(Silver Leader '84-'95, Alam United '95-'98, United '98-'00)							
	Orna	BC	1984	D	27,915	584' 08"	69' 03"	48' 05"
	(St. Catheriness 84-'90, Asian Erie '90-'92, Handy Laker '92-'98, Moor Laker '98-'03)							
	Pytheas	BC	1981	D	29,514	590' 01"	76' 00"	47' 07"
	(Yannis C. '81-'86, Pindos '86-'87, Ikan Selayang '97-'98, Kakawi '98-'00)							
	Toro	BC	1983	D	28,126	584' 06"	75' 07"	46' 09"
	(La Liberte '83-'87, Libert '87-'88, Astart '88-'93, Ulloa '93-'00)							
	Woody	BC	1984	D	25,166	593' 01"	75' 04"	35' 01"
	(High Light '84-'90, Scan Trader '90-'95, Asia Trader '95-'96, NST Challenge '96-'03)							
IS-5	**SEVEN SEAS CARRIERS A.S., BERGEN, NORWAY**							
	Lady Hamilton {2}	BC	1983	D	34,500	730' 01"	75' 09"	48' 00"
	(Saskatchewan Pioneer '83-'95)							
IS-6	**SHIH WEI NAVIGATION CO. LTD., TAIPEI, TAIWAN**							
	Excellent Pescadores	BC	2002	D	18,200	485' 05"	74' 08"	40' 00"
	Royal Pescadores	BC	1997	D	18,369	486' 01"	74' 10"	40' 00"
IS-7	**(THE) SHIPPING CORP. OF INDIA LTD., MUMBAI, INDIA**							
	Lok Maheshwari	BC	1986	D	26,728	605' 03"	75' 03"	47' 03"
	Lok Prakash	BC	1989	D	26,790	606' 11"	75' 04"	47' 03"
	Lok Pratap	BC	1993	D	26,718	605' 09"	75' 04"	47' 04"

Fleet #.	Fleet Name / Vessel Name	Type of Vessel	Year Built	Type of Engine	Cargo Cap. or Gross*	Overall Length	Breadth	Depth or Draft*
	Lok Prem	BC	1990	D	26,714	605' 08"	75' 04"	47' 03"
	Lok Rajeshwari	BC	1988	D	26,639	605' 08"	75' 04"	47' 03"
	(Jagat Rajeshwari '88-'88)							
IS-8	**SHUNZAN KAIUN CO. LTD., EHIME, JAPAN**							
	Spring Laker	BC	1996	D	30,855	606' 09"	77' 04"	48' 08"
IS-9	**SINGA STAR PTE. LTD., SINGAPORE, SINGAPORE**							
	Changi Hope	BC	2000	D	18,320	486' 01"	74' 10"	40' 00"
IS-10	**SIOMAR ENTERPRISES LTD., PIRAEUS, GREECE**							
	Island Gem	BC	1984	D	28,005	584' 08"	76' 02"	48' 05"
	Island Skipper	BC	1984	D	28,031	584' 08"	76' 02"	48' 05"
IS-11	**SOETERMEER, FEKKES' CARGADOORSKANTOOR B.V., ZWIJNDRECHT, NETHERLANDS**							
	Merwedelta	GC	2001	D	4,956	308' 03"	43' 02'	23' 04"
IS-12	**SPAR SHIPPING A.S., BERGEN, NORWAY**							
	FOLLOWING VESSELS UNDER CHARTER TO FEDNAV LTD.							
	Spar Garnet	BC	1984	D	30,686	589' 11"	75' 10"	50' 11"
	(Mary Anne '84-'93, Federal Vigra '93-'97)							
	Spar Jade	BC	1984	D	30,674	589' 11"	75' 10"	50' 11"
	(Fiona Mary '84-93, Federal Aalesund '93-'97)							
	Spar Opal	BC	1984	D	28,214	585' 00"	75' 10"	48' 05"
	(Lake Shidaka '84-'91, Consensus Atlantic '91-'92, Federal Matane '92-'97, Matane '97-'97)							
	Spar Ruby	BC	1985	D	28,259	584' 08"	75' 11"	48' 05"
	(Astral Neptune '85-'92, Liberty Sky ' 92-'98, Manila Bellona '98-'98, Solveig '98-'00)							
IS-13	**STOLT PARCEL TANKERS, INC., GREENWICH, CONNECTICUT, USA**							
	Stolt Accord	TK	1982	D	12,467	433' 01"	66' 04"	37' 09"
	(Rainbow '82-'89)							
	Stolt Alliance	TK	1985	D	12,674	404' 06"	65' 08"	36' 09"
	(Shoun Trader '85-'89)							
	Stolt Aspiration	TK	1987	D	12,219	422' 11"	66' 04"	36' 01
IS-14	**SUN BAY CRUISES LTD., NASSAU, BAHAMAS**							
	Orion	PA	2003	D	4,000*	334' 06"	45' 09'	19' 00"
IS-15	**SURRENDRA OVERSEAS LTD., CALCUTTA, INDIA**							
	APJ Anjli	BC	1982	D	27,192	577' 05"	75' 11"	47' 11"
	APJ Sushma	BC	1983	D	27,213	577' 05"	75' 11"	47' 11"
IT-1	**TACHIBANAYA CO. LTD., EHIME, JAPAN**							
	Panam Flota	TK	1999	D	11,642	384' 06"	65' 07"	36' 09"
	Panam Linda	TK	1998	D	10,300	410' 01"	61' 08"	32' 06"
	Panam Sol	TK	1998	D	12,756	406' 10"	66' 03"	36' 09"
IT-2	**TEO SHIPPING CORP., PIRAEUS, GREECE**							
	Antalina	BC	1984	D	28,082	584' 08"	75' 11"	48' 05"
	(Union Pioneer '84-'88, Manila Prosperity '88-'89, Consensus Sea '89-'92, Wiltrader '92-'94)							
	Marilis T.	BC	1984	D	28,097	584' 08"	75' 11"	47' 10"
	(Union Peace '84-'88, Manila Peace '88-'89, Consensus Sun '89-'92, Wilrider '92-'94)							
	Sevilla Wave	BC	1986	D	26,858	600' 08"	73' 08"	46' 08"
	Vamand Wave	BC	1985	D	28,303	580' 08"	75' 11"	47' 07"
IT-3	**TECHNOMAR SHIPPING INC., ATHENS, GREECE**							
	Dimitris Y	BC	1983	D	28,192	584' 06"	75' 08"	48' 05"
	(Kalliopi II '83-'88, Cineraria '88-'90, Consensus Star '90-'91, Federal Manitou '91-'95, Consensus Manitou '95-'99)							
IT-4	**THENAMARIS (SHIPS MANAGEMENT), INC., ATHENS, GREECE**							
	Seaguardian II	BC	1984	D	28,251	639' 09"	75' 10"	46' 11"
	(Sea Master II '84-'88, Sea Monarch '88-'97, Sealuck V '97-'00, Seaharmony II '00-'01, Seamonarch II '01-'02)							

Fleet #.	Fleet Name Vessel Name	Type of Vessel	Year Built	Type of Engine	Cargo Cap. or Gross*	Overall Length	Breadth	Depth or Draft*
	Sealink	BC	1983	D	28,234	639' 09"	75' 10"	46' 11"
	(Seaglory 83-'86, Sea Star II '86-'97)							
IT-5	**TOMASOS BROTHERS INC., PIRAUES, GREECE**							
	Alexis	BC	1984	D	27,048	599' 07"	75' 04"	46' 05"
	Ocean Crony '84-'88, Linda K '89-'91, Bold Champion '91-'91)							
IU-1	**UNION MARINE ENTERPRISES S.A. OF PANAMA, PIRAEUS, GREECE**							
	Capetan Michalis	BC	1981	D	28,600	593' 03"	75' 11"	47' 07"
	(Vasiliki '81-'85)							
IV-1	**VERGOS MARINE MANAGEMENT, PIRAEUS, GREECE**							
	Verdon	BC	1981	D	26,350	594' 09"	75' 00"	47' 01"
	(El Challenger '81-'85, Voyager '85-'86, Atlantica '86-'91, Sinem Uzundemir '91-'95)							
	Verily	BC	1982	D	26,450	594' 09"	75' 00"	47' 01"
	(Ingenious '82-'91, C Filyos '91-'95)							
IV-2	**VIKEN SHIPPING AS, BERGEN, NORWAY**							
	FOLLOWING VESSELS UNDER CHARTER TO FEDNAV LTD.							
	Daviken	BC	1987	D	34,752	729' 00"	75' 11"	48' 05"
	(Malinska '87-'97)							
	Federal Fuji	BC	1986	D	29,536	599' 09"	75' 11"	48' 07"
	Federal Polaris	BC	1985	D	29,536	599' 09"	75' 11"	48' 07"
	Goviken	BC	1987	D	34,752	729' 00"	75' 11"	48' 05"
	(Omisalj '87-'97)							
	Inviken	BC	1984	D	30,052	621' 05"	75' 01"	47' 11"
	(Bar '86-'97)							
	Sandviken	BC	1986	D	34,685	728' 09"	75' 11"	48' 05"
	(Petka '86-'00)							
	Utviken	BC	1985	D	30,052	621' 05"	75' 01"	47' 11"
	(Bijelo Polje '87-'92, C.Blanco '92-'95)							
IW-1	**W. BOCKSTIEGEL REEDEREI KG, EMDEN, GERMANY**							
	BBC Chile	GC	2001	D	7,616	353' 05"	59' 07"	33' 01"
	BBC Italy	GC	2001	D	7,612	353' 00"	60' 00"	33' 00"
	(BBC Italy '99-'01, Buccaneer '01-'03)							
	BBC Spain	CG	2001	D	7,598	351' 00"	59' 07"	33' 01"
	Malte B.	GC	1998	D	3,440	283' 06"	42' 00"	23' 04"
	Nils B.	GC	1998	D	3,440	283' 06"	42' 00"	23' 04"
IW-2	**WAGENBORG SHIPPING B.V., DELFZIJL, NETHERLANDS**							
	Dongeborg	GC	1999	D	9,000	437' 08"	52' 02"	32' 02"
	Drechtborg	GC	1998	D	9,100	441' 04"	54' 02"	32' 02"
	(Drechtborg '98-'00, MSC Skaw '00-'02))							
	Egbert Wagenborg	GC	1998	D	9,100	441' 04"	54' 02"	32' 02"
	(Maasborg '98-'98, Egbert Wagenborg '98-'02, MSC Bothnia '02-'03)							
	Kasteelborg	GC	1998	D	9,025	428' 08"	52' 01"	33' 06"
	Keizersborg	GC	1996	D	9,025	428' 08"	52' 01"	33' 06"
	Koningsborg	GC	1999	D	9,067	428' 08"	52' 01"	33' 06"
	Kwintebank	GC	2002	D	9,900	433' 07"	52' 01"	31' 04"
	Maineborg	GC	2001	D	9,100	441' 04"	54' 02"	32' 02"
	Medemborg	GC	1997	D	9,400	441' 02"	54' 01"	32' 01"
	(Arion '97-'03							
	Merweborg	GC	1997	D	9,400	441' 02"	54' 01"	32' 01"
	Merweborg '97-'00, MSC Bothnia '00-'02)							
	Michiganborg	GC	1999	D	9,200	441' 03"	54' 02"	32' 02"
	Missouriborg	GC	2000	D	9,100	441' 04"	54' 02"	32' 02"
	MSC Baltic	GC	1998	D	9,100	441' 04"	54' 02"	32' 02"
	(Munteborg '98-'00)							
	MSC Dardanelles	GC	1999	D	8,865	437' 08"	52' 02"	32' 02"
	(Dintelborg '97-'01)							

Fleet #.	Fleet Name Vessel Name	Type of Vessel	Year Built	Type of Engine	Cargo Cap. or Gross*	Overall Length	Breadth	Depth or Draft*
	MSC Suomi *(Markborg '96–'02)*	GC	1996	D	9,200	441' 03"	54' 02"	32' 02"
	Prinsenborg	GC	2003	D	16,615	467' 05"	72' 01"	39' 03"
	Vaasaborg	GC	1999	D	8,300	434' 00"	52' 01"	31' 07"
	Vancouverborg	GC	2000	D	8,300	433' 08"	52' 01"	31' 07"
	Varnebank	GC	2000	D	8,667	433' 08"	52' 01"	31' 07"
	Vechtborg	GC	1998	D	8,300	434' 00"	52' 01"	31' 07"
	Veerseborg	GC	1998	D	8,300	433' 09"	52' 01"	31' 07"
	Victoriaborg *(Volgaborg '01–'01)*	GC	2001	D	9,000	437' 08"	52' 02"	32' 02"
	Virginiaborg	GC	2001	D	9,000	437' 08"	52' 02"	32' 02"
	Vlieborg	GC	1999	D	8,300	434' 00"	52' 01"	31' 07"
	Vlistborg	GC	1999	D	8,300	434' 00"	52' 01"	31' 07"
	Volmeborg	GC	2001	D	9,000	437' 08"	52' 02"	37' 07"
	Voorneborg	GC	1999	D	8,300	434' 00"	52' 01"	31' 07"
	Zeus	GC	2000	D	9,100	428' 08"	52' 01"	33' 06"
IW-3	**WEALTH OCEAN SERVICES, HONG KONG, HONG KONG** ***FOLLOWING VESSEL UNDER CHARTER TO FEDNAV LTD.***							
	Federal Agno *(Federal Asahi {1} '85–'89)*	BC	1985	D	29,643	599' 09"	75' 09"	48' 07"
IY-1	**YAOKI SHIPPING S.A., PANAMA CITY, PANAMA**							
	North Challenge *(Queen of Montreaux '98–'99)*	TK	1998	D	12,180	406' 11"	67' 07"	36' 09"
	North Defiance	TK	2001	D	17,396	443' 09"	74' 08"	41' 00"
IZ-1	**Z. & G. HALCOUSSIS CO. LTD., PIRAEUS, GREECE**							
	Alexandria	BC	1981	D	29,372	589' 11"	76' 00"	47' 00"

Bulgarian-flag *Milin Kamak* heads for Lake Superior. *(Roger LeLievre)*

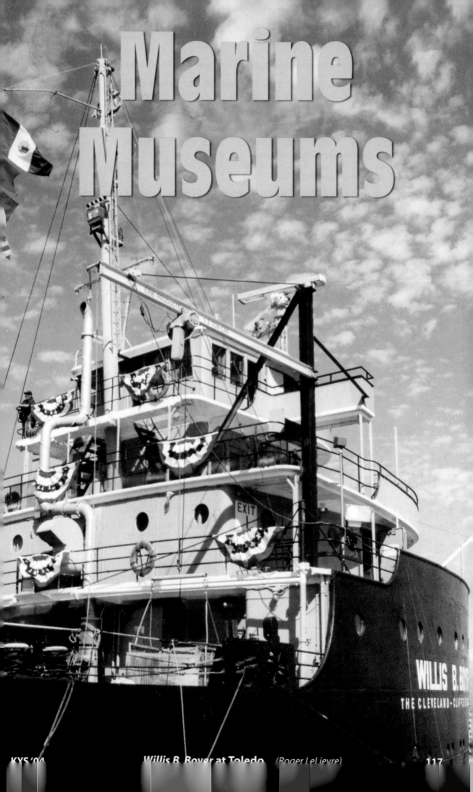

Marine Museums

Willis B. Boyer at Toledo   *(Roger LeLievre)*

Information can change without notice. Call ahead to verify times and hours.

MU-1   BERNIER MARITIME MUSEUM, L' ISLET-SUR-MER, QC – (418) 247-5001

Daniel McAllister		TB	1907	D	268*	115'00"	23'02"	12'00"

(Helena '07-'57, Helena M. B. '57-'66) (Former McAllister Towing & Salvage, Inc. vessel)

Detector		SV	1915	R	584*	147'00"	35'00"	10'00"*

(Former Canadian Coast Guard survey vessel)

Ernest Lapointe		IB	1941	R	1,179*	185'00"	36'00"	22'06"

(Former Canadian Coast Guard icebreaker)

Jean Yvan		GC	1958	D	200	84'00"	24'00"	8'00"

(Former "Goelette" type cargo vessel)

MU-2   BUFFALO AND ERIE COUNTY NAVAL AND MILITARY PARK, BUFFALO, NY – (716) 847-1773

Croaker	[IXSS-246]		1944	D	1,526*	311'07"	27'02"	33'09"

(Former U. S. Navy "Emergency Program (Gato)" class submarine [SS / SSK / AGSS / IXSS-246])

Little Rock	[CLG-4]		1945	T	10,670*	610'01"	66'04"	25'00"*

(Former U. S. Navy "Cleveland / Little Rock" class guided missile cruiser [CL-92 / CLG-4])

PTF-17	[PTF-17]		1968	D	69*	80'04"	24'07"	6'10"*

(Former U. S. Navy "Trumpy" class fast patrol/torpedo boat)

The Sullivans	[DD-537]		1943	T	2,500*	376'06"	39'08"	22'08"

(Launched as USS Putnam [DD-537]) (Former U. S. Navy "Fletcher" class destroyer)

MU-3   CANAL PARK MARINE MUSEUM, DULUTH, MN – (218) 727-2497

Bayfield		TB	1953	D	23*	45'00"	13'00"	7'00"*

(Former U.S. Army Corps of Engineers tug is an on-shore exhibit not open for tours)

MU-4   CITY OF KEWAUNEE, KEWAUNEE, WI – (920) 388-5000

Ludington		TB	1943	D	249*	115'00"	26'00"	13'08"

(Major Wilbur F. Browder [LT-4] '43-'47) (Former U.S. Army Corps of Engineers vessel)

MU-5   ERIE MARITIME MUSEUM, ERIE, PA – (814) 452-2744

Niagara		2B	1988	W	295*	198'00"	32'00"	10'06"

(Reconstruction of Oliver Hazard Perry's U. S. Navy brigantine from the War of 1812)

MU-6   GREAT LAKES CENTER FOR MARINE HISTORY, ST. IGNACE, MI

Maple	[WAGL-234]		1939	D	350*	122'03"	27'00"	7'06"*

(USCGC Maple [WLI / WAGL-234] '39-'73, Roger R. Simons '73-'94)
    (Former U.S. Coast Guard "122-Foot" class lighthouse tender [WLI / WAGL-234] / EPA vessel)

MU-7   GREAT LAKES CLIPPER PRESERVATION ASSOCIATION, MUSKEGON, MI – (231) 755-0990

Milwaukee Clipper		PA	1904	Q	4,272	361'00"	45'00"	28'00"

(Juniata '04-'41) (Former Wisconsin & Michigan Steamship Co. vessel last operated in 1970)

MU-8   GREAT LAKES HISTORICAL SOCIETY, CLEVELAND, OH – (800) 893-1485

Cod	[IXSS-224]		1943	D/V	1,525*	311'08"	27'02"	33'09"

(Former U.S. Navy "Albacore (Gato)" class submarine [SS / AGSS / IXSS-224])

MU-9   GREAT LAKES NAVAL MEMORIAL AND MUSEUM, MUSKEGON, MI – (231) 755-1230

Captain George		TB	1929	D	61*	63'00"	17'00"	7'08"

(USCOE Captain George '29-'68, Captain George '68-'73, Kurt R. Luetdke '73-'91)

LST-393			1942	D	2,100	328'00"	50'00"	25'00"

(USS LST-393 '42-'47, Highway 16 '47-'99)
    (Former U.S. Navy / Wisconsin & Michigan Steamship Co. vessel last operated July 31, 1973)

McLane	[WMEC-146]		1927	D	289*	125'00"	24'00"	12'06"

(USCGC McLane [WSC / WMEC-146] '27-'70, Manatra II '70-'93)
    (Former U.S. Coast Guard "Buck & A Quarter" class medium endurance cutter)

Silversides	[AGSS-236]		1941	D/V	1,526*	311'08"	27'03"	33'09"

(Former U.S. Navy "Albacore (Gato)" class submarine)

MU-10   H. LEE WHITE MARINE MUSEUM, OSWEGO, NY (315) 342-0480

LT-5		TB	1943	D	305*	115'00"	28'00"	14'00"

(Major Elisha K. Henson '43-'47, U.S. Army LT-5 '47-'47, Nash '47-'95)
    (Former U.S. Army Corps of Engineers vessel last operated in 1989)

Lightship museum *Huron* celebrates Christmas at Port Huron. *(Roger LeLievre)*

Fleet #.	Fleet Name Vessel Name	Type of Vessel	Year Built	Type of Engine	Cargo Cap. or Gross*	Overall Length	Breadth	Depth or Draft*
MU-11	**HARBOR HERITAGE SOCIETY, CLEVELAND, OH – (216) 574-6262**							
	William G. Mather {2}	BC	1925	T	13,950	618' 00"	62' 00"	32' 00"
	(Former Cleveland-Cliffs Steamship Co. vessel last operated Dec. 21, 1980)							
MU-12	**HMCS FRASER MUSEUM, BRIDGEWATER, NS – (902) 543-3925**							
	Fraser **[DDH-233]**		1957	T	2,858*	366' 00"	42' 00"	19' 08"*
	(Former Royal Canadian Navy "St. Laurent (River)" class helicopter-carrying frigate)							
MU-13	**IRVIN ORE BOAT TOURS, DULUTH, MN – (218) 722-7876**							
	Lake Superior	TB	1943	D	248*	114' 00"	26' 00"	13' 08"
	(Major Emil H. Block '43-'47, U. S. Army LT-18 '47-'50)							
	(Former U.S. Army Corps of Engineers vessel last operated in 1995)							
	William A. Irvin	BC	1938	T	14,050	610' 09"	60' 00"	32' 06"
	(Former United States Steel Corp. vessel last operated Dec. 16, 1978)							
MU-14	**LAKE COUNTY HISTORICAL SOCIETY, TWO HARBORS, MN – (218) 834-4898**							
	Edna G.	TB	1896	R	154*	102' 00"	23' 00"	14' 06"
	(Former Duluth, Missabe & Iron Range Railroad tug last operated in 1981)							
MU-15	**LE SAULT DE SAINTE MARIE HISTORIC SITES, INC., SAULT STE. MARIE, MI – (906) 632-3658**							
	Valley Camp {2}	BC	1917	R	12,000	550' 00"	58' 00"	31' 00"
	(Louis W. Hill '17-'55) (Former Republic Steel Corp. vessel last operated in 1966)							
MU-16	**MARINE MUSEUM OF THE GREAT LAKES AT KINGSTON, KINGSTON, ON – (613) 542-2261**							
	Alexander Henry	IB	1959	D	1,674*	210' 00"	44' 00"	17' 09"
	(Former Canadian Coast Guard vessel was retired in 1985)							
MU-17	**MARINE MUSEUM OF UPPER CANADA, TORONTO, ON – (416) 392-1765**							
	Ned Hanlan	TB	1932	R	105*	79' 06"	19' 00"	9' 09"
	(Former Municipality of Toronto vessel last operated in 1965)							
MU-18	**MARITIME MUSEUM OF THE ATLANTIC, HALIFAX, NS - (902) 424-7490**							
	Acadia	RV	1913	R	846*	170' 00"	33' 06"	12' 00"*
	(Former Royal Canadian Navy research vessel)							

Fleet #.	Fleet Name / Vessel Name		Type of Vessel	Year Built	Type of Engine	Cargo Cap. or Gross*	Overall Length	Breadth	Depth or Draft*
MU-19	**MUSEUM OF SCIENCE AND INDUSTRY, CHICAGO, IL – (773) 684-1414**								
	U-505			1941	D/V	1,178*	252' 00"	22' 04"	15' 05"*
	(Former German Type IX-C submarine, captured by the U. S. Navy Task Group 22.3 in the Atlantic Ocean off Africa on June 4, 1944)								
MU-20	**MUSEUM SHIP WILLIS B. BOYER, TOLEDO, OH – (419) 936-3070**								
	Willis B. Boyer		BC	1911	T	15,000	617' 00"	64' 00"	33' 01"
	(Col. James M. Schoonmaker '11-'69)								
	(Former Cleveland-Cliffs Steamship Co. vessel last operated in 1980)								
MU-21	**SS NORISLE HERITAGE PARK, MANITOWANING, ON – (705) 859-3905**								
	Norisle		PA	1946	R	1,668*	215' 09"	36' 03"	16' 00"
	(Former Ontario Northland Transportation Commission vessel last operated in 1974)								
MU-22	**NORTHEASTERN MARITIME HISTORICAL FOUNDATION INC., SUPERIOR, WI**								
	Mount McKay		TB	1908	D	99*	80' 00"	21' 06"	9' 00"
	(Walter F. Mattick '08-' 19, Merchant '19-'24, Marinette '24-'47, Esther S. '47-'66)								
MU-23	**HCMS HAIDA NATIONAL HISTORICAL SITE, HAMILTON, ON – (905)523-0682**								
	Haida	**[G-63]**		1943	T	2,744*	377' 00"	37' 06"	15' 02"
	(Former Royal Canadian Navy "Tribal" class destroyer [G-63 / DDE-215].								
MU-24	**PETERSEN STEAMSHIP CO., DOUGLAS, MI – (269) 857-2464**								
	Keewatin {2}		PA	1907	Q	3,856*	346' 00"	43' 08"	26' 06"
	(Former Canadian Pacific Railway Co. vessel last operated Nov. 29, 1965)								
	Reiss		TB	1913	R	99*	80' 00"	20' 00"	12' 06"
	(Q. A. Gillmore '13-'32) (Former Reiss Steamship Co. tug last operated in 1969)								
MU-25	**PORT HURON MUSEUM OF ARTS & HISTORY, PORT HURON, MI – (810) 982-0891**								
	Bramble	**[WLB-392]**	BT	1944	D	1,025*	180' 00"	37' 00"	17' 04"
	(USCGC Bramble **[WLB-392]** *'44-'03) Former U.S. Coast Guard vessel was retired in 2003)*								
	WLV-526	**[HURON]**		1920	D	392*	96' 05"	24' 00"	10' 00"*
	(Former U.S. Coast Guard 96-foot-class lightship was retired Aug. 25, 1970)								
MU-26	**S.S. CITY OF MILWAUKEE-NATIONAL HISTORIC LANDMARK, MANISTEE, MI – (231) 723-3587**								
	City of Milwaukee		TF	1931	R	26 rail cars	360' 00"	56' 03"	21' 06"
	(Train ferry sailed for the Grand Trunk Railroad '31-'78 and the Ann Arbor Railroad '78-'81)								
MU-27	**S.S. METEOR MARITIME MUSEUM, SUPERIOR, WI**								
	Meteor {2}		TK	1896	R	40,100	380' 00"	45' 00"	26' 00"
	(Frank Rockefeller 1896-'28, South Park '28-'43)								
	(Former Cleveland Tankers, Inc. vessel last operated in 1969)								
MU-28	**ST. MARYS RIVER MARINE CENTRE, SAULT STE. MARIE, ON – (705) 256-7447**								
	Norgoma		PA	1950	D	1,477*	188' 00"	37' 06"	22' 06"
	(Former Ontario Northland Transportation Commission vessel last operated in 1974)								
MU-29	**STE. CLAIRE FOUNDATION, CLEVELAND, OH**								
	Ste. Claire		PA	1910	R	870*	197' 00"	65' 00"	14' 00"
	(Last operated Sept.2, 1991; Not open to the public – undergoing restoration at Lorain, OH)								
MU-30	**STEAMER COLUMBIA FOUNDATION, DETROIT, MI**								
	Columbia {2}		PA	1902	R	968*	216' 00"	60' 00"	13' 06"
	(Last operated Sept. 2, 1991 – Laid up at Ecorse, MI.)								
MU-31	**THE CANADIAN NAVAL MEMORIAL TRUST, HALIFAX, NS – (902) 429-2132**								
	Sackville	**[K-181]**		1941	T	1,170*	208' 00"	33' 00"	17' 06"
	(Former Royal Canadian Navy "Flower" class corvette)								
MU-32	**WISCONSIN MARITIME MUSEUM, MANITOWOC, WI – (920) 684-0218**								
	Cobia	**[AGSS-245]**		1944	D/V	1,500*	311' 09"	27' 03"	33' 09"
	(Former U. S. Navy "Emergency Program (Gato)" class submarine)								

Discover the beauty
of Lake Superior & its shoreline,
the life of the light keeper,
and the haunting world of shipwrecks

- Oldest Active
  Lighthouse on Lake Superior
- Museum with Interpretive Exhibits
- Restored Light Station, Surf Boat & Historical Buildings
- Edmund Fitzgerald Exhibit featuring the Ship's Bell

Open Daily May-October

- Whitefish Point Bird Observatory
- Boardwalk Overlooking the Lake Superior Shoreline
- Museum Store with Quality Prints, Collectibles & Nauticals
- Overnight Accommodations at the Restored Crews Quarters

SHIPWRECK MUSEUM
AT WHITEFISH POINT

On Lake Superior's Shoreline
In Michigan's Eastern
Upper Peninsula
800-635-1742

WWW.SHIPWRECKMUSEUM.COM

MUSEUMS ASHORE

Information can change without notice. Call ahead to verify location and hours.

ANTIQUE BOAT MUSEUM, 750 MARY ST., CLAYTON, NY – (315) 686-4104: A large collection of freshwater boats and engines. Annual show is the first weekend of August. Open May 15-October 15.

ASHTABULA MARINE & U.S. COAST GUARD MEMORIAL MUSEUM, 1071 WALNUT BLVD., ASHTABULA, OH – (440) 964-6847: Housed in the 1898-built former lighthouse-keeper's residence, the museum includes models, paintings, artifacts, photos, the world's only working scale model of a Hullett ore unloading machine and the pilothouse from the steamer *Thomas Walters*. Open April-October.

BAYFIELD MARITIME MUSEUM, FIRST STREET, BAYFIELD, WI – (715) 779-9919: Exhibits explore commercial fishing, boatbuilding, lighthouses and shipwrecks. Memorial Day-early October.

CANAL PARK MARINE MUSEUM, ALONGSIDE THE SHIP CANAL, DULUTH, MN – (218) 727-2497: Museum provides displays, historic artifacts and programs that explain the roles of Duluth and Superior in Great Lakes shipping as well as the job of the U.S. Army Corps of Engineers in maintaining the nation's waterways. Many excellent models and other artifacts are on display. Open all year.

COLLINGWOOD MUSEUM, MEMORIAL PARK, COLLINGWOOD, ON – (705) 445-4811: More than 100 years of shipbuilding, illustrated with models, photos and videos. Open all year.

DOOR COUNTY MARITIME MUSEUM & LIGHTHOUSE PRESERVATION SOCIETY, INC., 120 N. MADISON AVE., STURGEON BAY, WI – (920) 743-5958: Many excellent models help portray the role shipbuilding has played in the Door Peninsula. Refurbished pilothouse on display. Open all year.

DOSSIN GREAT LAKES MUSEUM, 100 THE STRAND, BELLE ISLE, DETROIT, MI – (313) 852-4051: Models, photographs, interpretive displays, the smoking room from the 1912 passenger steamer *City of Detroit III,* an anchor from the *Edmund Fitzgerald* and the pilothouse from the steamer *William Clay Ford* are on display. Open weekends.

FAIRPORT HARBOR MUSEUM, 129 SECOND ST., FAIRPORT, OH – (440) 354-4825: Located in the Fairport Lighthouse, displays include the pilothouse from the lake carrier *Frontenac* and the mainmast of the first *U.S.S. Michigan.* Open late May-Labor Day.

GREAT LAKES HISTORICAL SOCIETY, 480 MAIN ST., VERMILION, OH – (800) 893-1485: Museum tells the story of the Great Lakes through ship models, paintings, exhibits and artifacts, including engines and other machinery. Pilothouse of retired laker *Canopus* and a replica of the Vermilion lighthouse are on display. Museum open all year. An affiliated operation is the *U.S.S. Cod,* on display in Cleveland.

GREAT LAKES SHIPWRECK MUSEUM, WHITEFISH POINT, MI – (906) 635-1742 or (800)-635-1742: Located next to the Whitefish Point lighthouse, the museum includes lighthouse and shipwreck artifacts, a shipwreck video theater, the restored lighthouse-keeper's quarters and an *Edmund Fitzgerald* display that includes the ship's bell. Open May 15-October 15.

LE SAULT DE SAINTE MARIE HISTORIC SITES, INC., 501 EAST WATER ST., SAULT STE. MARIE, MI – (906)-632-3658: The 1917-built steamer *Valley Camp* is the centerpiece of this extensive museum. Dedicated in 1968, the Valley Camp's three cargo holds house artifacts, ship models, aquariums, photos and other memorabilia, as well as a tribute to the *Edmund Fitzgerald* that includes the ill-fated vessel's lifeboats. Extensive gift shop offers a large selection of nautical books and other items. Tours available. Open May 15-October 15.

LOWER LAKES MARINE HISTORICAL MUSEUM, 66 ERIE ST., BUFFALO, NY – (716) 849-0914: Exhibits explore local maritime history. Open all year (Tuesday, Thursday and Saturday only).

MARITIME MUSEUM OF SANDUSKY, 125 MEIGS ST., SANDUSKY, OHIO – (419) 624-0274: Exhibits explore local maritime history. Open all year.

MARQUETTE MARINE MUSEUM, EAST RIDGE & LAKESHORE DR., MARQUETTE, MI – (906) 226-2006: Located in an 1890s waterworks building, the museum re-creates the offices of the first commercial fishing and passenger freight companies. Displays also include charts, photos, models and maritime artifacts. Open May 31-September 30.

MICHIGAN MARITIME MUSEUM, 260 DYCKMAN AVE., SOUTH HAVEN, MI – (269) 637-8078: Exhibits dedicated to the U.S. Lifesaving Service and U.S. Coast Guard. Displays tell the story of various kinds of boats and their uses on the Great Lakes. Open all year.

OWEN SOUND MARINE – RAIL MUSEUM, 1165 FIRST AVE., OWEN SOUND, ON – (519) 371-3333: Museum depicts the history of each industry (but leans more toward the marine end) through displays, models and photos. Seasonal.

PORT COLBORNE MARINE & HISTORICAL MUSEUM, 280 KING ST., PORT COLBORNE, ON – (905) 834-7604: Wheelhouse from the steam tug *Yvonne Dupre Jr.*, an anchor from the propeller ship *Raleigh* and a lifeboat from the steamer *Hochelaga* are among the museum's displays. Open May-December.

U.S. ARMY CORPS OF ENGINEERS MUSEUM, SOO LOCKS VISITOR CENTER, E. PORTAGE AVE., SAULT STE. MARIE, MI – (906) 632-3311: Exhibits include a working model of the Soo Locks, historic photos and a 25-minute film. Also, three observation decks adjacent to the MacArthur Lock provide an up-close view of ships locking through. No admission; open May-November. Check at the Visitor Center information desk for a list of vessels expected at the locks.

WELLAND CANAL VISITOR CENTRE, AT LOCK 3, THOROLD, ON – (905) 984-8880: Museum traces the development of the Welland Canal. Museum and adjacent gift shop open year 'round. Observation deck open during the navigation season. Check at the information desk for vessels expected at Lock 3.

WISCONSIN MARITIME MUSEUM, 75 MARITIME DRIVE, MANITOWOC, WI – (920) 684-0218: Displays explore the history of area shipbuilding and also honor submariners and submarines built in Manitowoc. The World War II submarine *Cobia* is adjacent to the museum and open for tours. Open all year.

Extra Tonnage

Algorail **at Windsor.** *(Roger LeLievre)*

Joseph L. Block **takes on a cargo of iron ore pellets at Two Harbors, Minn.** *(Roger LeLievre)*

MEANINGS OF BOAT WHISTLES

1 SHORT: I intend to leave you on my port side (answered by same if agreed upon)
2 SHORT: I intend to leave you on my starboard side (answered by same if agreed upon)
  (Passing arrangements may be agreed upon by radio. If so, no whistle signal is required.)
5 OR MORE SHORT BLASTS SOUNDED RAPIDLY: Danger.
1 PROLONGED: Vessel leaving dock
3 SHORT: Operating astern propulsion
1 PROLONGED, SOUNDED AT INTERVALS OF NOT MORE THAN 2 MINUTES: Vessel moving in restricted visibility

1 SHORT, 1 PROLONGED, 1 SHORT: Vessel at anchor in restricted visibility (optional). May be accompanied by the ringing of a bell on the forward part of the ship and a gong on the after end.
3 PROLONGED and 2 SHORT:
Salute (formal)
1 PROLONGED and 2 SHORT:
Salute (commonly used)
3 PROLONGED and 1 SHORT: International Shipmasters' Association member's salute

Some of the above signals are listed in the pilot rules.
Others have been adopted through common use.

Fred R. White Jr. loading limestone at Rogers City, Mich.

(Don Coles Great Lakes Aerial Photos, www.aerialpics.com)

MAJOR GREAT LAKES LOADING PORTS

Iron Ore
Duluth, Minn.
Superior, Wis.
Two Harbors, Minn.
Marquette, Mich.
Escanaba, Mich.

Petroleum
Sarnia, Ont.
E. Chicago, Ill.

Limestone
Port Inland, Mich.
Cedarville, Mich.
Drummond
  Island, Mich.
Calcite, Mich.
Rogers City, Mich.
Stoneport, Mich.
Marblehead, Ohio

Coal
Superior, Wis.
Chicago, Ill.
Toledo, Ohio
Sandusky, Ohio
Ashtabula, Ohio
Conneaut, Ohio

Grain
Thunder Bay, Ont.
Duluth, Minn.
Milwaukee, Wis.
Superior, Wis.
Sarnia, Ont.
Toledo, Ohio

Cement
Charlevoix, Mich.
Alpena, Mich.

Salt
Goderich, Ont.
Windsor, Ont.
Cleveland, Ohio
Fairport, Ohio

MAJOR UNLOADING PORTS

The primary U.S. iron ore and limestone receiving ports are Cleveland, Chicago, Gary, Burns Harbor, Indiana Harbor, Detroit, Toledo, Ashtabula and Conneaut. Nanticoke, Hamilton and Sault Ste. Marie, Ont. are major ore-receiving ports in Canada. Coal is carried by self-unloaders to power plants in the U.S. and Canada. Most grain loaded on the lakes is destined for export via the St. Lawrence Seaway. Cement is delivered to terminals from Lake Superior to Lake Ontario. Tankers bring petroleum products to cities as diverse in size as Cleveland, Detroit, Escanaba and Muskegon. Self-unloaders carry limestone, road salt and sand to cities throughout the region.

'For less than the cost of a fast-food meal, we can move one ton of cargo from Duluth to Chicago or Cleveland.'

– Jim Weakley, president of the Cleveland-based Lake Carriers' Association

THE SOO LOCKS

American Locks

MacArthur Lock

Named after World War II Gen. Douglas MacArthur, the MacArthur Lock is 800-feet long (243.8 meters) between inner gates, 80-feet wide (24.4 meters) and 31-feet deep (9.4 meters) over the sills. The lock was built by the U.S. in the war years 1942-'43 and opened to traffic July 11, 1943. The maximum-sized vessel that can transit the MacArthur Lock is 730-feet long (222.5 meters) by 76-feet wide (23 meters). In emergencies, this limit may be exceeded for vessels up to 767-feet in length (233.8 meters).

Poe Lock

The Poe Lock is 1,200-feet long (365.8 meters), 110-feet wide (33.5 meters) and has a depth over the sills of 32-feet (9.8 meters). Named after Col. Orlando M. Poe, it was built by the U.S. in the years 1961-'68. The lock's vessel limit is 1,100 feet long (335.3 meters) by 105 feet wide (32 meters). There are currently more than 30 vessels sailing the lakes restricted by size to the Poe Lock.

Davis Lock

Named after Col. Charles E.L.B. Davis, the Davis Lock measures 1,350-feet long (411.5 meters) between inner gates, 80 feet-wide (24.4 meters) and 23-feet deep (7 meters) over the sills. It was built in the years 1908-'14 and now sees limited use due to its shallow depth.

Sabin Lock

Measuring the same as the Davis Lock, the Sabin Lock was built from 1913-'19. Named after L.C. Sabin, the lock is currently inactive.

St. Marys River

Connecting Lake Superior with Lake Huron, the 80-mile (128.7 km) long St. Marys River includes breathtaking scenery, picturesque islands and its share of hazardous twists and turns.

Remote Isle Parisienne marks the river's beginning; the equally-lonely DeTour Reef Light marks its end. Between are two marvels of engineering, the West Neebish Cut, a channel literally dynamited out of solid rock, and the Soo Locks, which stand where Native Americans in dugout canoes once challenged the St. Marys Rapids.

Vessels in the St. Marys River system are under control of the U.S. Coast Guard at Sault Ste. Marie, MI, and are required to check in with Soo Traffic on VHF Ch.12 (156.600 Mhz) at various locations in the river. In the vicinity of the locks, they fall under jurisdiction of the Lockmaster, who must be contacted on VHF Ch. 14 (156.700 Mhz) for lock assignments. Many vessels are also equipped with Automated Information System (AIS) transponders which electronically transmit their positions and other data.

The first lock was built on the Canadian side of the river by the Northwest Fur Co. in 1797-98. That lock was 38-feet (11.6 meters) long and barely 9-feet (2.7 meters) wide.

The first ship canal on the American side, known as the State Canal, was built from 1853-55 by engineer Charles T. Harvey. There were two tandem locks on masonry, each 350-feet (106.7 meters) long by 70-feet (21.3 meters) wide, with a lift of about 9-feet (2.7 meters).

The canal was destroyed in 1888 by workers making way for newer and bigger locks. ▶

Oglebay Norton passes under the International Bridge and railway bridge after leaving the Poe Lock at the Soo. *(Neil Schultheiss)*

Michipicoten **at the upper level in the MacArthur Lock.** *(John Chomniak)*

A New Soo Lock?

Discussion continues about building a new lock in the space now occupied by the Davis and Sabin locks. It would relieve the pressure on the Poe, the only lock now able to handle vessels more than 730-feet (222.5 meters) long and/or 76-feet (23 meters) wide.

Cost of such a lock was estimated at $225 million in 1999. If built, it would be paid for by the U.S. federal government and the states surrounding the Great Lakes.

Although it looked like construction might start on a new lock in 2003, an economic downturn and other factors have led to further postponement of the project.

The Canadian Canal

The present Canadian Lock has its origins in a canal constructed during the years 1887-'95 through the red sandstone rock of St. Marys Island on the north side of the St. Marys Rapids. The most westerly canal on the Seaway route, the waterway measures 7,294-feet (2,223.4 meters), or about 1.4 miles (2.2 km) long, from end to end of upper and lower piers. A 900-foot (274.3 meters) long lock served vessels until the collapse of a lock wall in 1987 closed the waterway.

In 1998, after $10.3 million in repairs, a much smaller lock opened, built inside the old lock chamber. Operated by Parks Canada, it is used mainly by pleasure craft, tugs and tour boats.

All traffic through the Soo Locks passes toll-free.
Locks in the Seaway system operate on gravity – no pumps are used.

You Can't Get ~~Much~~ (ANY) Closer Than This!

LOCK TOURS CANADA

M/V Chief Shingwauk

SIGHTSEEING CHARTER & DINNER CRUISES

Soo Locks Tours Departing Daily from **ROBERTA BONDAR PARK SAULT STE. MARIE, ONTARIO**

1-800-226-3665 **locktours.com**

THE WELLAND CANAL

The 27-mile long (43.7 km) Welland Canal, which was built to bypass nearby Niagara Falls, overcomes a difference in water level of 326.5 feet (99.5 meters) between lakes Erie and Ontario.

The first Welland Canal opened in 1829; the present (fourth) canal opened officially on Aug. 6, 1932, with the passage of the steamer *Lemoyne*. Each of the seven Welland Canal locks has an average lift of 46.5 feet (14.2 meters). All locks (except Lock 8) are 859-feet (261.8 meters) long, 80-feet (24.4 meters) wide and 30-feet (9.1 meters) deep. Lock 8 measures 1,380 feet (420.6 km).

The maximum sized vessel that may transit the canal is 740-feet (225.5 meters) long, 78-feet (23.8 meters) wide and 26-feet (7.9 meters) in draft. Connecting channels are kept dredged to a minimum of 27-feet (8.2 meters).

John D. Leitch leaves Lock 8 at Port Colborne and heads out into Lake Erie. (Gerry Ouderkirk)

Locks 1, 2 and 3 are at St. Catharines, on the Lake Ontario end of the waterway. At Lock 3, the Welland Canal Viewing Center and Museum houses an information desk (which posts a list of vessels expected at the lock), a gift shop and restaurant. At Thorold, **locks 4, 5** and **6**, twinned to help speed passage of vessels, are controlled with an elaborate interlocking system for safety. These locks (positioned end to end, they resemble a short flight of stairs) have an aggregate lift of 139.5 feet (42.5 meters) and are similar to the Gatun Locks on the Panama Canal. Just south of locks 4, 5 and 6 is **Lock 7**. **Lock 8**, seven miles (11.2 km) upstream at Port Colborne, completes the process, making the final adjustment to Lake Erie's level.

In 1973, a new channel was constructed to replace the section of the canal that bisected the city of Welland. The Welland bypass eliminated long delays for ship navigation, road and rail traffic.

The average passage time for the Welland Canal is about 12 hours, with the majority spent transiting locks 4-7. Vessels passing through the Welland Canal and St. Lawrence Seaway must carry a qualified pilot.

There are also 11 railway and highway bridges crossing the Welland Canal. The most significant are the landmark vertical-lift bridges that provide a clearance of 126 feet (36.6 meters) for vessels passing underneath. Tunnels at Thorold and South Welland allow vehicle traffic to pass beneath the waterway.

All vessel traffic though the Welland Canal is regulated by a control center. Upbound vessels must call Seaway Welland off Port Weller, on VHF Ch. 14 (156.700 Mhz), while downbound vessels are required to make contact off Port Colborne. Cameras keep vessels under constant observation, and individual locks (and most bridges over the canal) are controlled from the center.

THE ST. LAWRENCE SEAWAY

The St. Lawrence Seaway is a deep waterway extending some 2,038 miles (3,701.4 km) from the Atlantic Ocean to the head of the Great Lakes at Duluth, including Montreal harbor and the Welland Canal. More specifically, it is a system of locks and canals (U.S. and Canadian), built between 1954 and 1958 at a cost of $474 million and opened in 1959, that allow vessels to pass from Montreal to the Welland Canal at the western end of Lake Ontario. The vessel size limit within this system is 740-feet (225.6 meters) long, 78-feet (23.8 meters) wide and 26-feet (7.9 meters) draft.

Closest to the ocean is the **St. Lambert Lock**, which lifts ships some 15 feet (4.6 meters) from Montreal harbor to the level of the Laprairie Basin, through which the channel sweeps in a great arc 8.5 miles (13.7 km) long, to the second lock. The **Cote St. Catherine Lock**, like the other six St. Lawrence Seaway locks, is built to the dimensions shown in the table at left. The Cote St. Catherine lifts ships from the level of the Laprairie Basin, 30 feet (9.1 meters) to the level of Lake St. Louis, bypassing the Lachine Rapids. Beyond it, the channel runs 7.5 miles (12.1 km) before reaching Lake St. Louis.

LOCK DIMENSIONS	
Length	766' (233.5 meters)
Width	80' (24 meters)
Depth	30' (24.4 meters)

The **Lower Beauharnois Lock**, bypassing the Beauharnois Power House, lifts ships 41 feet (12.5 meters) and sends them through a short canal to the **Upper Beauharnois Lock**, where they are lifted 41 feet (12.5 meters) to reach the Beauharnois Canal. After a 13 mile (20.9 km) trip in the canal, and a 30-mile (48.3 km) passage through Lake St. Francis, vessels reach the U.S. border and the **Snell Lock**, which has a lift of 45 feet (13.7 meters) and empties into the 10-mile (16.1 km) Wiley-Dondero Canal.

After passing through the Wiley-Dondero, ships are raised another 38 feet (11.6 meters) by the **Dwight D. Eisenhower Lock**, after which they enter Lake St. Lawrence, the pool upon which nearby power-generating stations draw for their turbines located a mile to the north.

At the Western end of Lake St. Lawrence, the **Iroquois Lock** allows ships to bypass the Iroquois Control Dam. The lift here is only about one foot (.3 meters). Once in the waters west of Iroquois, the channel meanders through the Thousand Islands to Lake Ontario and beyond.

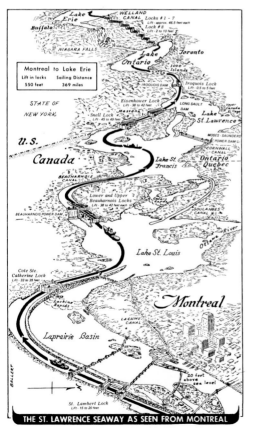

THE ST. LAWRENCE SEAWAY AS SEEN FROM MONTREAL

Freshly-painted *Wilfred Sykes* at the ore dock in Marquette Jan. 4, 2004.   *(Chris Winters)*

PLIMSOLL MARKS

   The Plimsoll Mark is a load line on the side of a ship's hull. It shows how much cargo the ship can carry safely under different conditions. The position of the marking depends on the type and size of the vessel. A ship "loaded down to her marks" carries capacity cargo – any more would lessen the chance of a safe voyage. Load lines on American ships were established by the American Bureau of Shipping, provided by the Load Line Act of 1929, and apply to deep sea vessels of 150 tons or more. The distance between the Plimsoll Mark and the deck is the ship's "freeboard." Special markings were established in 1935 for Great Lakes /Atlantic/Pacific coast voyages.

Plimsoll Mark – Great Lakes/Seaway

The letters AB signify American Bureau of Shipping.
The letters LR signify Lloyd's Registry of Shipping.
The letters FW signify load line in fresh water.
The letters SW signify load line in salt water*.
The letters MS signify midsummer load (May 1- Sept. 15).
The letter S signifies summer load line (April 26-30 and Sept. 16-30).
The letter I signifies intermediate load line (April 1-15 and Oct. 1-31).
The letter W signifies winter load line (Nov.1 to March 31).

*The salt water marks are assigned only to vessels intending to load in salt water of the St. Lawrence River.

Additional Plimsoll Marks Seen on Saltwater Vessels

The letters LL signify Lloyd's of London.
The letter T signifies load line in tropical waters.
The letters TF signify load line in tropical fresh water.
The letters WNA apply to winter, North Atlantic load line.

Other Frequently Seen Hull Markings

Vessel has a bulbous bow that may be hidden beneath the waterline.

A bow or stern thruster is directly below and beneath the waterline. Keep clear.

Colors of the Great Lakes & Seaway Smokestacks

A.B.M. Marine
Thunder Bay, ON

Algoma Central Marine Group
Div. of Algoma Central Corp.
St. Catharines, ON

Algoma Tankers Ltd.
Div. of Algoma Central Corp.
Dartmouth, NS

American Canadian Caribbean Line, Inc.
Warren, RI

American Marine Construction
Benton Harbor, MI

American Steamship Co.
Williamsville, NY

Andrie, Inc.
Muskegon, MI

Apostle Island Cruise Service
Bayfield, WI

Arnold Transit Co.
Mackinac Island, MI

Atlantic Towing Ltd.
St. John, NB

Basic Towing, Inc.
Escanaba, MI

Bay City Boat Lines
Bay City, MI

Bay Shipbuilding Co.
Sturgeon Bay, WI

Beaver Island Boat Co.
Charlevoix, MI

Bigane Vessel Fueling Co.
Chicago, IL

Billington Contracting Inc.
Duluth, MN

Blue Circle Cement Co.
Detroit, MI
Toronto, ON

Blue Heron Co.
Tobermory, ON

Buffalo Public Works Dept.
Buffalo, NY

Busch Marine, Inc.
Carrollton, MI

Canada Steamship Lines, Inc.
Montreal, QC

Canadian Coast Guard
Ottawa, ON

Central Marine Logistics, Inc.
Griffith, IN

Chicago Fire Department
Chicago, IL

**City of Toronto
Parks & Recreation
Dept.**
Toronto, ON

Cleveland Fire Department
Cleveland, OH

Cleveland Tankers (1991), Inc.
Algoma Tankers, Ltd. Mgr.
Cleveland, OH

Clipper Cruise Line
St. Louis, MO

Columbia Yacht Club
Chicago. IL

Croisieres AML Inc.
Quebec, QC

Croisieres Marjolaine, Inc.
Chicoutimi, QC

Dan Minor & Sons, Inc.
Port Colborne, ON

Dean Construction Co.
Belle River, ON

Detroit City Fire Department
Detroit, MI

Diamond Jack's River Tours
Grosse Ile, MI

Duc D'Orleans Cruise Boat
Corunna, ON

Durocher Marine
Cheboygan, MI

Eastern Canada Towing Ltd.
Halifax, NS

Eastern Upper Peninsula Transportation Authority
Sault Ste. Marie, MI

Edward E. Gillen Co.
Milwaukee, WI

Erie Sand Steamship Co. M/V J.S. St John
Erie, PA

Essroc Canada, Inc. Upper Lakes Group, Mgr
Downsville, ON

Federal Terminals Ltd.
Port Cartier, QC

Ferriss Marine Contracting Inc.
Detroit, MI

Fraser Shipyards, Inc.
Superior, WI

Goderich Tug Boat Co.
Grosse Ile, MI

Gananoque Boat Line
Gananoque,ON

Gardiner Marine
Sault Ste. Marie, ON

Geo. Gradel Co.
Toledo, OH

Geo. Gradel Co.
Toledo, OH

Goderich Elevators, Ltd.
Goderich, ON

Goodtime Transit Boats, Inc.
Cleveland, OH

Gravel & Lake Services, Ltd. M/V Wolf River
Thunder Bay, ON

Gravel & Lake Services, Ltd. Tug Peninsula
Thunder Bay, ON

Great Lakes Associates, Inc.
Rocky River, OH

Great Lakes Fleet, Inc.
Duluth, MN

Great Lakes International Towing & Salvage Ltd.
Burlington, ON

Great Lakes Maritime Academy
Northwestern Michigan College
Traverse City, MI

Great Lakes Towing Co.
Cleveland, OH

Great Lakes Transport Ltd.
Halifax, NS

HMC Ship Managment
Lemont, IL

Hamilton Port Authority
Hamilton, ON

Hamilton Marine & Engineering Ltd. Div. of ULS Corp.
Port Colborne, ON

Hannah Marine Corp.
Lemont, IL

Heritage Cruise Lines
Parry Sound, ON

Holly Marine Towing
Chicago, IL

Inland Bulk Transfer
Cleveland, OH

Inland Lakes Management, Inc.
Alpena, MI

The Interlake Steamship Co. Lakes Shipping Co.
Richfield, OH

International Steel Group
Burns Harbor Inc.
Chesterton, IN

Jacobs Investments
Cleveland, OH

Kadinger Marine Service, Inc.
Milwaukee, WI

Kent Line Ltd
St. John, NB

Keystone Great Lakes, Inc.
Bala Cynwyd, PA

Kindra Lake Towing Co.
Downer's Grove, IL

King Company Inc.
Holland, MI

Lafarge Cement Corp.
Toronto, ON

Lafarge Cement Corp.
Alpena, MI

Lake Michigan Carferry Service, Inc.
Ludington, MI

Lake Michigan Contractors, Inc.
Holland, MI

Le Groupe C.T.M.A. Navigation Madeline Inc.
Cap-Aux-Meules, QC

Le Groupe Ocean Inc.
Quebec, QC

Le Groupe Ocean Inc.
Montreal, QC

Lee Marine, Ltd.
Sombra, ON

Les Equipment Verreault, Inc.
Les Mechins, QC

Lock Tours Canada
Sault Ste. Marie, ON

**Lower Lakes Towing, Ltd.
Grand River Navigation Co.**
Port Dover, ON

Luedtke Engineering Co.
Frankfort, MI

M.C.M. Marine Inc.
Sault Ste Marie, MI

MacDonald Marine Ltd.
Goderich, ON

Madeline Island Ferry Line, Inc.
LaPointe, WI

Maid of the Mist Steamboat Co., Ltd.
Niagara Falls, ON

Malcom Marine
St. Clair, MI

Marine Atlantic, Inc.
Moncton, NB

Marine Tech Inc.
Duluth, MN

Mariposa Cruise Line
Toronto, ON

McAsphalt Marine Transportation
Scarborough, ON

**McKeil Marine Ltd.
M/V Capt. Ralph Tucker**
Hamilton, ON

McKeil Marine Ltd.
Hamilton, ON

McKeil Marine Ltd.
Hamilton, ON

McNally Marine, Inc
Toronto, ON

Miller Boat Line, Inc.
Put-In-Bay, OH

**Museum Ship
CCGC Alexander Henry**
Scarborough, ON

Museum Tug Edna G
Two Harbors, MN

**Museum Ship
HMCS Haida**
Hamilton, ON

**Museum Ship
Keewatin**
Douglas, MI

**Museum Ships
USS Little Rock
USS The Sullivans**
Buffalo, NY

**Museum Ship
Meteor**
Superior, WI

**Museum Ship
City of Milwaukee**
Manistee, MI

**Museum Ship
Milwaukee Clipper**
Muskegon, MI

**Museum Ships
Norgoma** (Sault Ste. Marie,ON)
Norisle (Manitowaning,ON)

**Museum Ship
Valley Camp**
Sault Ste. Marie, MI

**Museum Ship
William A. Irvin**
Duluth, MN

**Museum Ships
Willis B. Boyer** (Toledo,OH)
William G. Mather (Cleveland,OH)

Muskoka Lakes Navigation & Hotel Co.
Gravenhurst, ON

Nadro Marine Services
Port Dover, ON

Northern Transportation Co.
Edmonton, AB

Neuman's Kelly's Island Ferry
Sandusky, OH

Oglebay Norton Marine Services Co.
Cleveland, OH

Ontario Ministry of Transportation & Communication
Kingston, ON

Osborne Materials Co.
Mentor, OH

Owen Sound Transportation Co. Ltd.
Owen Sound, ON

Pelee Island Transportation Services
Pelee Island, ON

Pere Marquette Shipping Co. Tug Undaunted
Ludington, MI

Provmar Fuels, Inc. Div. of ULS Corporation
Toronto, ON

Purvis Marine Ltd.
Sault Ste. Marie, ON

Purvis Marine Ltd.
Sault Ste. Marie, ON

Rigel Shipping Canada, Inc. Rigel Shipping Co., Inc
Shediac, NB

Roen Salvage Co.
Sturgeon Bay, WI

Sea Fox Thousand Islands Tours
Kingston, ON

Selvick Marine Towing Corp.
Sturgeon Bay, WI

Shoreline Sightseeing Co.
Chicago, IL

Sivertson's Grand Portage Isle Royale Transportation Lines
Superior, WI

Societe des Traversiers du Quebec
Quebec, QC

Society Quebecoise D'Exploration Miniere Algoma Central Corp.-Mgr.
Sault Ste. Marie, ON

Soo Locks Boat Tours
Sault Ste. Marie, MI

St. Lawrence Cruise Lines, Inc.
Kingston, ON

St. Lawrence Seaway Management Corp.
Cornwall, ON

St. Lawrence Seaway Development Corp.
Massena, NY

Three Rivers Boatmen, Inc.
Trois Rivieres, QC

Thunder Bay Marine Services Ltd.
Thunder Bay, On

Thunder Bay Tug Services
Thunder Bay, ON

Transport Desgagnes, Inc.
Quebec, QC

Transport Iglooik, Inc.
Montreal, QC

Upper Lakes Group Jackes Shipping, Inc.
Toronto, ON

United States Army Corps of Engineers Great Lakes and Ohio River Division
Chicago, IL

United States Coast Guard 9th Coast Guard District
Cleveland, OH

United States Environmental Protection Agency
Bay City, MI

United States Department of the Interior
Ann Arbor, MI

United States National Park Service
Houghton, MI

University of Michigan Center for Great Lakes & Aquatic Sciences
Ann Arbor, MI

Upper Lakes Towing, Inc.
Escanaba, MI

Verreault Navigation Inc.
Les Mechins, QC

Wendella Boat Tours Co.
Chicago, IL

Zenith Tugboat Co.
Duluth, MN

Colors of Saltwater Fleets

Atlantska Plovidba
Dubrovnik, Croatia

Aurora Shipping, Inc.
Manila, Philippines

B&N Moorman B.V.
Ridderkerk, Netherlands

Blystad Tankers
Oslo, Norway

Briese Schiffahrts GMBH & Co. KG
Leer, Germany

Canadian Forest Navigation Co. Ltd.
Montreal, QC

Canada Maritime Ltd.
Hamilton, Bermuda

Carisbrooke Shipping PLC
Cowes, UK

Catsambis Shipping Ltd.
Piraeus, Greece

Commercial Fleet of Donbass
Donetsk, Ukraine

Commercial Trading & Discount Co., Ltd.
Athens, Greece

Compagnie des Iles du Ponant M/V LeLevant
Nantes, France

Densan Shipping Co. Ltd.
Istanbul, Turkey

Det Nordenfjeldske D/S AS
Trondheim, Norway

Diana Shipping Agencies S.A.
Piraeus, Greece

ER Denizcilik Sanayi Nakliyat ve Ticaret A.S.
Istanbul, Turkey

Elmira Shipping & Trading S.A.
Athens, Greece

Enzian Shipping AG
Berne, Switzerland

Far-Eastern Shipping Co.
Vladivostok, Russia

Fednav International Ltd.
Montreal, QC

Fednav International Ltd.
Montreal, QC

Flinter Groningen B.V.
Groningen, Netherlands

Fortum Oil & Gas
Espoo, Finland

Great Lakes European Shipping A.S.
Ornskoldsvik, Sweden

Hapag Lloyd Cruises M/V c. Columbus
Hamburg, Germany

Harbor Shipping & Trading Co. S.A.
Chios, Greece

Hilal Shipping, Trading & Industry Co.
Istanbul, Turkey

Holland Ship Service
Rotterdam, Netherlands

Indochina Shipmanagement Ltd.
Hong Kong, Hong Kong

Intersee Schiffahrts-Gesellschaft MbH & Co.
Herren-Ems, Germany

J.G. Goumas (Shipping) Co.
Piraeus, Greece

Jo Tankers, B.V.
Spijkenisse, Netherlands

Jumbo Shipping Co. S.A.
Geneva, Switzerland

Knutsen O.A.S. Shipping
Haugesund, Norway

Krey Schiffahrts GMBH & Co.
Simonswolde, Germany

Laurin Maritime, Inc
Houston, TX

**Lietuvos Juro Laivininkyste
(Lithuanian Shipping Co.)**
Klaipeda, Lithuania

**Malaysia International
Shipping Corp.**
Selangor, Singapore

**Marbulk Shipping Inc.
CSL International Inc., Mgrs.**
Beverly, MS

Murmansk Shipping Co.
Murmansk, Russia

**Navigation Maritime
Bulgare Ltd.**
Varna, Bulgaria

NB Two Shipping Ltd.
Limassol, Cyprus

Novoship (UK) Ltd.
London, England

Oceanbulk Maritime S.A.
Athens, Greece

Oceanbulk Maritime S.A.
Athens, Greece

Oceanex Partnership Ltd.
Quebec, QC

**Oldendorff Carriers
GMBH & Co.**
Luebeck, Germany

**Olympic Shipping and
Management S.A.**
Athens, Greece

Orion Schiffahrts-Gesellschaft
Hamburg, Germany

Polish Steamship Co.
Szczecin, Poland

Primal Ship Management
Athens, Greece

**Reederei Hans-Peter
Eckhoff Co., H.G.**
Hollenstedt, Germany

Scandia Shipping Hellas, Inc.
Athens, Greece

**Scanscot Shipping Services
GmbH**
Hamburg, Germany

Seastar Navigation Co. Ltd.
Athens, Greece

Seven Seas Carriers A.S.
Bergen, Norway

**Shih Wei Navigation Co.
Ltd.**
Taipei, Taiwan

Shipping Corp. of India Ltd.
Mumbai, India

Shunzan Kaiun Co., Ltd.
Ehime, Japan

Spar Shipping A.S.
Bergen, Norway

**Spliethoff's
Bevrachtingskantoor Ltd.**
Amsterdam, Netherlands

Stolt Parcel Tankers
Greenwich, CT

Sun Bay Cruises Ltd.
Nassau, Bahamas

Surrendra Overseas Ltd.
Calcutta, India

Tachibanaya Co. Ltd.
Ehime, Japan

Teo Shipping Corp.
Piraeus, Greece

**Thenamaris Ships
Management, Inc.**
Athens, Greece

Tomasos Brothers, Inc.
Piraeus, Greece

Triton Bereederungs GMBH & Co.
Leer, Germany

Union Marine Enterprises S.A.
Piraeus, Greece

Vergos Marine Management
Piraeus, Greece

Viken Shipping AS
Bergen, Norway

W. Bockstiegel Reederei KG
Emden, Germany

Wagenborg Shipping B.V.
Delfzijl, Netherlands

Z&G Halcoussis Co. Ltd.
Piraeus, Greece

House Flags of Great Lakes & Seaway Fleets

**Algoma Central
Marine Group**
Sault Ste. Marie, ON

American Steamship Co.
Williamsville, NY

Atlantic Towing Ltd.
St. John, NB

**Canada Steamship
Lines, Inc.**
Montreal, QC

**Cleveland Tankers,
(1991) Inc.**
Cleveland, OH

Fednav Ltd.
Montreal, QC

Gaelic Tug Boat Co.
Grosse Ile, MI

**Great Lakes
Associates Inc.**
Rocky River, OH

**Great Lakes
Fleet, Inc.**
Duluth, MN

Great Lakes Towing Co.
Cleveland, OH

**Inland Lakes
Management, Inc.**
Alpena, MI

**Interlake Steamship Co.
Lakes Shipping Co.**
Richfield, OH

International Steel Group
Chesterton, IN

J.W. Westcott Co.
Detroit, MI

**LaFarge Cement
Corp.**
Montreal, QC

**Lake Michigan Carferry
Service, Inc.**
Ludington, MI

**Lower Lakes
Towing Ltd.**
Port Dover, ON

**McAsphalt Marine
Transportation Ltd.**
Scarborough, ON

McKeil Marine Ltd.
Hamilton, ON

McNally Marine, Inc.
Toronto, ON

**Oglebay Norton
Marine Services Co.**
Cleveland, OH

**Owen Sound
Transportation Co. Ltd.**
Owen Sound, ON

Purvis Marine Ltd.
Sault Ste. Marie, ON

Rigel Shipping Canada, Inc.
Shediac, NB

Seaway Marine Transport
Toronto, ON

**Transport
Desgagnes, Inc.**
Quebec, QC

Upper Lakes Group, Inc.
Toronto, ON

Wagenborg Shipping B.V.
Delfzijl, Netherlands

Flags of Nations in the Marine Trade

Antigua & Barbuda

Argentina

Australia

Austria

Azerbaijan

Bahamas

Bahrain

Barbados

Bermuda

Bosnia & Herzevovinia

Brazil

Canada

Cayman Islands

Chile

China

Cote D'Ivoire

Croatia

Cyprus

Czech Republic

Denmark

Dominican Republic

Ecuador

Egypt

Estonia

Fiji

Finland

France

Germany

Ghana

Greece

Guinea

Haiti

Honduras

Hong Kong

Hungary

Iceland

India

Indonesia

Ireland

Isle of Man

Israel

Italy

Japan

Korea-South

Latvia

Liberia

Lithuania

Luxembourg

Malaysia

Malta

 Marshall Islands

 Mexico

 Monaco

 Morocco

 Myanmar

 Netherlands

 Netherlands Antilles

 New Zealand

 Nicaragua

 N. Mariana Islands

 Norway

 Pakistan

 Panama

 Peru

 Philippines

 Poland

 Portugal

 Republic of South Africa

 Romania

 Russia

 Singapore

 Solomon Islands

 Spain

 St. Kitts Nevis

 St. Vincent & The Grenadines

 Sweden

 Switzerland

 Syria

 Taiwan

 Thailand

 Trinidad & Tobago

 Tunisia

 Turkey

 Ukraine

 United Kingdom

 United States

 Vanuatu

 Venezuela

 Yugoslavia

Other Flags of Interest

International Shipmaster's Association – Member Pennant

Canadian Coast Guard Ensign

Dangerous Cargo On Board

Pilot On Board

U.S. Coast Guard Auxiliary Ensign

U.S. Coast Guard Ensign

U.S. Army Corps of Engineers

St. Lawrence Seaway Development Corp.

St. Lawrence Seaway Management Corp.

Cement carrier *Southdown Challenger* and tug at Sturgeon Bay, Wis. *(Chris Winters)*

FOLLOWING THE FLEET

These prerecorded messages help track vessel arrivals and departures.

Algoma Central Marine	**(905) 708-3873**	ACM vessel movements
Boatwatcher's Hotline	**(218) 722-6489**	Superior, Duluth, Two Harbors, Taconite Harbor and Silver Bay traffic
CSX Coal Docks/Torco Dock	**(419) 697-2304**	Toledo, OH, vessel information
DMIR Ore Dock	**(218) 628-4590**	Duluth, MN, vessel information
Eisenhower Lock	**(315) 769-2422**	Eisenhower Lock vessel movements
Michigan Limestone docks	**(989) 734-2117**	Calcite, MI vessel information
Michigan Limestone docks	**(906) 484-2201**	Ext. 503 - Cedarville, MI vessel info.
Oglebay Norton Co.	**(800) 861-8760**	O-N Vessel movements
Presque Isle Corp.	**(989) 595-6611**	Stoneport, MI, vessel information
Soo Traffic	**(906) 635-3224**	Previous day's traffic – St. Marys River
Superior Midwest Energy Terminal	**(715) 395-3559**	Superior, WI, vessel information
Thunder Bay Port Authority	**(807) 345-1256**	Thunder Bay, ON, vessel information
USS Great Lakes Fleet	**(218) 628-4389**	USS vessel movements
Upper Lakes Group	**(905) 688-5878**	ULG vessel movements
Welland Canal	**(905) 688-6462**	Welland Canal traffic update

With an inxpensive VHF scanner, boatwatchers can tune to ship-to-ship and ship-to-shore traffic, using the following frequency guide.

Commercial vessels only	**Ch. 13** (156.650 Mhz)	Bridge-to-Bridge Communications
Calling / Distress ONLY	**Ch. 16** (156.800 Mhz)	**Calling / Distress ONLY**
Commercial vessels only	**Ch. 06** (156.300 Mhz)	Working Channel
Commercial vessels only	**Ch. 08** (156.400 Mhz)	Working Channel
Supply boat at Sault Ste. Marie, MI	**Ch. 08** (156.400 Mhz)	Supply boat Ojibway
Detour Reef to Lake St. Clair Light	**Ch. 11** (156.550 Mhz)	Sarnia Traffic - Sector 1
Long Point Light to Lake St. Clair Light	**Ch. 12** (156.600 Mhz)	Sarnia Traffic - Sector 2
Montreal to about mid-Lake St. Francis	**Ch. 14** (156.700 Mhz)	Seaway Beauharnois - Sector 1
Mid-Lake St. Francis to Bradford Island	**Ch. 12** (156.600 Mhz)	Seaway Eisenhower - Sector 2
Bradford Island to Crossover Island	**Ch. 11** (156.550 Mhz)	Seaway Iroquois - Sector 3
Crossover Island to Cape Vincent	**Ch. 13** (156.650 Mhz)	Seaway Clayton - Sector 4 St. Lawrence River portion
Cape Vincent to mid-Lake Ontario	**Ch. 13** (156.650 Mhz)	Seaway Sodus - Sector 4 Lake Ontario portion
Mid-Lake Ontario to Welland Canal	**Ch. 11** (156.550 Mhz)	Seaway Newcastle - Sector 5
Welland Canal	**Ch. 14** (156.700 Mhz)	Seaway Welland - Sector 6
Welland Canal to Long Point Light	**Ch. 11** (156.550 Mhz)	Seaway Long Point - Sector 7
St. Marys River Traffic Service	**Ch. 12** (156.600 Mhz)	Soo Traffic, Sault Ste. Marie, MI
Lockmaster, Soo Locks	**Ch. 14** (156.700 Mhz)	Soo Lockmaster (call WUE-21)
Coast Guard traffic	**Ch. 21** (157.050 Mhz)	United States Coast Guard
Coast Guard traffic	**Ch. 22** (157.100 Mhz)	United States Coast Guard
U.S. Mailboat, Detroit, MI	**Ch. 10** (156.500 Mhz)	Mailboat J. W. Westcott II

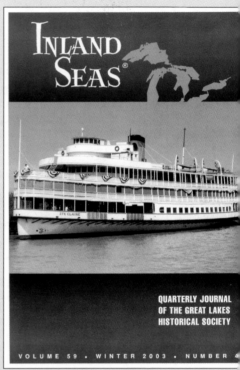